Cambridge Studies in Social Anthropology

GENERAL EDITOR: JACK GOODY

30

Minangkabau social formations

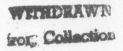

Minangkabau social formations

Indonesian peasants and the world-economy

JOEL S. KAHN

Lecturer in Anthropology
University College London

CAMBRIDGE UNIVERSITY PRESS

CAMBRIDGE
LONDON   NEW YORK   NEW ROCHELLE
MELBOURNE   SYDNEY

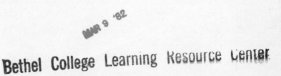

Published by the Press Syndicate of the University of Cambridge
The Pitt Building, Trumpington Street, Cambridge CB2 1RP
32 East 57th Street, New York, NY 10022, USA
296 Beaconsfield Parade, Middle Park, Melbourne 3206, Australia

First published 1980

Printed in Great Britain at the University Press, Cambridge

British Library Cataloguing in Publication Data
Kahn, Joel S
Minangkabau social formations. − (Cambridge studies
in social anthropology; 30).
1. Minangkabau (Indonesian people)
2. Social structure − Indonesia − Sumatera Barat
I. Title II. Series
301.4′009598′1   DS632.M4   79-41605
ISBN 0 521 22993 6

To my parents

Contents

Contents

Maps, figures and tables

Tables

Maps

Figures

Preface

This book is the product of almost eight years of work, during which time I prepared to go to Indonesia, did fieldwork in West Sumatra, wrote up the research as a doctoral dissertation and finally transformed the dissertation into a more readable form. I am indebted to a great many people at each step of the way.

The late Professor Maurice Freedman supervised my M. Phil. thesis and directed me to Minangkabau. Before I went to the field I was supervised by Clive Kessler who helped me formulate my research problems. Most of all I am indebted to Maurice Bloch who supervised me from the time I went to the field until the dissertation was finished. He provided me not only with intellectual guidance but with the moral support and encouragement without which this book would never have been finished.

The fieldwork in West Sumatra was generously supported by a grant from the London Cornell Project for South-east Asian Studies, and sponsored in Indonesia by L.I.P.I., the Indonesian Academy of Sciences. While in Indonesia I received help from a large number of people. I owe an enormous debt of gratitude to Dr Amelijoes Sa'danoer and his wife Dr Kartini Sa'danoer. They provided me with a home away from home in Padang, shared with me their substantial knowledge of the area, and were generally so hospitable and helpful that I can only hope that one day I will be able to do the same for them. I received help from such a large number of people at Andalas University and in government offices in Padang, that it would be impossible to mention them all by name. But most of all I am grateful to the people of Bungus and Sungai Puar who allowed me to live among them and to pry into their affairs, and who, in many cases, freely shared with me their knowledge of Minangkabau village life. Although I would dearly like to thank some of these people by name, for the sake of their privacy I shall not. Suffice it to mention my adopted mother and my assistants in Sungai Puar and from Andalas. Perhaps if they ever see this book they will know how much I owe them.

While I was in the field I was visited by Professor George Kahin and his wife Audrey. They took me around the province and gave me a chance to indulge in my anthropological ravings. Because they also were very kind to me later when I was out of the field I would like to register my gratitude here.

Last but not least I want to thank Maila Stivens for coming with me to Sumatra and helping me at all stages of the research.

In writing up the dissertation and then trying to make it into a book I accrued many debts. Again the advice and encouragement of Maurice Bloch was invaluable. I benefited greatly from discussions, formal and informal, with colleagues at University College, particularly Professors M. G. Smith and Mary Douglas, Jonathan Friedman and Mike Gilsenan. The theoretical approach was shaped through extended discussion with fellow postgraduates J. R. Llobera, Felicity Edholm, Maila Stivens, Kate Young and Julian Clark, and other members of the editorial collective of *Critique of Anthropology*. James Siegel of Cornell University made many helpful suggestions, as did Chandra Jayawardena. I should also like to thank the staff of C.U.P. for help in preparing the manuscript.

Finally I should like to thank my family for all the help, encouragement and editorial advice they have given me. My father, Alfred E. Kahn, performed an heroic task in reading through almost the whole of the manuscript and attempting to make it as readable and clear as his own writing. Much of the better writing is due to him, much of the worse occurs where I resisted his good advice.

While I received a large amount of help, I hope that some of what is in this book is my own, including all of the mistakes.

The language of everyday conversation in West Sumatra is Minangkabau, a fairly closely related dialect of the national language, Bahasa Indonesia. In citing most local terms and place names I have used Minangkabau, based on the spelling adopted by the only provincial newspaper written in dialect – *Singgalang*. Since I carried out my fieldwork the national languages of Indonesia and Malaysia have undergone spelling changes for the sake of regional uniformity. I have used the new spellings where appropriate.

The Indonesian unit of currency is the *rupiah*. The exchange rate at the time of my fieldwork was approximately 1,000 *rupiah* (Rp. 1,000) to £1 sterling.

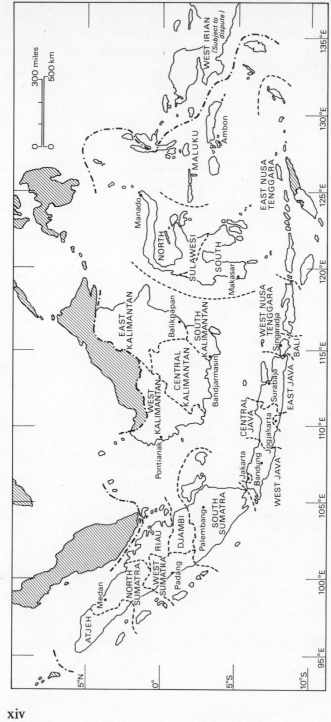

Map 1   First-level administrative regions of Indonesia, 1960 (after Legge, *Central Authority and Regional Autonomy in Indonesia*, 1961)

xiv

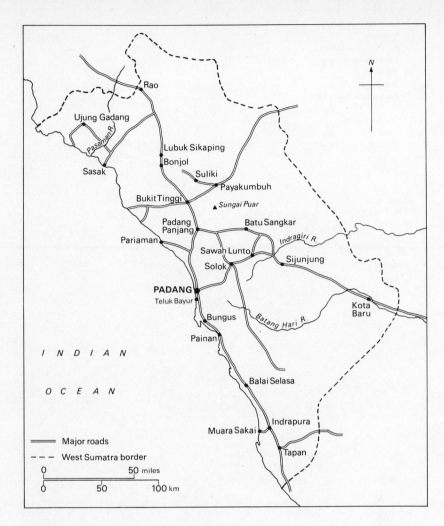

Map 2   Major towns and roads of West Sumatra

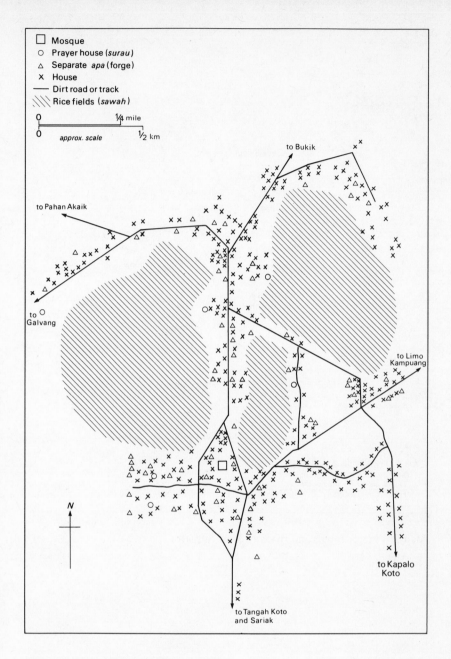

Map 3   The main areas of Limo Suku

xvi

1
Introduction

This book is primarily about a form of peasant economic activity predominant among the Minangkabau of the modern Indonesian province of West Sumatra during the period of field research between 1970 and 1972, that is to say, the production and distribution of commodities on a small, often individual scale. It is at the same time an attempt to account for the predominance of this economic form in a specific place and time.

This focus on the economy I feel needs little justification in the context of modern Indonesia, and indeed questions of poverty and underdevelopment are central concerns of the people themselves. A study of the rural peasant economy is particularly relevant when estimates have it that as much as 60 per cent of national income is derived from rural areas, and 85 per cent of the people earn their living outside the towns (see Mackie in Glassburner, 1971, p. 22).

Any study of Indonesian peasant economy must inevitably come up against a number of particularly thorny questions. Why, for example, in spite of the relative richness of Indonesia's natural resource base, has rural income failed often to keep pace even with population growth? What are the reasons for the relative technological backwardness of peasant enterprises and the general absence, at least in the modern period, of large-scale enterprise in the peasant sector? Is class differentiation among the peasantry an inevitable result of contact with a capitalist economy? These questions lead one to consider the origins of this form of economic activity and, a more central political problem, the conditions under which the peasant economy may be transformed to yield a better living to the millions of small-scale producers and traders who eke out a living at a standard many times lower than that enjoyed in the capitalist metropolis, much of the wealth of which

1

has nonetheless been derived from countries like Indonesia. It is particularly important here to assess the degree to which conditions in West Sumatra are and have been the product of the integration of the region into a world capitalist system. This is indeed a more general problem for anthropologists and other social scientists who base their analyses on findings in a particular region.

For anthropologists especially the application of techniques designed to build a deep understanding of relatively self-contained social units, presuming these ever existed, to discontinuous segments of societies of ever-increasing scope has given rise to a large number of ethical, methodological and theoretical problems. The difficulty has, of course, long been recognised. Redfield, for example, asked: 'What forms of thought are available to us for conceiving and describing a whole that is both inclosed [*sic*] within other wholes and is also in some part permeated by them?' (1955, p. 114). Leach in his classic study (1954) of the oscillation between egalitarian and hierarchical forms of political organisation in highland Burma attacked the idea of neat cultural, social and tribal boundaries posited in the approach of writers like Radcliffe-Brown who had argued in 1940 that anthropologists could build up models of social structure of any particular society on the basis of research in 'any convenient locality of a suitable size' (in Radcliffe-Brown, 1963, p. 193).

In the twenty years since Redfield, Leach and others raised these questions, however, it does not seem as though anthropology has provided satisfactory answers. As evidence for this conclusion I would simply draw attention to the term used to describe societies like Minangkabau — 'peasant society'. The use of this term has given it the status of an evolutionary stage, while in fact the 'peasantries' described by anthropologists are no such thing, but have rather developed in conjunction with other classes in feudal, colonial and neo-colonial social systems.

In itself this is not a particularly interesting or original conclusion. Pick up almost any monograph and you will find an introductory statement about the outside society, the total social whole in which the village is embedded, the importance of extra-local ties, etc. And yet I would argue that in most of such cases this holistic view is set aside, and the total social structure ignored in favour of detailed analyses of purely local phenomena. The anthropologist

2

in many cases accepts the peasants' own equation of physical space — the world outside — with social distance. Marriot, for example, was content to treat the Indian village of Kishan Garhi as a 'definable structure . . . a system' in itself in the light of 'the concerns and emphases that the people of the village express' (1955, p. 171), demonstrating only that while economic and political structures may not be geographically bounded, ideologies often are.

It may well be that anthropology, as a discipline which almost always requires fieldwork as a necessary exercise for its practitioners, is not likely to produce an unbiased answer to this question. And it is perhaps significant that more recently the question has been raised in other quarters. Andre Gunder Frank's radical rejection of the 'dualism' of modernisation theory is in many ways a sign of a period when some classes in the newly independent nations found they were not as independent as they had imagined. Similarly the liberation struggles of recent decades have both sought inspiration in, and inspired in turn, Marxist theory — hence giving rise for some Marxist theorists to the problem of reconciling the appearance of pre-capitalist social forms in a predominantly capitalist world-economy with the classical imperialism theories of Lenin, Bukharin and Luxemburg.

The recent debate between so-called world-systems theorists and those who advocate a concept of the articulation of modes of production has again brought to the fore the question of internal versus external influence on socio-economic organisation in the Third World.

Marxists themselves, of course, differ quite significantly on this issue. Friedman, for example, in taking issue with the concepts of mode of production and social formation maintains that the proper starting-point in such analyses is what he terms the 'system of total reproduction'. Local conditions within such a totality are said only to 'constrain and limit local variation, determine the limits of productivity, surplus extraction, intensification etc. in the short run' (1976, p. 10). Similarly Wallerstein, in positing a 'world-economy', maintains that it allows him to 'explain changes in the sovereign states as consequent upon the evolution and interaction of the world system' (1974).

In opposition to this one-sided emphasis on the totality, others give a greater role to the effectiveness of local modes of production. Pierre-Phillipe Rey, for example, one of the few writers to take the concept of the articulation of modes of production to its logical conclusion, implies that in transitional periods in the development of capitalism, certain branches of the economy remain largely outside the capitalist system, resisting as it were the impulse of capitalism towards the proletarianisation of the direct producer (see Rey, 1973). Any attempt to go beyond an internal description of the peasant economy, to attempt to account for its emergence, reproduction and transformation, clearly must consider this issue.

While, therefore, in one sense this book is extremely specific, in that it is a monograph in anthropology describing a particular form of economic organisation in a remote corner of the world within a brief span of time, in another sense it expresses more general concerns with the problems of underdevelopment, as well as with the pertinence of Marxist concepts like mode of production, social formation, relations of production and value in the analysis of a concrete situation.

The organisation of the book reflects this concern. The first part is an attempt to get at the nature of the West Sumatran economy, and will seek particularly to establish the primary importance of petty commodity production in the period of research. This is done largely through a detailed discussion of a single village in the highlands of West Sumatra, the home of an important blacksmithing industry. At the same time these chapters will place the blacksmithing industry in its social and economic context. After an introduction to the region, Chapter 2 presents a general survey of the village of Sungai Puar. In Chapter 3 I turn to village society, and particularly to the relation between kinship and subsistence agriculture. Chapter 4 takes up the theme of subsistence production, while in Chapter 5 I turn to the analysis of blacksmithing as an example of petty commodity production. In Chapter 6 I present a general discussion of the organisation of commodity production in the local and regional economy in order to demonstrate the significance of this particular form of peasant economic organisation.

The following part of the book turns to the problem of accounting for the emergence and reproduction of petty commodity production. Chapter 7 presents an abstract and structural analysis of petty commodity production in order to establish the structural conditions necessary to its emergence, as well as the conditions necessary to its reproduction. Chapters 8 and 9 are concerned with the historical development of this economic form. The former chapter attempts to lay out the historical baseline, as it were, not in a traditional and timeless society, as modernisation theory would have it, but in a 'traditionalised' society which was in fact a product of colonial mercantilism. The latter chapter then considers the breakdown of this system and the transition to the modern economy, still tied to a larger system, but in different ways and with different consequences, one of which is the emergence of petty commodity production as if not the dominant form of economic organisation certainly the *pre*-dominant one. This means taking issue with those who see differentiation of the peasantry as the inevitable product of capitalist expansion, as well as those who would characterise the peripheries of the world-economy as simply capitalist. While Chapter 9 considers the historical conditions under which petty commodity production emerged in West Sumatra, the final chapter takes up its reproduction within a world capitalist social formation, as well as attempting to look at the conditions under which petty commodity production has been and may be transformed. While therefore the second part of the book begins with an abstract structural analysis, it returns to the concrete historical situation of Minangkabau peasants in the 1970s through an examination of the historical and structural conditions of existence of the peasant economy.

Before turning to the analysis of the specific economy of the village of Sungai Puar, it is necessary to say a brief word on the region as a whole. The Minangkabau represent, in many ways, a typical object of anthropological study. Although the Minangkabau people today are just so many citizens of the Republic of Indonesia, in their own eyes, and in the eyes of observers, they have often been depicted as a unique ethnic group, sharing a language, a sub-culture, a religion, a homeland and apparently a rather special position within the Indonesian economy. The Minangkabau language is a dialect of the national language, Bahasa Indonesia. The subculture is known as *adat* Minangkabau, an often vague term taken to refer to that complex of matrilineal custom taken by Minangkabau and ethnographers alike to be a heritage from a 'traditional' past. Their religion is Islam, which, although often said to claim the adherence of 90 per cent of Indonesians, is said to be found in Minangkabau in a purer form known among In-donesianists as *santri* (cf. Geertz, 1960). Their homeland is the Indonesian province of West Sumatra (Sumatera Barat) with a population of some two million, the overwhelming majority of which is said to be ethnically Minangkabau. Some writers, however, estimate that almost as many Minangkabau live outside West Sumatra in other parts of Indonesia and overseas. As for their economic position, the Minangkabau are said to be active small-scale entrepreneurs, migrants in search of profitable trade and one of the few ethnic groups capable of competing successfully with Chinese traders and shopkeepers in Indonesia.

Not only do the Minangkabau represent in popular ideology and in the writings of scholars a unique ethnic group, eminently suitable for anthropological study, they are also seen to be undergoing processes of change typical in many ways of the changes experienced by other 'traditional' peoples in the modernising Third World. Matrilineal custom has been breaking down in the face of the pressures of colonialism and then national independence. Matrilineal *adat* is also seen to be in conflict with the demands of a purist Islam. Corporate groups are disintegrating in the face of Western-induced commercial pressures, and the power of 'traditional' elites is waning under new political conditions.

The radical changes brought by the twentieth century have, it is argued, brought forth often violent response from the Minangkabau themselves. The anti-tax rebellions of the first decade of this century, the abortive communist uprisings of the 1920s, the sweeping tide of nationalism in the period of the war for independence and the regionalist movement of the late 1950s are all taken to be responses, however incoherent, to the pressures of modernisation and commercialisation. The Minangkabau have also responded at the level of national politics. Numerous prominent national politicians are and have been ethnic Minangkabau.

In short the Minangkabau seem to provide us with an ideal subject for the study both of a traditional society, and of social change as it is at present being experienced in the newly independent nations of the Third World.

This rather facile impression of Minangkabau seems to provide the modern researcher with easy explanations for much of what is observed in the field. Ethnographers such as this one, with an

6

interest in analysing both the reasons for the relative economic success of Minangkabau entrepreneurs and the causes of the under-development of the region as a whole, might be tempted by explanations which rely on the cultural characteristics of the Minang-kabau as an ethnic group subjected to rapid social change in the twentieth century.

However, this book is an attempt to dissolve the simplistic accounts offered above, or, to use the terminology of structuralists and Marxists, to penetrate behind the appearances in order to understand them.

Before this attempt I will present here and in Chapters 2—6 a discussion of modern Minangkabau, with particular emphasis on the economy.

The homeland of the Minangkabau

The traditional homeland of the Minangkabau is the highland area of western Sumatra — the second largest of some 3,000 islands which make up the present-day Republic of Indonesia. The modern province of West Sumatra is bordered on the north by Sumatera Utara, homeland of the Batak peoples, on the south by Jambi, on the east by Riau, and on the west by the Indian Ocean. Sumatra itself straddles the Equator, which runs just to the north of the old Dutch town of Fort de Kock, now known by its indigenous name of Bukit Tinggi.

The provincial capital and largest city in West Sumatra with a population of just under 200,000 is Padang on the west coast, which can be reached by air from Jakarta and Singapore or by boat to its near-by port of Teluk Bayur.

The Minangkabau highlands are part of a mountain chain (the Bukit Barisan) which runs from north to south along the western side of the island, rarely more than thirty-five miles from the Indian Ocean. The mountains are dotted with longitudinal rift valleys which form a discontinuous trough along their length. Blockage by volcanic debris in some of the deeper depressions in the trough has led to the formation of spectacular mountain lakes like Maninjau and Singkarak in West Sumatra. Rainfall and water from mountain springs flow through the trough, which is drained primarily by rivers which flow eastwards towards the broad alluvial lowlands of Sumatra's east coast and then into the Straits of Malacca. The highland valleys and plains are the site of much of the irrigated rice cultivation that is carried out in scattered areas throughout the island.

Today the province is divided into eight districts (*Kabupaten*) and six municipalities (*Kota Madya*). The districts are further divided into subdistricts known as *Kecamatan* which are in turn composed of villages called *nagari*.

Minangkabau was traditionally divided into two main regions known as Darat and Rantau. Darat refers to a geographical area as well as to a cultural phenomenon − the highlands and the culture core respectively. Rantau is taken to mean the outlying districts to the south, east and west of the Darat. This includes the coastal plain on the Indian Ocean side of West Sumatra, and the hilly regions to the south and east. The term *rantau* can also be taken to refer to any area outside the Darat populated by large numbers of Minangkabau migrants.

Early political and economic history

According to *adat*, or customary law, the Darat is divided into three main regions known as *luhak*. These are called Agam, Tanah Datar and Limopuluah Koto and their boundaries correspond largely to those of the modern districts of the same name. This division of the highlands appears to date from the period of the Minangkabau kingdom, of which not a great deal is known from the time of its founding in the fourteenth century. Traditional history maintains that the first king of Minangkabau was a Javanese aristocrat known as Adityawarman, while Minangkabau myth has it that the kingdom, and indeed Minangkabau itself, was founded by Maharajo Dirajo, one of the three sons of Iskandar Zulkarnain or Alexander the Great.

In the myth the modern forms of Minangkabau *adat* originate from two Culture Heroes − Datuak Katumangguangan and Datuak Parapatiah nan Sabatang − the former a direct patrilineal descendant of the original king, and the latter his half-brother whose father was a commoner or a sage. It was in the period of the Culture Heroes that Minangkabau was divided into village settlements known as *nagari*, that the matriclans or *suku* were formed and clan heads known as *panghulu* are said to have been installed as representatives of the king in the *nagari*.

Introduction

Elsewhere (Kahn, forthcoming) I have dealt in more detail with the significance of this myth in terms of the little history we know of the Minangkabau kingdom. I have attempted to show that Minangkabau, like other important kingdoms in the region, was an offshoot of the large trading empire of Srivijaya centred on South Sumatra, that in fact a system of dual descent was in operation, whereby royal power passed in the patriline while control of land and inheritance lay with localised matriclans, and that royal power was based on an extensive regional, and indeed overseas, trade in gold, spices, cloth and forest produce.

Contrary to the picture presented in the opening pages, Sumatra has long had contact with the West. Marco Polo apparently visited North Sumatra in the thirteenth century, and Portuguese travellers like Tomé Pires visited other parts of the island. Pires collected information on Minangkabau from other visitors in the sixteenth century. By the early seventeenth century ships from the Netherlands had become involved in the pepper and gold trade on the west coast, an involvement which resulted in a series of contracts with local rulers in the latter half of the century which aimed to preserve a trade monopoly, with a charter from the Minangkabau king, for the Netherlands East India Company (V.O.C.). The British also visited the west coast, and governed their possessions from Fort Marlborough Benkulu. It was these possessions in West Sumatra which they traded to the Dutch in exchange for the port of Malacca on the Malay peninsula in the early 1800s.

When the V.O.C. was dissolved, and a colonial government took control of its possessions in the East Indies, West Sumatra again became an important focus of colonial activity. In 1847 West Sumatra was one of the few places outside Java to be subjected to the infamous *Cultuurstelsel*, or Culture System as it has been rendered in English. This was a system of forced extraction of export crops, and in the latter half of the nineteenth century the highlands of Minangkabau became a major exporter of coffee.

While the restrictions on private capitalism imposed under the Culture System were lifted in Java in 1870, West Sumatra remained closed to the expansion of plantation capitalism until just after 1910. The abolition of the Culture System in Minangkabau was followed by the rapid growth of a commercialised peasantry, and we are fortunate to have a detailed report by a Dutch sociologist on this period (cf. Schrieke, 1955) which describes at

9

length both economic and social changes which followed this shift in the economics of colonialism.

Apart from being an important centre for indigenous commercial development in this century, Minangkabau has also exhibited in concentrated form the basic political changes and conflict found in other parts of Indonesia. Commercial development led to a growing class of local entrepreneurs, merchants and petty capitalists who often found themselves in opposition to the colonial powers. At the political level this generated the so-called Kaum Muda (literally Young Group) movement influenced by the strong current of Muslim modernism in the early decades of this century. The Kaum Muda set themselves against the 'traditional' hierarchy of *adat* officials and religious teachers upon whom the Netherlands had relied for the administration of the Culture System. Not surprisingly, however, the growth of a modernist movement among Indonesians brought the Kaum Muda into conflict with the colonial authorities as well.

Sarekat Islam, founded in Java, which listed among its demands greater participation by Indonesians in the governing of the colony, found widespread support in West Sumatra after a branch was established in Padang in 1915, as did other modernist organisations like Muhammadiyah, Budi Baik (founded in Bukit Tinggi in 1918) and the Sarekat Combinatie Minangkabau founded in the following year (cf. Abdullah, 1971).

A more radical political movement emerged from the heart of Sarekat Islam itself, and in 1921 radical modernists were forced out of the party. They banded together in the Sarekat Rakyat (People's Union), which was to be the organisational base for the Indonesian Communist Party (the P.K.I.). In March 1923 a Padang branch of the P.K.I. was set up, and in the same period a certain Datuak Batuah turned the famous Sumatera Thwalib school in the highland town of Padang Panjang into a centre of 'Islamic communism'.

West Sumatra was a fertile ground for the P.K.I. in its early years, and the party had considerable success until the warnings of the national and provincial leadership were ignored and a revolutionary committee called on leaders at the local level to take up arms against the Dutch. The short-lived rebellion which broke out in the village of Silungkang in January 1927 was quickly put down, and this was followed by an extended period of political

10

repression by the colonial authorities (Schrieke, 1955; Banda and McVey, 1960).

Minangkabau, like many other parts of Indonesia, was occupied by the Japanese in the early 1940s and resisted the return of Dutch forces when the Japanese withdrew. In the immediate post-Independence period Minangkabau was strongly represented at the national level by political leaders, many of whom were bred within the modernist movements.

The post-Independence period: economy

In the years since Independence in 1949 there have been some changes in the nature of the economy. Although there is large-scale investment by foreign firms in certain sectors of the economy, most notably in the oilfields of Sumatra and Indonesian Borneo (Kalimantan), the large majority of Indonesians are peasant cultivators, small-scale craftsmen, fishermen and petty traders. Writing in 1963, Pelzer estimated that the 'primary production sector — which yields peasant food crops, smallholder and plantation export crops, livestock, fish, and forest products . . . — is a source of livelihood for more than 60 per cent of Indonesia's gainfully employed inhabitants' (in Glassburner, ed., 1971, p. 128). Moreover, according to another estimate about 85 per cent of the population live in rural villages and towns of fewer than 10,000 persons (Mackie in Glassburner, p. 21). These figures, as Mackie points out, show a distribution of national income which is highly unfavourable to the rural areas.

If anything, then, there has been an increasing 'peasantisation' of the Indonesian economy since the Independence, accentuated by the nationalisation of Dutch-owned plantations in 1957, although this has gone hand in hand with stagnation in most of the indices used by economists to calculate economic growth. In the case of cash crops like rubber there has been a steady increase in the proportion grown on peasant holdings. In 1938, for example, slightly over 50 per cent of Indonesia's rubber was grown on estates, while in 1960 about two-thirds came from smallholdings. Moreover, 'over 25 per cent of Indonesia's foreign exchange earnings has come from smallholders' rubber in the postwar years' (Mackie in Glassburner, p. 28). Only oil has outstripped the peasant sector in the table in Indonesian exports.

The importance of the commercial peasantry in Indonesia as a whole is exceeded by its significance in the economy of the so-called Outer Islands. Sumatra in particular has been known for the important contribution made by its peasant producers to Indonesian export earnings, which is itself a manifestation of the significance of peasant production and petty trade in regional income figures. For example, of a gross domestic product of just over 60 billion *rupiah* in West Sumatra in 1969, it is estimated that 28 billion derived from agriculture, forestry, and fishing and that over 15 billion came from the wholesale and retail trade (see Esmara, 1971); as Table 1.1 shows, the bulk of agricultural output came from very small peasant farms. According to statistics issued by the provincial government, which can be taken only as rough estimates, the average farm size in the province is just 0.85 hectares (Esmara, 1971, p. 119).

Similarly, the large majority of those involved in the wholesale and retail trade are self-employed or working for very small firms, a picture which emerges in the few studies on marketing done elsewhere in Indonesia (see Dewey, 1962; Siegel, 1969). Large-scale manufacturing has also been relatively unimportant in Indonesia in general and West Sumatra in particular. Manufactured goods are either imported from overseas, or produced locally by small-scale craft. In 1970 in West Sumatra as a whole there were only 20 factories employing 100 workers or more, and 139 workshops employed from 10 to 99 workers. Cloth, tools and other goods were either produced locally by peasant craftsmen, or imported into the region, mostly from overseas.

The economy of Minangkabau is, then, typical of Indonesia as a whole, or perhaps more accurately typical of the economy which supports 85 per cent of Indonesian citizens, based on peasant cash crops and handicrafts, and small-scale trading.

It is also typical in another sense, in that it is underdeveloped, if we use this term to refer to low *per-capita* income, economic stagnation and a standard of living drastically lower than that enjoyed in the West, or if we judge by the small proportion of Indonesians involved in high levels of the government or foreign-controlled enterprise. Most of the contributors to the Glassburner volume point out that economic growth has largely failed to keep pace with the growth of population since Independence, and that *per-capita* income is extremely low. The estimates of *per-capita*

Table 1.1 *Agricultural production in West Sumatra, 1971 (based on Esmara, 1972)*

Crop	Smallholder		Estate	
	Area (ha.)	Production (tons)	Area	Production
Rubber	43,070	25,355	5,135	679
Cassia vera	8,639	2,104	–	–
Coffee	9,115	2,119	–	–
Nutmeg	283	419	–	–
Cloves	9,315	2,590	–	–
Tobacco	760	304	–	–
Gambir	8,622	1,903	–	–
Coconuts	49,595	20,371	–	–
Pepper	214	134	–	–
Sugar-cane	6,438	7,370	–	–
Kapok	759	138	–	–
Chinchona	–	–	6,042	260
Tea	–	–	5,178	43

income made by the West Sumatran provincial government in 1970 are both higher than estimates for the country as a whole, and even at only about £100 per year are in all probability optimistic for West Sumatra itself. These estimates, moreover, include an estimate made for the value of rice produced for subsistence which is clearly too high (see below, Chapter 4).

Any understanding, therefore, of the Indonesian economy must be based on a detailed analysis of the nature of the peasant economy, and particularly the small-scale production and distribution of commodities within Indonesia and for export; this is the primary aim of this book. We shall see, however, that having looked in some detail at a single example of this peasant economy it will be necessary to return to the relation between small-scale production and distribution and the world-economy of which it is a part.

The post-Independence period: politics

There were, at least up to the horrendous massacre of communists and communist sympathisers in 1965, three major political forces in post-war Indonesia, all of which emerged in the colonial period: the nationalists, the communists and the various Muslim movements. Geertz has described these movements as streams or, to use the Indonesian term, *aliran* (see Geertz, 1960 and 1965). While the concept of *aliran* does not explain political conflict (see Kahn, 1978), it provides a useful idiom with which to describe what Geertz calls the 'cultural paradigm' according to which Indonesians themselves operate, or at least have frequently operated in the past.

All three streams of political alliance have been important at various times in Minangkabau, as we have seen. However, the post-war political situation is perhaps best characterised by the domination of regionalism and Islam in its *santri* or modernist form. I have elsewhere (Kahn, 1978) attempted to account for this, but for our purposes here it is sufficient to describe briefly the regional rebellions of the middle to late 1950s in order to provide something of the flavour of the present-day political situation. For while these rebellions were put down, the conditions which generated them were not abolished, and regionalist sentiments continue to run high in the province.

In the 1955 general elections Masjumi, the modernist Muslim party, was the most popular party in centres of Indonesian commercial interest such as West Sumatra. A split soon developed, however, between national leaders and the local movements. Frustrated by the lack of economic development in the Outer Islands, the local movement came into direct conflict with Jakarta. While this represented a reaction primarily to the growing political and economic hegemony of Sukarno and the nationalist party (P.N.I.), it could be argued that in the early years of the regional movements dissatisfaction was also felt with Masjumi for failing to come to grips with the economic problems faced by the Indonesian commercial classes.

In December 1956 a group known as the Dewan Banteng took over the reins of provincial government in West Sumatra.[1] The Dewan Banteng was a political group which emerged from the

---

1. There is a lack of good material on the regional rebellions *per se*. The following discussion is taken from material which I gathered during fieldwork, from an interesting thesis which discusses the rebellions (Alliband, 1970) and from reports in *Haluan*, a pro-Dewan Banteng newspaper published in Padang in this period.

Banteng division of the Indonesian Armed Forces under the command of a certain Colonel Ismail Lengah. The transition was bloodless, largely, it seems, because the regional administrators chose not to oppose the Dewan Banteng – indeed, many clearly favoured its action.

It is interesting to note that the demands of the Dewan Banteng on taking over the governing of West Sumatra were concerned largely with issues of economic centralisation and corruption. As a condition for the return to centralised administration, the supporters of the Dewan Banteng demanded an end to economic policies which were seen to discriminate against the exporting economy of the Outer Islands and against government corruption which also was blocking the development of the regional economy.

The Dewan Banteng proved remarkably popular in West Sumatra, drawing support from a wide spectrum of groups, including large numbers of peasant villagers (see reports published in *Haluan*, January to March 1957). Religious groups, Minangkabau ethnic organisations and even some local branches of the P.K.I. declared their support publicly.

In 1957, however, the direction of the regional movement changed, and confrontation with Jakarta was provoked. While modernism and Minangkabau ethnic identity, expressed through the Dewan Banteng movement, served to unite the commercial classes, including the peasantry, against external domination of the regional economy, in 1957 leadership of the movement passed from representatives of local interests to refugees from the central government. More concerned with their loss of power at the national level, these new leaders managed to change the main aims of the regionalists from the development of the local economy to an open battle with Sukarno and the Indonesian communists.

In mid-1957 Sumitro, the National Finance Minister, and Colonel Dahlan Djambek, Third Deputy Chief of Staff of the Army, fell in with the regionalists. It was men such as these who dominated the South Sumatra meeting of 5 October 1957, when an anti-communist movement (Gerakan Bersama Anti Kommunisme) was formed and an ultimatum issued that should demands not be met a separatist government would be installed in Padang. This duly occurred on 15 February 1958. The Dewan Banteng was ousted and the Revolutionary Government of the Republic of Indonesia (P.R.R.I.) was formed in Padang.

15

This move prompted quick central government action. Within a few months troops from the central government had seized control of the major towns in Sumatra previously loyal to the regionalists' cause. While fighting continued in the jungle, and even in villages in the Minangkabau highlands, the revolt was effectively over.

Since the defeat of the regionalist movement there has been a significant change in the balance of power at the national level. The P.K.I. has been at least temporarily wiped out and most of its leaders, supporters and sympathisers have been either killed or imprisoned without trial. And yet while the P.R.R.I. took as its main enemies Sukarno and the P.K.I., regional dissatisfaction has not abated. In my opinion this is not surprising, arguing as I do that it was the Dewan Banteng and not the P.R.R.I. which more closely reflected the dissatisfactions of most Minangkabau peasants and traders in the 1950s. Regional unrest developed not so much out of a concern with the balance of political power in Jakarta as with inequalities between largely rural producers and the government elites, and the local representatives of foreign enterprise, inequalities which persist today in spite of the fact that 85 per cent of the population is rural.

Therefore, just as an understanding of the modern Indonesian economy must rest on a knowledge of the organisation and determinants of this small-scale rural economy, so such knowledge will also give us a key to understanding the formation of classes and political struggle in the 1970s. It is necessary to penetrate behind the appearance of streams of political alliance and of the economic statistics before we can understand the modern economic and political conjunctures which I have outlined above.

My main aim in this book is to explore the relationship between the concrete world of a Minangkabau village in the highlands of West Sumatra and the abstract concepts of historical materialism in an attempt to generate this understanding of local forms of economic organisation and political struggle. In my presentation of the material I have followed anthropological convention by first giving a description of the village (in the following five chapters). Because of the importance of small-scale commodity production in the Indonesian economy, particularly in West Sumatra, I have chosen to focus on a discussion of the local blacksmithing industry, although an attempt is made to place this in its social

16

context and, particularly in Chapter 5, to show that this example is in many ways typical of the organisation of commodity production and distribution in general.

2

The internal and the external in a Minangkabau village: an introduction to the world of the concrete

The *nagari*, or village, of Sungai Puar is located in the Agam district in the cultural heartland of Minangkabau territory near Bukit Tinggi, the district capital. The Agam plateau is one of the larger of the cultivable areas in the highlands about 1,000 metres above sea level and located at the base of the three mountains of Marapi, Singgalang and Sago, the peaks of which tower a further 2,000 metres above the valley floor. Sungai Puar rests at the foot of Mount Marapi, a tame but still active volcano whose lower slopes are sufficiently gradual to allow villagers to cultivate irrigated rice on terraced fields.

Agam district, with a population of some 340,000 in 1970, is administered from the town of Bukit Tinggi, which grew up on the site of the nineteenth-century Dutch Fort de Kock. Bukit Tinggi is the seat of the regional assembly, and the district is administered by an executive group and a single appointed head, the *Bupati*, whose appointment is subject to the approval of the provincial government (Said, 1970).[1]

The provincial capital, Padang, lies on the west coast, about 90 kilometres to the south-west of Bukit Tinggi. Access is by either the main Padang–Medan road, which passes through the district capital, or a narrow-gauge railway. While the train is slow and the service relatively infrequent, there is a heavy lorry and bus traffic between the two towns.

The district of Agam is made up of 10 subdistricts known as *Kecamatan*. These in turn are subdivided into 73 villages. Sungai Puar is in the *Kecamatan* Banuhampu/Sungai Puar, which covers about 70 square kilometres with a population of some 40,000 people. The village, six kilometres from Bukit Tinggi, is reached by

1. For a more detailed account of the Indonesian system of regional administration see Legge, 1961.

a partially paved narrow road which branches off the main Bukit Tinggi–Padang road four kilometres south of the district capital. The crossroads is the site of the subdistrict office, which houses the office of the *camat* as well as small police and army posts.

While Sungai Puar has a resident population of some 9,000 people, it remains a village in appearance. There is no population centre, nor is there a street of shops. At the centre there is simply a small market, a lower secondary school (*Sekolah Menengah Pertama*), and a ramshackle building which houses the office of the village mayor (*Wali Nagari*). The village itself is divided into five sections, the largest of which is Limo Suku (Five Clans), the centre of the local blacksmithing industry. Limo Suku, like the other village sections, is administered by a locally appointed headman (*Kepala Kampung*).

All houses in the village are connected by a network of unpaved paths and roads, some passable to motor traffic, others only on foot. In fact these roads and paths form the focus of population. Most houses are strung out evenly on both sides of the roads. The road through Limo Suku is better than most, and this means that population is slightly denser than in other parts of the village. *Oplet* or small buses pass back and forth along the Limo Suku road to and from Bukit Tinggi carrying passengers and goods to market.

There is great variety in local house styles. Wooden and glass structures and small wooden bungalows stand side by side with small shacks and larger wooden constructions built up on high concrete foundations. The latter are often covered by the elegantly curved roof said to represent the horns of the buffalo – a symbol of Minangkabau culture which has penetrated throughout Malaysia and Indonesia. Although a few houses are thatched, the large majority are covered with the ubiquitous corrugated metal which is so popular in that part of the world.

Behind the housing clusters on both sides of the roads are the irrigated rice fields (*sawah*), invisible from the road because of the dense green foliage of trees which keep many houses in perpetual cooling shade. Below the road, paths lead out to the fields which slope gradually down and away towards the Bukit Tinggi plain.

The occupied parts of Limo Suku are quiet in the middle of the day, except for the sound of steel being forged in the numerous

19

small workshops and the occasional rattle of a sewing machine in the houses. The small coffee shops or *lapau* are almost empty at this time. In the shaded areas around the houses children play, and women may be outside pounding rice in broad wooden or stone mortars. Occasionally an *oplet* passes by on its way to Bukit Tinggi, honking its horn to the tune of some popular song to attract passengers. A few young men may be sitting in the coffee shops, or walking along the road arm in arm. But otherwise the village seems deserted. Solitary farmers can be seen in the *sawah* hoeing, ploughing, weeding or harvesting the highly prized rice crop.

Only later in the day does social life become busier. Blacksmiths who have finished work sit in the coffee shops, farmers return from the fields, and women and children go to the coffee shops to buy paraffin, eggs, chillies, or dried fish. People don sarongs and head for the pools around the mosque or prayer houses for their evening bath. Drums beat for evening prayer and people return home for the evening meal. Lamps are lit and the sun sets abruptly. Few people go out of their houses in the evening, except for the card players in the coffee shops.

The start of the day is marked before sunrise by the beating of prayer-house drums, and people are soon up and around – women to the nearest market, to the pools to do the family washing and then either to the fields or the house for cooking, sewing and mat-making, men usually to their workshops to begin the morning's forging.

According to villagers, a *nagari* is an independent, self-sufficient community. Tradition requires that a *nagari* contain *sawah* (irrigated rice land), *ladang* (unirrigated land for dry cultivation), house plots and houses, pools, gardens, a mosque, a *balai adat* or meeting hall for the village council and numerous lineage houses. These symbolise a community self-sufficient in terms of lineage structure, economics, religion and government. The religious congregation, the unity of kin groups, the political unit and the economic structure are seen as coterminous, making up an independent community bound together and set off from other similar communities.

In fact, as we shall see, a Minangkabau village is neither autonomous nor coherent. Neither is this an adequate conception of the Minangkabau *nagari* of the past. In one sense the village is made up of segments which are in some ways more cohesive than the village itself, and in another it is, and was, simply a part of a more comprehensive social universe.

Administrative and political structure

The Minangkabau village is the smallest in a hierarchy of territorial units within the Indonesian State, just as the mayor and the village council are at the bottom of an administrative hierarchy reaching up to the President and the National Assembly. In theory the mayor is a village official, elected by the village council and subject only to the will of the villagers. There is no doubt, however, that on important issues the mayor is expected to follow the policies laid down by political forces outside the village. In the period leading up to the general elections of 1971, for example, the mayor of Sungai Puar was dismissed by the *Bupati* because he refused to support the dominant political alliance, Golkar, in the campaign. He was replaced by a member of the council more in favour with Golkar authorities. The village mayor is, then, a sort of go-between, acting as a mediator between villagers and official, salaried members of the State bureaucracy. He and his secretary are usually approached first by villagers with any problem that requires contact with government offices outside the village. They give advice, write letters, and direct people to the right place.

It is also the duty of the mayor and his assistants to collect taxes, to ensure village security through the supervision of a local unofficial police force, to issue radio licences, and to assist all outsiders, administrative officials in particular, with business in the village. The mayor's office also acts as a court of appeal for disputes which cannot be settled within kin or local groups.

Apart from his office assistants, the *Wali Nagari* relies on the help of the section headman as well as neighbourhood leaders to see that the village is administered smoothly. During the elections, for example, these men were expected to control the registration and voting in their areas. At the same time the mayor's office and outsiders exerted considerable pressure on these officials to drum up support for Golkar.

The majority of village officials — from the mayor to the neighbourhood leaders — are selected from the ranks of retired petty bureaucrats, or pensioned servicemen and policemen. There was thus a close parallel between power relations within the village and political developments in Indonesia as a whole in the late 1960s and early 1970s, for it was in this period that the so-called Golongan Karya was taking form. In its attempt to build up a stable power base the predominantly military government of General Suharto formed this supposedly non-political alliance of what they called 'service' or 'functional' groups. This rather thinly veiled attempt to build up a single State party, solidly behind the group which had ousted Sukarno and destroyed the communist movement, was conducted by organising members of the armed forces and a group in Indonesia loosely known as the *pegawai* class – a term which means 'civil servant' and applies to anyone from the lowliest clerk to government ministers. Golkar thus reached down to the village level in Sumatra, seeking to control villagers through their local leaders, themselves ex-servicemen and civil servants.

Village politics, from what I could gather, reflected this national movement. The unofficial as well as official village elite was made up predominantly of government and military officials, most of whom were retired. At the same time West Sumatra, and par-ticularly the highland villages like Sungai Puar, has a long tradition of opposition to the rule from Jakarta. This political confrontation, as we have seen, reached a head in the late 1950s with the outbreak of the P.R.R.I. rebellions. Masjumi, the modernist Muslim party implicated in these rebellions, had a strong following in the village. Even when it was banned, this political force did not disappear. Rather it seems that the Partai Muslimin Indonesia inherited much of its support in West Sumatra.[1] In spite of the over-all clampdown on political activity during the period of my research, the pre-election ban on campaigning and the general reluctance of villagers to discuss any politics with me, it became clear that the P.M.I. had considerable support in Sungai Puar. The P.M.I. meeting held just before the election was the largest public meeting I saw while I lived in the village.

While I have argued that the dominant group in the adminis-tration of village affairs was made up of pensioned *pegawai*, a number of wealthy villagers had some considerable influence as well. It was perhaps the strength of the commercial interests which

1. For a recent discussion of the Partai Muslimin Indonesia see Ward, 1970.

gave the P.M.I. a majority over Golkar in Sungai Puar, one of the few villages in West Sumatra to vote against the new State party.

In terms of both political and administrative structures, therefore, Sungai Puar cannot be considered in isolation. Political splits within the village are closely related to those throughout the nation. And in terms of administrative structure the village government is far from being independent of the Indonesian State administrative apparatus.

Religion

The village forms a religious unit in only a very loose sense. Sungai Puar has not one but five mosques, one in each section. By and large villagers draw no sharp religious boundaries. At the highest level they all consider themselves to be members of the worldwide community of Muslims. Being a Muslim means different things to different people. Mostly it means that the believer has confessed the faith by repeating, in Arabic: 'There is no God but Allah and Muhammed is his prophet.' It means ideally that the adherent observes the five daily prayers (only the Friday midday prayer need be in a mosque). People usually pray in their homes, although some go to one of the many prayer houses (*surau*) in the village. Being a Muslim also means, ideally, that during the month of Ramadhan the believer fasts from sunrise to sunset. It means theoretically that he or she gives alms (*zakat* and *fitrah*) both during the fasting month and at other times. Only for the very few does it mean making the pilgrimage to Mecca (the *haj*).[1] The returned pilgrim is addressed by the honorific *haji*, used in Sumatra for both men and women.

Those who are considered to have a special knowledge of Islam, which includes a rudimentary knowledge of Arabic, are considered to be holy men (*urang siak*) or *ulama*. Their advice may be sought on religious issues. But each individual believer is his own expert. He needs no priest or intermediary to validate his faith.

In fact being a Muslim may mean none of these things. It was my impression that very few people prayed five times a day. Only the very old, the extremely devout, and perhaps more women than men observed the rule. Others simply never said that they did *not* do so. The Friday sermon at the Limo Suku mosque was attended

1. These are the so-called Five Pillars of Islam (cf. Gibb, 1969).

by not even half the adult male population. The fast was observed by many, and yet a large number of people took the fast to mean that they should not be seen to break it. Coffee shops closed down, and eating and smoking took place only behind closed doors. And yet in spite of all these breachings of the formal ritual, no one questioned his own religious conviction.

To be a Muslim in Minangkabau certainly does not mean to take a fatalistic attitude towards any endeavour.[1] The word 'fate' was never used spontaneously in my presence. There is some consensus over what good behaviour should be, particularly behaviour between the sexes, and while Islam combined with other cultural attitudes may inhibit any close interaction between young people of opposite sexes, it certainly does not seem to censure overtly independent attitudes on the part of women. Islam in Minangkabau is far from the patriarchal Islam of the Middle East.

Neither does Islam in Sungai Puar mean intolerance. People are ready to accept other religions on an equal footing. What is unacceptable to villagers is atheism, which they immediately equate with communism. Islam may be used to appeal to the solidarity of the Indonesian people, or to a section of the people. Thus political parties like the P.M.I. the Nahdatul Ulama, Perti, I.P.K.I. and others make appeals for votes on the basis of Muslim solidarity. In certain historical periods religious feeling has run high, and this may account for the seemingly inaccurate reputation of the modern Minangkabau as fanatical Muslims.

The Limo Suku mosque is an impressive stone structure, flanked by a large pool used for ritual washing before prayer, and also for everyday bathing and washing. The mosque has a small staff: the *Imam*, the leader of prayers; the *Khatib*, who delivers some sermons; the *Kadi*, who performs the Muslim marriage ceremonies (*nikah*); and the *Bilal*, who calls the people to prayer. Similarly each clan leader is supposed to have a holy man on his staff who advises group members on religious matters. This office is rarely filled today.

1. Islamic fatalism is often cited as an obstacle to economic development in Malaysia and Indonesia. Swift, for example, makes this point for Islam in Negeri Sembilan (Swift, 1965), and Parkinson attempts to revive this sort of explanation of underdevelopment (Parkinson, 1967). Minangkabau seems, however, to provide an important case in the argument that it is misleading to read off social structure in Muslim societies directly from religious teachings, a point made well by Kessler (1972) at the general level, and by Geertz who shows the variety of interpretations of Islamic doctrine in Java (in Geertz, 1960).

Adat and kinship

An important element in local ideology is the concept of *adat*. The term itself, although in constant use, is highly ambiguous. It is usually translated by anthropologists with the gloss 'customary law'. In its most general form of reference *adat* can mean simply 'the way' — as in 'the way we as Minangkabau do things', or 'the way you as a westerner do things'. In this sense the meaning of the term is remarkably close to such anthropological concepts as 'culture'. More often when *adat* is discussed the speaker is drawing attention to what he takes to be unique about Minangkabau society — in particular to the rules of conduct, inheritance and management of property associated with the system of matrilineal kinship. In this sense *adat* could be translated loosely as tradition, i.e. a single portion of modern culture thought to be derived from the past, and hence set aside from other aspects of culture. Here *adat* serves both to emphasise the importance of matrilineal organisation in Minangkabau, both now and in the past, and to distinguish this body of custom from modern influences, and even from Muslim religious law. In the traditional sayings of the Minangkabau (*papatah*), *adat* is sometimes said to encompass *syarat* (religious law).

While all societies are thought to have their own *adat*, Minangkabau *adat* is said to be special because it is based on principles of matrilineal organisation into clans and lineages known as *suku*. In the following chapter I shall discuss kinship organisation in more detail, particularly as it relates to economic relations in subsistence agriculture. Suffice it to say here that *adat* forms a crucial part of local cosmology and that it is related to property concepts. The vagueness of the term is in part related to the changing role of subsistence agriculture within the Minangkabau social formation (see Kahn, 1976). It would, for example, be unwise to use the modern conception of *adat* as evidence of pre-colonial Minangkabau social organisation, even though it is conceived of in this way by villagers. It is clear, for example, that colonial economic, political and legal organisation of Minangkabau, particularly under the so-called Culture System in the nineteenth century, resulted in a basic reorientation of village life. The Dutch legal system in the East Indies had an important formative influence on modern conceptualisation of *adat*.

25

The economy of Sungai Puar

In later chapters I shall describe in detail the forms of local economic organisation. Here I wish to provide an overview of economic activities in the modern Minangkabau village. There are two
main forms. The first consists of the production and distribution
of commodities, using the term in the sense given to it by Marx,
i.e. goods which are produced for exchange (exchange by the
owner of the product). The second form of economic activity
consists of the production of goods for immediate consumption.
The main commodities produced in Limo Suku are steel tools and
clothing. The former are forged by blacksmiths, all of whom are
men. The latter are made by the large number of women who sew
in their own homes. Subsistence production is represented by the
cultivation of rice on irrigated fields (*sawah*). Property relations
in the two sectors differ. Commodities are in almost all cases
produced by individuals or small groups. The means of production
are individually owned. The blacksmiths' tools and workshops,
and the sewing machines, are of a type of property known as
harto pancarian, or 'earned property'. Rice as a subsistence
product, on the other hand, is grown on terraced fields classified
as *harto pusako*, or ancestral property.

The two forms of property are subject to different systems of
inheritance. *Harto pancarian* can be passed on to children of either
sex. While it is commonly assumed that such property is divided
according to Muslim law, it seems rather to be subject to a more
general bilateral system of kinship found in many parts of
Malaysia and Indonesia. Thus villagers argue that acquired property
owned by women is passed on to their daughters, while men's
property is inherited by their sons. The rules for the inheritance
of acquired property seem to be relatively flexible. The owner,
should he choose, is free to sell acquired property.

Ancestral property, however, is always in the possession of
women, and almost always passes from mother to daughter(s).
As we shall see in the next chapter, all transfers of rights in
ancestral property are closely supervised by the kin group as a
whole.

In Sungai Puar, and in Limo Suku in particular, certain characteristics of both subsistence and commodity production serve to
link the local economy directly to the outside world. Subsistence

26

rice cultivators produce only enough rice to feed the villagers for two months out of every year. There are a large number of families completely without access to irrigated rice land. Except for a few families, therefore, the people of Limo Suku must buy the bulk of their rice in the market – rice which is grown both elsewhere in Indonesia and overseas.

The production of commodities for the market is highly specialised. Blacksmiths turn out primarily agricultural implements, while seamstresses make children's clothes. Some fruits and vegetables are locally grown. Otherwise villagers rely heavily on the market for their consumption needs. Apart from rice, villagers buy a wide variety of foodstuffs, cloth, paraffin, stoves, lanterns, bicycles, house-building materials, clothing, shoes, and radios in local and Bukit Tinggi markets. The Wednesday and Saturday market days in Bukit Tinggi see a large-scale exodus of villagers to the town both to sell locally produced commodities and to shop for food and other goods.

Commodities produced in Limo Suku have a primarily local market – extending at most only throughout the island of Sumatra. Commodities produced in other parts of Minangkabau, however, are exported. Rubber, coffee, coconut oil, copra and tea are some of the main exports. Goods purchased by villagers come both from Indonesia itself and from overseas. Even the simplest of manufactured goods are imported into Indonesia from Hong Kong, Singapore, Japan and the West.

While the only obvious direct contact with the world-economy is through the market, it is clear that the village is closely linked economically to the outside world because of a national and international division of labour. Only when we consider this system as a whole can we fully understand the nature and forms of local economic organisation.

Demographic patterns and migration

The statistics on demography, occupation, land tenure and the like presented here and in later chapters are compiled from a census which I carried out after about six months of research in Sungai Puar. The census covered a total of 394 households and included questions on a wide range of characteristics of household composition, household economic activities, migration and demography. This census was confined to the section of Limo Suku, which alone had a population of more than 3,000 residents. A preliminary survey covered about 10 per cent of households. The census — both because the preliminary 10 per cent sample was eliminated, and because a certain number of people either refused to cooperate, or were unavailable for questioning — covered just over 75 per cent of the population of Limo Suku. At the end of the year I carried out a re-census of the same sample of 394 households in order to gather material on changes in composition, but also to ask some additional questions. Unless otherwise stated, statistics presented below are based on these two censuses.

Data gathered by the Sungai Puar mayor's office give some picture of the total population (see Table 2.1). These figures can be compared with data from my own sample in the section of Limo Suku. A total of 394 occupied houses were included in the census with a total resident population of 2,568, i.e. a survey of 76 per cent of the resident population of Limo Suku.

Demographic data were collected from each individual household. In most cases this meant constructing a genealogy of household members, so as to include in the census all those migrants still remembered by occupants. Migration, as the figures show, has an important effect on the composition of the resident population.

Minangkabau villagers today almost all adhere to the cultural preference for uxorilocal residence. In many cases this means that a single house is occupied by members of a joint family. In such instances it is usual for married sisters to remain in their parental home together. It is unusual for more distantly related female kin to live together. Even when a newly married couple builds a new house together, the general tendency is to build next to or close to the house of the wife's mother. This accounts for the pattern of clustering of households whose female and unmarried occupants form a matrilineage segment. It should be noted that while this tendency may be stronger in Minangkabau, it is not untypical of Indonesia and Malaysia as a whole, even in non-matrilineal areas (see Siegel, 1969, who describes a similar situation for Aceh).

Married men in the sample were in most cases recorded twice. They were recorded both in their parental homes and in their wives' homes, when both were included in the sample. The purpose of this procedure was to establish affinal links between

28

Table 2.1 *Population of Sungai Puar**

Section	Number of houses	Occupied	Empty	Total population
Galung	207	160	25	937
Tangah Koto	249	194	33	1,249
Limo Suku	708	599	86	3,376
Limo Kampuang	325	227	19	1,482
Kapalo Koto	486	390	67	2,236
Total	1,975	1,570	230	9,280

*Source: Kantor Wali Nagari Sungai Puar, 20 January 1971. The disparities in these figures, when pointed out to the mayor, were never satisfactorily explained.

households. However, the population figures given here are calculated using only the recording of married men in their wives' homes.

Table 2.2 summarises these data. It is a breakdown of the total population, both residents and migrants, by age.

The total population in the sample is 5,002. While I have not calculated birth and death rates, and while there are no reliable figures on which to base an estimate of population growth rate for the village, the age breakdown presented here gives a good picture of the rapid growth in over-all population. More than half the total population is under the age of twenty. The two largest cohorts are those aged four years and under, and those aged between five and nine.

This over-all total can be broken down along lines of sex and residence. Of the total population of 5,002 recorded above, 52 per cent are female and 48 per cent male. Tables 2.3 and 2.4 give a picture of the different nature of resident and migrant populations.

Of residents of Limo Suku, 42.1 per cent are male and 57.9 per cent are female. The relative preponderance of female residents in almost all age groups is in contrast to the relatively greater numbers of males in the migrant population.

These figures on migration from a single Minangkabau village can serve to illustrate some general points about the pattern known as *marantau*, described by Mochtar Naim, a Minangkabau sociologist (Naim, 1971). *Marantau* is a verb which means, literally,

29

Table 2.2 *Population of village sample (residents and migrants) by age*

Age	Absolute frequency	Relative frequency (per cent)	Cumulative frequency (per cent)
0–4	775	15.5	15.5
5–9	773	15.5	31.0
10–14	611	12.2	43.2
15–19	542	10.8	54.0
20–24	354	7.1	61.1
25–29	287	5.7	66.8
30–34	262	5.2	72.0
35–39	282	5.6	77.6
40–44	262	5.2	82.8
45–49	179	3.6	86.4
50–54	191	3.8	90.2
55–59	99	2.0	92.2
60–64	150	3.0	95.2
65–69	75	1.5	96.7
70–74	76	1.5	98.2
75–79	23	0.5	98.7
80–84	25	0.5	99.2
85–89	6	0.1	99.3
90–94	11	0.2	99.5
95+	19	0.4	99.9
Total	5,002		

to go to the Rantau or outlying territories of Minangkabau. Today it is used to refer to migrants from highland villages and, more broadly, to all those people who, while they may be resident elsewhere, retain social and economic links with the village itself. Included in this cultural category, then, are both long-term and temporary migrants, as well as some people who were not born in the village at all.

Naim has estimated that there are as many Minangkabau living outside the home province of West Sumatra as there are living in their traditional homeland. Migrants from Minangkabau preserve a firm feeling of cultural identity. There is a strong association of

Table 2.3 *Village residents by age and sex*

Age	Frequency		Relative frequency		Cumulative frequency	
	Male	Female	Male	Female	Male	Female
0–4	187	183	17.3	12.3	17.3	12.3
5–9	206	206	19.1	13.9	36.4	26.2
10–14	165	166	15.3	11.2	51.6	37.4
15–19	111	166	10.3	11.2	61.9	48.6
20–24	69	79	6.4	5.3	68.3	53.9
25–29	46	77	4.3	5.2	72.7	59.1
30–34	41	73	3.8	4.9	76.3	64.0
35–39	51	89	4.7	6.0	81.0	70.0
40–44	52	85	4.8	5.7	85.8	75.7
45–49	38	56	3.5	3.8	89.4	79.5
50–54	26	71	2.4	4.8	91.8	84.3
55–59	25	39	2.3	2.6	94.1	86.9
60–64	22	81	2.0	5.4	96.1	92.3
65–69	14	31	1.3	2.1	97.4	94.4
70–74	11	43	1.0	2.9	98.4	97.3
75–79	7	11	0.6	0.7	99.1	98.0
80–84	3	19	0.3	1.3	99.4	99.3
85–89	3	2	0.3	0.1	99.6	99.4
90–94	3	6	0.3	0.4	99.9	99.8
95+	1	4	0.1	0.3	100.0	100.1
Total	1,081	1,487				

Minangkabau migrants with Islam, particularly in its modernist forms. Migrants express a preference for certain cultural trappings as well as for specific occupations, most notably petty trading. They make frequent visits to their home village and maintain close contact with kin and fellow villagers in the place of migration. Identification with the home community often results in migrants buying a house and land in the home village. In this way they retain a social identity in the village even after many years' absence, and many return to their village to retire.

It should be stressed that these features of the so-called Minangkabau *marantau* are by no means distinctly Minangkabau. Nor do they apply to all Minangkabau migrants. They represent a cultural ideal and do not correlate strictly with actual practice.

It has been estimated (Naim, 1971) that several hundred thousand people of Minangkabau origin are living in Jakarta, the Indonesian capital. Some familiarity with patterns of dress, occu-

Table 2.4 *Migrants by age and sex*

Age	Frequency		Relative frequency		Cumulative frequency	
	Male	Female	Male	Female	Male	Female
0–4	184	202	14.2	18.4	14.2	18.4
5–9	171	188	13.2	17.2	27.3	35.6
10–14	162	117	12.5	10.7	39.8	46.3
15–19	144	120	11.1	10.9	50.9	57.2
20–24	120	86	9.2	7.8	60.2	65.1
25–29	93	69	7.2	6.3	67.3	71.4
30–34	75	72	5.8	6.6	73.1	77.9
35–39	71	70	5.5	6.4	78.6	84.3
40–44	77	47	5.9	4.3	84.5	88.6
45–49	52	33	4.0	3.0	88.5	91.6
50–54	59	34	4.5	3.1	93.1	94.7
55–59	19	16	1.4	1.5	94.5	96.2
60–64	29	18	2.2	1.6	96.8	97.8
65–69	20	10	1.5	0.9	98.3	98.7
70–74	16	5	2.2	0.5	99.5	99.2
75–79	1	3	0.1	0.3	99.6	99.5
80–84	2	1	0.2	0.1	99.8	99.5
85–89	0	1	0.0	0.1	99.8	99.6
90–94	1	1	0.1	0.1	99.9	99.7
95+	1	3	0.1	0.3	100.0	100.0
Total	1,298	1,096				

pational specialisation, eating habits and the like allows the observer to pick them out of the crowd. The small pedlars selling their wares on the pavement – a style of selling known as *manggaleh kaki limo* – are more often than not Minangkabau. Minangkabau migrants, with other Sumatrans, prefer a style of dress which they take to be more Islamic than that of the Javanese. The city abounds with small restaurants known as *Nasi Padang* (Padang Rice), in which the hot, spicy Minangkabau food is prepared and served by Minangkabau migrants. Many of the small shops in Jakarta's market-place are owned and run by Minangkabau merchants. It is perhaps these migrants who are most immediately noticeable by non-Minangkabau, who have given the Minangkabau, or *orang Padang* (men of Padang) as they are known, their stereotyped image.

There are others, however, who are less prominent. They work as highly successful merchants owning and managing larger establishments modelled on Western shops. Others are active in the religious movements, such as Muhammadiyah, or in political parties and the government. Minangkabau also work in the arts and entertainment, in factories and shops, in schools and universities as teachers and students, as doctors and nurses – in short, in all occupational categories.

While many Minangkabau migrants bring their children up to follow the cultural pattern, speaking the highly valued regional dialect, some have largely given up their cultural identity. These have either joined a growing group of people whose primary association is national rather than ethnic, or adopted the traits of one of Indonesia's other ethnic groups.[1] While many people keep in close contact with their home villages, others do not. It was my impression in Jakarta that cultural identification varied greatly among Minangkabau there, and that the identification took different forms among different groups of people. The middle traders seemed to feel the identity most strongly, and acted the role of devout yet tolerant Muslims, and of rather boisterous and impolite people in contrast with the refined and obsequious Javanese. Those in the higher realms of the civil service, and particularly those with a higher education, took a great interest in Minangkabau *adat* and history. Indeed, West Sumatra seems to have produced more than its share of anthropologists. On the other hand, poor labourers and the like considerably underplayed their part as Minangkabau, often perhaps concealing their ethnic affiliation.

Migrants from a number of different parts of West Sumatra have formed associations in Jakarta of *nagari*-mates. The Sungai Puar association is not very active, and yet it manages to collect funds annually to send back to aid projects like school- and mosque-building in the village.

Large numbers of people from Sungai Puar migrate to other parts of Java, to East Indonesia, West Irian, Kalimantan and to places outside Indonesia altogether. Minangkabau also make up a sizeable proportion of the population of most cities in Sumatra outside their home province. Medan, Pakan Baru, Jambi and Palembang all have large numbers of Minangkabau residents.

1. For one view of the importance of ethnicity in Indonesian cities see Bruner, 1974, although elsewhere I have taken issue with the tendency to treat ethnic differentiation as a principle of social structure (Kahn, 1978).

The movement of people out of their home villages is illustrated in Table 2.5. This describes all those people recorded in the census living outside the village section according to place of residence.

Minangkabau residents in urban Indonesia, as we have seen, exhibit varying degrees of ethnic identity. Similarly, migrants differ according to the relative length of time they spend outside their home villages. It is not unusual, for example, for a person born and brought up in Padang, the provincial capital, to answer a question about his home town (*kampuang*) by referring to a village in the Minangkabau highlands which he may have either never seen or only visited briefly. At the other extreme is a large bloc of town residents whose stay is only temporary. They may be villagers trying their luck in the market as small traders. Many of them return to their village after a short period of town residence. Some townspeople are traders or merchants who travel from place to place, buying things in one part of the province and selling them in another. In the smaller market towns Minangkabau traders rent shops or stalls to which they come only on market days. The rest of the time they may spend in their home villages, or in travelling to other markets. According to villagers, traders in the past were constantly on the move. Men left their wives and children behind while they made the rounds of markets in the area.

Table 2.5 *Migrants from Limo Suku by place of migration*

Place of migration	Number	Relative frequency (per cent)
Sungai Puar (outside Limo Suku)	23	1.0
Agam District, including the municipality of Bukit Tinggi	294	12.3
Other parts of West Sumatra	882	36.8
Other parts of Sumatra	892	37.3
Java	288	12.0
Indonesia, other than Java and Sumatra	6	0.3
Outside Indonesia	2	0.1
No information	7	0.3

Internal and external in a Minangkabau village

If Padang remains in many ways a temporary base for Minang-kabau migrants, many of whom consider themselves to be members of a village community elsewhere, this is even more the case for Bukit Tinggi. Because it is in the cultural heartland, it is even easier for people to work in Bukit Tinggi while retaining close links with one of the *nagari* of the Agam district. This is especially true for the people from Sungai Puar who live so close to the district capital. The mobility of these people is illustrated by the following cases:

Bakar is the principal of a school in Bukit Tinggi. His wife, Ati, is a school-teacher. They return almost once a week to Limo Suku, to the home of Ati's parents. Her father, a retired government employee, spent most of his working life out of the village. Bakar and Ati are present in Limo Suku for all important family occasions. They were present, for example, throughout the period of the wedding of Ati's brother. When Ati had a bicycle accident in Bukit Tinggi, she returned to her parents' home to recover. She returned to the village after the birth of her third child to stay with her parents, who looked after all three children during the day when Ati went off to Bukit Tinggi to teach.

Edi works as a blacksmith in Bukit Tinggi, and lives there with his wife. He moved about five years ago, and returns about twice a year to visit his widowed mother. Edi's father was also a smith, with a workshop in Bukit Tinggi. His mother moved back to Limo Suku when her husband stopped working. Edi also sends money to help his mother out when he can.

Azwar has worked in the past as a petty trader, selling bits of stamped metal decorations produced by friends in Limo Suku. He returned to Limo Suku every evening, and spent nights and free days with his wife and children. At that time Azwar's son accompanied him to Bukit Tinggi daily; the son attended a technical school there. Both have now stopped going daily to Bukit Tinggi, and they now work together making the goods they previously only sold. Azwar now goes to Bukit Tinggi only twice a week, on market days, to sell his wares.

Djon is 32 and his wife Rosna is 29. Djon has, for eight years, sold cloth and clothing in the Bukit Tinggi market. His wife and three children now live with him in a rented house in the market town, but his second child, a boy, lives with Rosna's parents in Limo Suku. The family visits the village frequently, and they occasionally leave other children to stay with Rosna's parents. In fact the mobility between the two households makes it extremely difficult to treat them as separate domestic units. It would be more accurate to describe

35

this as a three-generation joint family divided between two essentially common or shared residences.

Svan went to Bukit Tinggi five years ago to find some sort of work. He found a smith who made aluminium spoons to sell in the market. Svan went to work for this man, and has worked there ever since. He has married a woman from Bukit Tinggi, yet he still returns to Limo Suku about once every month to visit his mother, father and younger sister. Since his father has taken a second wife, Svan also helps his mother by sending her extra money when he can spare it. She cannot support herself and her daughter on their small plot of land and the small amount of money she can earn from weaving mats.

Afril and his wife lived for a number of years in Bukit Tinggi. He sold odds and ends in the street. Two years ago he got together enough money to rent a small shop in the East Sumatran town of Pakan Baru, and he now sells steel goods, some of which are produced in Sungai Puar. Now that they have moved to Pakan Baru they do not return to Limo Suku so often.

These cases are quite typical. They show how difficult it is to differentiate the rural from the urban, at least in West Sumatra. Towns differ from villages largely because towns are both bureaucratic and distributive centres for the surrounding regions. As I shall have occasion to note in later chapters, the structure of the distributive network does not differ greatly from the organisation of production in the rural areas. Particularly for those people who work as traders, the social cleavage between town and country – between migrants and non-migrants – is not great.

Some of these general points about the Minangkabau pattern of *marantau* are illustrated in the statistics on the Limo Suku sample census (see Tables 2.3 and 2.4). The figures show that men are more likely than women to migrate. While many male migrants take their families with them, and while there are working female migrants as well, a large number of migrants are men who leave the village on their own to seek work in towns and cities both in West Sumatra and in other parts of the country. Young, unmarried men leave the village as a matter of course in search of employment, although many return within a short time. Many other men live and work at a considerable distance from the village, and leave their wives and children behind.

The data also show that the migrant population is, on the whole, younger than the resident. This is because the migrant population

is composed mainly of working people, i.e. of people in the productive age groups. The older migrants frequently return to the
village as soon as they stop working. The village in a way, then,
serves as a kind of domestic base for migrants. Many leave their
children behind in the care of grandparents or other kin. Old
people retire to the village where they live on kin aid as well as
subsistence rice cultivation. In demographic, social and economic
terms it is impossible to speak of the migrant population in
isolation from its village base, just as the village cannot be
conceived of without taking into account the role of migrants.[1]
Finally, migration has served as an outlet for surplus population
for at least the past ten to twenty years, and probably since the
turn of the century, resulting in very low growth rates in the rural
area. This is in marked contrast to the rapid rate of population
increase in urban areas — a result of migration as much as, if not
more than, of natural increase in these areas.

To the anthropologist and to the residents the West Sumatran
a *nagari* appears to be an autonomous social whole. Physical
boundaries appear to coincide with social reality. The ideal Minangkabau community is both isolated and self-sufficient, its autonomy
symbolised in the mosque, the lineage houses, the rice fields and
the dry land. It is true that contact is frequently established with
the world outside. Migrants leave in search of a living, goods are
bought and sold in the regional market, and yet these links appear
to be unstable, impermanent and relatively unimportant. Minangkabau migrants appear to form an extension of the village community, temporary residents at best in the external world. Traders
in the market themselves belong to the local community, and hence
market relations themselves are rarely impersonal.

Yet even such a cursory analysis of religion, politics, administration and economics in a Minangkabau village shows such
boundaries to be artificial. To say that the village is incorporated
within a wider society is itself an unhelpful metaphor which
preserves the dichotomy between internal and external and hence
accepts the primacy of these two physically bounded spheres

---

1. I shall have occasion to return to this aspect of the village economy. I have elsewhere
(Kahn, 1974) tried to argue that a transfer of surplus through unequal exchange is the
result, at least in the first instance, of the fact that labour power is partially reproduced
through the subsistence sector of the peasant economy. More recently Meillassoux has
made a similar point about migrant labour in Africa (Meillassoux, 1975).

of social interaction. This is not to say that the village of Sungai Puar can be taken as a microcosm of the wider society, the great tradition writ small. The national and world system of which Sungai Puar forms a part is clearly not made up of homogeneous units or peasant villages alone.

Before we can properly consider the nature of this totality, as well as the specific set of structures which relate villages like Sungai Puar to other segments, we must look more closely at other aspects of local social organisation and seize the concrete situation in all its complexity. I turn first, therefore, to a consideration of kinship and land tenure in Sungai Puar before looking at other aspects of local economic organisation.

3

Adat, kinship and marriage: the constitution of the subsistence community

To render intelligible the concrete world of a modern Minangkabau village, to say nothing of the world of Minangkabau scholarship, is to enter the discourse on *adat* and matrilineal kinship. This is no less important for the world of concrete economic behaviour than for the realm of ritual. While, therefore, my main aim in the following chapters is to present a preliminary analysis of the peasant economy of the Minangkabau, in this chapter it is necessary to deal with the relations between local models of social organisation and the basic economic relations in a Minangkabau *nagari*.

I have pointed out that it is useful to distinguish between two sectors of the peasant economy, one concerned with subsistence production and the other with the production and distribution of commodities. Little sense can be made, at least of the former, without an understanding of the local models of kinship organisation, the relation between kinship and residence patterns and the role of *adat* in the system of land tenure.

Adat as conceptual system

The role of kinship and *adat* in defining property relations for the Minangkabau villager has changed considerably in this century. The change, as we shall see in a later chapter, is not simply one from a 'traditional' to a modern system. Instead, kinship has played a number of different roles in the history of Minangkabau, its form having evolved in accordance with these functional changes. The role of kinship organisation during the period of the Minangkabau kingdom, in the period of mercantile domination and in the modern context, has been a constantly changing one.

These changes are not entirely accounted for within the modern conceptualisation of kinship and *adat* in the Minangkabau village

39

(see Figure 3.1). People of Sungai Puar conceive of their kinship system as a relatively eternal, systematic and symmetrical mode of social organisation based on the matrilineal kin group or *suku*. *Suku* is a broad term and can be used to refer to any of a number of different levels of kin grouping. At its most inclusive a *suku* is one of four pan-Minangkabau phratries founded by the matrilineal descendants of the two Culture Heroes: Datuak Parpatiah nan Sabatang and Datuak Katumangguangan. These four *suku* are named Koto, Piliang, Bodi and Caniago and grouped into two moieties. Although neither the moieties nor the phratries correspond to discrete territorial units, every village in Minangkabau is associated with one or other moiety. Moiety affiliation has certain consequences for modern local organisation, although none of the villagers is very clear on the differences (cf. Josselin de Jong, 1951, 51f.).

At the next level down, the system of segmentation becomes more complicated. Each *nagari* is associated with one of the moieties but is also made up of members of a number of *suku*, which represent, in some sense, segments of the four phratries. In Sungai Puar there are five such village-level *suku* which I have called clans: Koto, Piliang, Sikumbang, Pisang and Malayu. Again these are not territorially distinct. Each section of the village has representative segments of each of the five village clans. Limo Suku (Five Clans), as the name implies, has lineages from each of the five *suku*.

I have suggested that clans are segments of the pan-Minangkabau phratries because it is said by some villagers that each of these clans is linked to one of the four phratries. At least today, however, these links are tenuous, and no one was able to trace them, with the exception of the clans Koto and Piliang, which were obviously linked with the phratries of the same names. Interpretations of the phratry affiliations of the other three clans – Pisang, Sikumbang and Malayu – were confusing as well as confused. Some people went so far as to deny any such link.

Different *nagari* have different clans, and the number is not a constant five. In Bungus, a coastal fishing village, there were seven clans.

In Sungai Puar today the clans are little more than ideally exogamous, named units. The two largest of these – Koto and Piliang – are divided into subclans, referred to by the clan name with the addition of a qualifying term. Koto Gobah, Koto Musajik and Koto Salek Batuang, for example, are three subclans within the clan Koto. The subclans are neither territorially distinct nor politically corporate.

The clans and subclans are further divided into unnamed segments, also termed *suku*, each headed by a chief or *panghulu* (term of address: *Datuak*). These segments, which I choose to call lineages,[1] are groups of people related matrilineally and, in Sungai Puar, with a single office of leadership. The pattern is slightly different elsewhere. In Bungus each village-level clan is headed by a *panghulu*, while in Sungai Puar there are no clan leaders. Even the lineage may not be territorially distinct. A lineage of average size may consist of two or three household clusters and several isolated households in different parts of the village section. In almost all cases the households belonging to a single lineage were located in one of the five sections (*jorong*) of the village.

In Limo Suku section there are 64 such lineage groups. These may be distinguished from the clan, whose name they hold, by referring to the honorary title (*gala*) of the chief of the lineage group. This title remains the same even when a new chief is installed in office. In referring to his lineage someone might say: 'Kami kamanakan Datuak Rangkayo nan Gadang' This means: 'We are the sisters' children of the chief whose title is Richman the Big.' 'Sisters' children' is used in the classificatory sense here, without regard to generation, to refer to all lineage-mates of the chief, even though the chief himself may be of a junior generation. This lineage is one of the thirty segments of the clan Koto in Limo Suku, and is at the same time a segment of the subclan Koto Musajik.

The process may be explained by Figure 3.2, where I have outlined the way the villagers conceptualise the segmentation of the clan Koto. Across the whole village section this clan is divided into three subclans – Koto Gobah, Koto Musajik and Koto Salek

1. I use the term 'lineage' here to refer to the lowest level of kin group in Sungai Puar with a single leader, the *panghulu*. The term is traditionally used by anthropologists to refer to a unilineal descent group in which all kin ties among its members are known. This is not quite the case here – there is some disagreement over the exact ties to the common ancestress. Lineages are made up of smaller segments, in which the ties are clearer. However, these smaller groups are informal, they are not separately named, nor do they have a formal leadership structure. Hence I retain lineage for the higher-level group.

Minangkabau social formations

Territorial framework

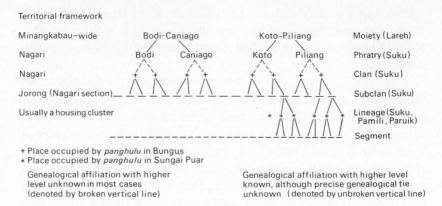

Figure 3.1 Levels of kinship organisation in Minangkabau (from Kahn, 1976)

Figure 3.2 Segmentation of Koto Clan in Sungai Puar (from Kahn, 1976)

Batuang — and each of these has representative lineages in each of the five village sections. The leaders of closely related lineages within the subclan often bear similar *gala*. This is presumed to be the result of fission in the recent past. When a lineage becomes too large, the villagers assert, a segment within it might elect its own *panghulu* and split away, with the permission of the members of the mother lineage. The new *panghulu* is then expected to retain the title of the mother segment, either in the same form or with the addition of a qualifier. For example, the lineage of Datuak Tumangguang split into two segments at some time in the past. The mother segment, it is thought, retained the title of Datuak Tumangguang for its *panghulu*. The daughter lineage retained the title but added the qualifier 'nan Kayo' (the Rich), presumably because the first holder of the office was thought to be exceptionally wealthy. In the other case illustrated in Figure 3.2

(descendants of Datuak Rangkayo nan Gadang), the segments all
retained the title unaltered. They are distinguished by using the
given name of the present holder of the *panghulu*-ship, e.g. 'We
are the sisters' children of Yahya Datuak Rangkayo nan Gadang'
(Yahya being the given name of the present *panghulu*). Whatever
may have been the case in the past, all lineage segments in Sungai
Puar today are, to all intents and purposes, of equal rank, regardless of their point of segmentation. This holds also for the various
panghulu. While it has been suggested that in some *nagari* one
panghulu from each clan was given the title *panghulu pucuak*,
denoting higher status, such is not the case for Sungai Puar. There
were vague rumblings about certain superior lines, as well as certain
especially respected *panghulu*, but I was never able to get a
coherent account of status differentials. My impression was that
at least in present circumstances such differences as may exist are
based not so much on formal status differentials as on the varying
personal qualities of office-holders. One *panghulu* in Sungai Puar
managed to preserve a high status because he claimed to know a
great deal about *adat* and history, and because he was able to
convince others of his esoteric knowledge through a certain
arrogance in bearing. When I tried to pin him down to a discussion
of particular *adat* esoterica he, like many others, suggested I have
a look at a book by a knowledgeable Dutchman who understood
the whole thing better than anyone.

It is recognised that fusion of *suku* may take place as well as
fission. When a lineage is reduced in size for some reason it may
then fuse with what is taken to be a closely related lineage. In the
past it is said groups came from outside the *nagari* and were
expected to attach themselves (*malakok*) to one of the original
lineages. Villagers from Sungai Puar living in neighbouring *nagari*
similarly join a lineage closely related to their own. While in the
past this process too may have implied important changes in status
(see Bachtiar, 1967), today such differentials are relatively insignificant.

With the declining importance of the *suku*, the office of *panghulu* is today not always filled after the death of the incumbent.
This situation arises if lineage members are not prepared to bear
the expense of the ceremony necessary to install a new *panghulu*
(the *baralek badatuak*), because there is no member of the lineage
willing to take on the duties of the *panghulu*-ship (which in most

cases go largely unrewarded), or because lineage members cannot agree among themselves upon a likely successor. A lineage without a living *panghulu* may still be referred to by the honorary title of the office, or it may fuse eventually with another lineage. For the *panghulu*-ship of Datuak Rangkayo nan Gadang there are two such cases, in which a separate lineage has been preserved in spite of the fact that the office of *panghulu* has not been filled.

This model of the formal aspects of *suku* organisation is consciously adhered to by almost every person in Sungai Puar. The description derives from my own fieldwork, and therefore depicts the present situation, not the past. It has of course evolved out of the past, but the nature of that evolution has been much more complex than is perceived by the villagers (see Kahn, 1976). For contained within the villagers' view of *adat* is a conception of change remarkably close to that of the social scientist when studying social change. The idea that *suku* are no longer as important as before, that therefore the office of *panghulu* is not always filled, that the egalitarianism of *adat* relations has tended to give way in the face of modernisation — these are all part of the way modern Minangkabau conceive of their tradition. While, as we shall see in later chapters, the role of the *panghulu* and the function of *suku* organisation have varied in important respects historically, in the eyes of the villagers the modern *suku* system has been essentially carried over from the past. As they see it, the aspects of life associated with *suku* organisation — the leadership of the *panghulu*, marriage ritual, and possession of ancestral property — are all aspects of their traditional system of organisation, which has undergone changes only recently, as a result of contact with the West.

This impression is strengthened by the work of a number of scholars who, in discussing matriliny in West Sumatra, attribute its changing role in village life to economic changes in this century. Maretin, for example, suggests (1961) that the decline of matrilineal organisation in Minangkabau resulted largely from twentieth-century historical processes. Schrieke (1955) argues similarly that the commercial changes following the end of the Culture System in West Sumatra led to a breakdown of *suku* structure. While I shall attempt to show that this oversimplifies the pre-twentieth-century situation, these analyses have the virtue of accurately describing the modern Minangkabau ideology of social change.

The villagers attribute certain virtues to *suku* solidarity. This idea of solidarity evidently does have some effect on interpersonal behaviour, by strengthening or relaxing general rules of interaction based on sex and age. For example, unmarried people of opposite sexes are expected to avoid each other as much as possible, although this rule is a little less strict for closely related girls and boys. Similarly, one is expected to show great deference and respect to people older than oneself. This respect is especially demanded by older lineage-mates, even in their absence, as the following extract from my notes shows:

Akmal is a young man of about 20 years old. He is not hesitant about revealing his frank opinion of older men in the village, although he is always respectful when he meets them face to face. One day a group of us were discussing his mother's brother, a man of about 50 who had been involved in a number of doubtful ventures, and was generally considered to be unreliable. Indeed many people openly gossiped about him when he was not around. While I felt that Akmal clearly had similar feelings about his uncle he never discussed them with me. In the critical discussion about his mother's brother Akmal refused to participate, although he was an active participant in similar gossip sessions about other people. I was later told by a neighbour of Akmal's that he would be embarrassed even to overhear anything derogatory about his mother's brother.

In general the mother's brother is thought to have a responsibility towards his sisters' children (*kamanakan*). Most older men in the village take this to mean that they must keep an eye on their sisters' household. When possible they make a special effort to pass by their sisters' house, although they rarely actually go inside. One man told me that this was in order to make himself available if his advice was needed without appearing to be interfering. This is in fact a very accurate picture of the true role of the mother's brother today. In spite of arguments to the contrary by villagers when discussing *adat* ideals, the mother's brother is no longer a guardian of his *kamanakan*, whether or not he may have been in the past. A father is thought to be responsible for the needs of his own children. School fees, for example, as well as responsibility for higher education, lie with the father. The only substantive role of the mother's brother has to do with the administration of his sister's ancestral property.

Interaction with kin is not restricted in any way to matrilineal ties. While uxorilocal residence means that female lineage-mates

45

see a good deal of each other, there is a tendency for people to make frequent visits to other kin in other parts of the village. During Hari Raya, the festival at the end of the fasting month, for example, visits are paid to a wide range of kin on both sides of the family, as well as to neighbours and friends. A man is expected to take his children often to his parents and sisters. In fact a good deal of emphasis is placed on these ties to the father's kin known as *bako*.

The importance of bilateral ties as well as ties of common residence is brought out in almost all *adat* ceremonies. Weddings, the most important of such ceremonies for the average villager, are the responsibility of the matrilineal kin. They are attended, however, by a wide range of kin from both sides of the family and by friends and neighbours. Similar, although smaller, gatherings are held to mark a death, when there are several evenings of Koran reading and group prayer (*basalawaik*).

A basic feature of all such ceremonies is that at least one meal is eaten by the guests in the house in which the ceremony takes place. Since all guests enter the house, eat a meal and usually leave quickly, it is rare for large numbers of guests to sit around together for any period of time. When they do, as for example during the ritualised speechmaking (*sambah-manyambah*) at weddings and *panghulu* installations, the lineage tie is rarely stressed to the exclusion of others. In fact, many people at weddings informed me that the main function of the practice of six people eating from a single plate (*makan bajambah*) is to allow a free mixing of people from different groups.

Adat and marriage

'People of the same *suku* may not marry' – this is perhaps the most frequently cited consequence of Minangkabau *adat*. As for other general statements about their *adat*, however, here too Minangkabau seem to delight in their ambiguity. As we have seen, the referent of *suku* itself is ambiguous, and informants saw little difficulty even if it were pointed out to them that there were many cases of clan endogamy. In practice marriages between members of the same clan, and indeed the same subclan, frequently occur. The real exogamous unit is the lineage.

Lineage exogamy is accompanied by a clearly stated preference

46

for village endogamy. In Sungai Puar no formal rule of endogamy exists, although other *nagari* do have such rules (cf. Junus, 1964). Nevertheless, of 838 marriages recorded in my census, 720 were between *nagari*-mates. The other 118 were between Sungai Puar women and men from elsewhere, since the recording of married men only in their wife's home was used in the analysis of data.

The preference for village endogamy is most strongly brought out when men from other localities come to live in the village with their Sungai Puar brides. In the mixed marriages cited above, only fifteen of the couples were resident in Limo Suku at the time of my census. Ninety-five other such couples lived outside the village altogether. The remaining eight were residing separately, the husbands living and working outside the village and the wives remaining behind.

It might be said that the function of village endogamy is to prevent outsiders from gaining access to village ancestral land, and indeed there is a close correlation between access to irrigated rice land in the village and a woman's marriage choice. Of the women in the Limo Suku sample who married men from outside the village, 67 per cent were landless, as compared with 48 per cent of all the women in that group. Moreover, while 26 per cent of all married women have access to land yielding 120 kilograms or more, this was true of only 12 per cent of the women who married outsiders. Of local men who have taken wives from outside the village, 71 per cent are landless in their parental home.

The Minangkabau follow Muslim marriage law, as well as the prescriptions of *adat*. It is therefore theoretically possible for a man to have up to four wives at one time. Polygyny is, however, rare today. Of 838 married women, only 21 are married to men who have at least one other wife. Of these, five husbands have taken their second wife from outside the village. Frequently a male migrant will take a second wife in the town in which he lives, and simply not bother to divorce his village wife, even if he has no intention of returning to her, or supporting her. These five cases are all of men who have lived outside the village for several years, and it seems likely that their first marriages had in fact broken up.

Of the 21 polygynous men, 16 had two wives, two had three wives, and for the remaining three information was not available. It is quite possible that there were more cases of polygyny than

I was able to record, as men are reluctant to admit it. However, it remains that polygyny is relatively rare.

Josselin de Jong, in his study of Minangkabau (1951), argues that, at least in the past, Minangkabau *suku* were linked by a system of prescribed or preferential cross-cousin marriage. The result, he suggests, was a system of circulating connubium (the result of marriage between a man and his matrilateral cross-cousin). Whatever the case in the past, there is no such general rule in Sungai Puar today. The occurrence is sufficiently frequent, however, for there to be a term to describe it. When a woman marries her FZS (father's sister's son) it is said that she has 'pulang ka rumah bako', i.e. returned to the home of her father's kin. This expression is used most frequently to refer to a woman's marriage either to a real patrilateral cross-cousin, or to a male member of her father's lineage segment (a man from her father's house of origin or housing cluster). It is used occasionally when a woman marries a more distantly related member of her father's lineage, and sometimes even to refer to a marriage into her father's clan. A man may also 'pulang ka rumah bako'. In this case the man marries either a real or a classificatory patrilateral cross-cousin, a practice directly in conflict with any system of asymmetrical exchange.

If we define cross-cousin marriage as marriage to a cousin in the mother's or father's lineage, then of the 838 marriages recorded in my census, 53 were between cross-cousins. Of these 43 were men marrying matrilateral cross-cousins, and the remaining 10 were between men and their patrilateral cross-cousins.

It would be misleading, however, to conclude that marriage in Sungai Puar is an entirely random affair. The existence of cross-cousin marriages indicates a possible link, over time, between different groups (in this case matrilineal kin groups). Marriage in Sungai Puar is still arranged. There is still some attempt to create such links. In a small number of cases there are relatively permanent links between kin groups, such that a significant proportion of women of one group are married to the men of the other.

If we assume that cross-cousin marriage serves to link groups over time, we must base our model on the existence of corporate, unilineal descent groups. If, however, the basic groups are *not* kin groups, but are defined by a variety of factors such as bilateral ties, social ties manifest in residential proximity, occupational and class similarities, then affinal alliances can be formed even without cousin marriage. It is my impression that the marriage pattern in Sungai Puar does perform the function of linking groups, informally defined, of approximately equal status. There is a tendency for marriages to take place between such groups and for the links to be perpetuated over time.

Take the case of a man looking for a husband for his daughter. He may choose to take a young man from his own circle of close matrilineal kinsmen, in which case we would have a MBD—FZS (mother's brother's daughter—father's sister's son) marriage. He may, however, choose instead a man from among his circle of acquaintances, workmates or people who live close to his parental home. The combination of these factors, through time, indeed seems to result in a series of alliances similar to those created by the rule of preferential cross-cousin marriage.

In Sungai Puar today, then, the system of marriage preferences has two main effects. First, it serves to tie men and women from broadly similar backgrounds. Second, it servsed to create links between groups defined in other than kinship terms.

Equally significant, therefore, from the point of view of sub-sistence agriculture, is the pattern of marriage alliances. While — as we shall see — for a woman access to subsistence land derives from her membership of a kin group, for a man access to the sub-sistence product is defined through marriage. Since marriage is not random but rather serves to link non-kin groups, it is through membership in these groups that a man acquires a wife within the village, gains access to ancestral land and to rice, the main product of labour on subsistence land.

Residence patterns

According to villagers, the traditional residential group consisted of a group of matrilineal kinswomen, their husbands and children. The traditional Minangkabau house, only a few of which still remain, was a large structure, raised above the ground, with a characteristic sloping roof. This house, known as the *rumah adaik* or *rumah bagonjong*, served as the symbol of the matrilineage. The large lineage house, according to tradition, has a long inner chamber running down the centre, which serves both as living space for the occupants and as a ceremonial hall for weddings, *panghulu* installations and the like. Grouped around the central chamber is a series of family rooms (*bilek*), all of which have doors that give onto the centre of the house. A shared kitchen area is usually attached to one of the long sides of the rectangular house at ground level. Traditionally, entry to the house and the central chamber was through the kitchen, although this is rare today.

Each *bilek* is occupied by a single family. The best room is reserved for the most recently married girl, and after each marriage families were therefore expected to move from one room to another. The most senior women of the group were often expected to move entirely outside the lineage house into a small shack built in the grounds when there were no more available *bilek*. Even today it is not uncommon for very old women to move right out of the family home and live in a small hut within the compound.

According to Josselin de Jong (1951), the Minangkabau had a form of natalocal residence. He asserts that husbands, called *urang sumando* (visitors), were not thought to reside permanently with their wives. However, the evidence does not entirely support this contention. In any case it would be difficult to argue that the modern Minangkabau husband is a mere visitor in his wife's house. It is here that he eats, sleeps and spends most of his free time.

In Sungai Puar today uxorical residence is therefore the rule. After marriage a woman will, in all cases, stay either in her parents' home or in a new house close by on ancestral land (except, of course, when she accompanies a migrant husband). If at marriage the couple cannot afford to build a new house, it is always the man's aim eventually to build a new house for his wife and children. While the money for a new home frequently comes from the husband, it too passes to his daughters, and eventually becomes ancestral property (*harto pusako*). In fact all houses built in Sungai Puar are said by a man to be 'for my children' or 'for my daughters' and never 'for my wife and myself'. This is true even when a man's children are still very young.

Even in larger residential households, with several women and their husbands, the elementary family remains a separate social and economic unit. Cooking facilities may be shared, but the elementary family eats, cooks and sleeps together. Food, even when stored in the kitchen, is kept separate. Even basic food items like salt and chillies are not shared among married sisters.

The only exception to this residential isolation of the elementary family is when an older widowed or divorced kinswoman also lives in the house. She will join the consumption unit of her closest younger kinswoman or, if she is an elderly mother with several married daughters in residence, she may 'rotate' among her children. If an older man is widowed or divorced he usually returns to live in the home of his sisters and their children.

It is considered best today for elementary families to live on their own. The existence of a large number of extended family households is due to the fact either that the husband is unable to afford a separate house, or that, sometimes, men leave the village to work, leaving behind wives who prefer living with kin to living on their own.

It is difficult to generalise about the patterns of domestic authority. It is clear today that a married man will have a greater degree of authority over his wife and children than does any man of her own matrilineage. While men frequently complained that they felt oppressed by the solidarity of their wife's kinswomen, and by the interference of their wife's real and classificatory brothers, there is no doubt that their accounts tended to exaggerate all challenges to their authority. The fact that they complained openly is an indication of the extent to which a husband's right to exercise such authority is accepted.

It is also difficult to generalise about female authority. Obviously the fact that Minangkabau women own rice land, house plots and, in most cases, the houses themselves gives them a certain authority lacking among women in other parts of Indonesia. Older women with married children in particular have an air of assurance and self-sufficiency about them in the surroundings of their own homes that is difficult to miss. Women also have an important role in lineage affairs (see Tanner, 1974). Older women in particular have no hesitation about joining in male conversation, and women do not seem to stand in perpetual fear of a husband's rebuke. At the same time both men and women told me that a husband has the last word in domestic decisions except when these are concerned with ancestral property. It would be almost impossible, therefore, to make any definite statement about the relative 'status' of Minangkabau women because of the impossibly subjective nature of the concept.

51

Adat and land tenure

The pattern of kinship and marriage is closely related to the subsistence sector of the economy. The system described above both contains a set of prescriptions by which villagers gain access to rice land, and defines a social community which stands between an individual cultivator and her land. These relations at the same time play a role in determining the pattern of labour organisation in rice cultivation. In effect *adat*, under modern conditions, provides a model of and for economic behaviour in the subsistence sector, while the community, through ties of kinship, common residence, marriage links and overlapping group rights in ancestral property, serves to organise access to the basic means of production, i.e. irrigated rice land known as *sawah*.

In different historical circumstances *adat* in Minangkabau has had a broader referent. Most of these earlier prescriptions, contained and preserved in the traditional sayings known as *papatah*, have remained. They remain, however, by and large in the minds of a small number of experts, whose knowledge has become both esoteric and private. The average villager's knowledge of such *adat* esoterica is limited. Most villagers are quite happy to leave such intellectualising to the few self-proclaimed experts, who can be counted on to assist in the organisation of weddings and other rituals.

In contrast, every villager needs to understand those *adat* prescriptions which relate to ancestral property known as *harto pusako*. Rules of inheritance, regulations on alienation of ancestral property, prescriptions concerning the relations between husbands and wives, and brothers and sisters — all these are part of the cultural system within which most adults operate. Ignorance of *adat* prescriptions which regulate access to rice land and other ancestral property can easily exclude a person from access to land. To some extent a *panghulu* can be expected to offer advice to his *kamanakan*. Villagers acknowledge, however, that there is no substitute for personal knowledge and ability to manipulate the system. The dangers of relying on others are pointed up by the following case:

Amik was chosen by his lineage to become their *panghulu* 15 years ago. He persuaded three classificatory sisters to pawn a piece of their jointly owned land in order to raise enough money to pay the cost of installation. They agreed and eventually the land was pawned. Perhaps unusually, Amik himself took up the pawn. It was therefore Amik's personal money which was used to finance the ceremony. Ever since he has been the *panghulu* Amik has treated the land as the personal property of his elementary family.

In 1970 the three women had saved up what they thought was enough money to reclaim the pawned land from Amik. But Amik was unwilling to give up the land, which he had farmed for fifteen years. As a result he raised the reclamation price to a level he knew the women could not afford. He was in this way able to block the return of the land.

The three sisters in this case were outmanoeuvred by their own *panghulu*, who might normally have been expected to back them up. They were not able to press their case because the normal route of appeal was blocked. It is of course highly unethical for a person to treat a piece of lineage land, even if it is held on pledge, as personal property. It is also unethical to raise the original price in any significant way. The three sisters were, however, unable to do much about it. They might have appealed to the office of the village mayor, or even to a court in Bukit Tinggi. The original transaction, however, was an informal one, and they could not offer any proof. Among other things, this case illustrates the need for all villagers to be familiar with the rules concerning the pawning of ancestral land.

Access to *sawah pusako* (ancestral rice land) is gained in a number of ways. In most cases land is held by women, who inherit this right from their mothers. Less frequently, access is gained through a system of pawning known as *paggang-gadai*. Even less frequently, a villager can buy a piece of irrigated land. While land is held by women, men also exercise certain rights with respect to it. As husbands, they both help to work their wife's land and share in the harvest. As brothers, men represent the lineage group in their capacity as administrators of the land and supervisors of its alienation.

Women in Sungai Puar, and indeed in most Minangkabau communities, exercise individual rights of possession in irrigated rice land. A woman works the land, usually with the assistance of her husband and children. Individual women enjoy full rights to rice they produce on it. Women also receive the money when the land is sold or pawned.

In most cases, as I have said, women exercise these rights individually. Land is passed regularly from mother to daughter, either when the mother becomes too old to exercise her rights, or on her death. Most villagers think that it is the duty of a mother to divide her land before her death among her daughters, or at least to allocate some of it to them when they marry. When a woman allocates land to her daughters before her death, the division is usually considered informal. In effect the land in this case is held by the women of the extended family as a group. In spite of this communal possession, women in most of such cases work their allocations individually. Communal cultivation is extremely rare in Sungai Puar.

In some cases communal forms of possession remain after a woman's death. Either by choice or because of excessive fragmentation, daughters may elect not to divide the land permanently. Indeed, in some cases the land remains undivided even into a second generation. This explains the existence of communal possession among sisters or first matrilateral parallel cousins in Sungai Puar.

While female possession of land may in some cases be communal, the working of the land, as I have pointed out, is almost always individual. In the case of an undivided estate shared among a group of closely related kin, the women usually elect to exercise rotating rights to cultivation, a system known as *sawah balega*. Here sisters work the land in alternate years, or land passes from one set of sisters to another every two or three years. Again, within the sibling group land is worked in alternate years.

There are a few cases of male possession of land. Men sometimes cultivate a piece of ancestral land of their own kin group with and for their own elementary families. In such cases disputes are almost inevitable. They usually revolve around the issue of a man who is said to have 'taken lineage land to his wife's house' (*dibao karumah padusi*). Men sometimes manage to take possession of lineage land, at least temporarily, either when their mother dies without daughters, or as a reward for financial aid which they have given to a sister. Normally, when a woman dies without heirs, her land is supposed to be redistributed within the lineage, preferably within her own segment. The confusion which follows the death of a woman without female heirs usually gives an enterprising son or brother an opportunity to work the land. Whenever the legal heirs are financially able to do so, this form of male possession can be successfully challenged. Men with money and influence can, how-

54

ever, prolong the arrangement for a considerable period of time. The general absence of written records and the connivance of the *panghulu* in rare cases mean that a man can successfully take complete possession of such land so that it eventually becomes the property of his wife's *suku*.

A woman's brothers, and other senior men of the lineage and lineage segment, more frequently play the role of administrators of ancestral property. They have a good deal of power to control both its pawning and its sale.

There are a number of obstacles to free alienation of land. A person in need of cash is more likely to pawn her land — or other forms of ancestral property — in exchange for a cash loan, than to sell it. The pawner gives up the right to cultivate: as long as the loan is not paid, the pawnee treats the land as his or her own. While *adat* sets out regulations for pawning, it is now commonly agreed that land can be pawned if the welfare of a particular family is involved. This option is interpreted broadly by the villagers. According to *adat*, for example, a person can pawn ancestral land in order to pay for a girl's wedding, if her father or other kin have not saved up enough money to pay for it. Regardless of the fact that a man may have sunk all his ready money into a business venture, he can still plead that he has no free cash to pay for a wedding. In effect, then, a family in need of cash can in most cases find a justifiable reason to pawn ancestral land.

People are supposed to pawn or sell land only to close kin 'within the *suku*'. The practice is therefore to offer it first to close kin, then to lineage and clan-mates and only then to fellow villagers. Pawning and selling ancestral land is a lineage matter. Male relatives of the owner, as well as the *panghulu*, thus have considerable power to negotiate the pawning or sale, to block a transaction, or to take the land themselves.

Because *adat* permits pawning, the ancestral land provides a form of insurance against hard times. Those who have access to it can risk their money more freely, for they know that they can always fall back on pawning to tide them over financial difficulties. While a husband has no formal rights in his wife's land, and may not pawn it himself, he benefits in the same way: he can rely on his wife to do so if he is not able to provide for his children.

A man of the lineage may benefit even more directly from the pawning of land. One man, for example, was able to build up a large business in retailing steelware in the Bukit Tinggi market in the 1950s because a large proportion of his lineage land was pawned to provide him with capital. The merchant was able to persuade both his female lineage-mates and, more importantly, the *panghulu*, to help him in this way. Young men are sometimes able to persuade their mother to pawn their share of lineage land in order to obtain capital for trade. Because such arrangements are not in accord with the *adat* ideal, people are extremely reluctant to discuss them. For this reason, while I am sure pawning under such circumstances is a not infrequent occurrence, I was not able to document more than a few such cases.

As we shall see, the subsistence rice crop is very important. Access to land can have a considerable effect on a man's position in the commodity economy. For this reason, marriage serves an important economic function in Sungai Puar. For while land is owned by women, marriage serves at the same time to allow men to benefit from the subsistence cultivation of rice.

The rights of a man in his wife's land are not precisely defined. In fact they vary from family to family. If a man is a full-time farmer he may work his wife's rice land. Since villagers frequently plant vegetable cash crops on irrigated land after the rice harvest, it is useful to a farmer to have access to land through his wife for this purpose. Usually a full-time farmer will have access to land by a number of different arrangements. Some land he may rent, some he may share-crop, and some he may use because it belongs to his wife.

Ilyas, a blacksmith, for example, plants a crop of chillies on his wife's land after the rice harvest. He sells the chillies in the Bukit Tinggi market, and uses the proceeds both for the consumption needs of his elementary family and to finance his blacksmithing when cash is short. Abas, on the other hand, is a full-time farmer. He grows rice and cash crops and works for a wage as a ploughman. He rents some land, and also has share-cropping arrangements. At the same time he does much of the heavy work on his wife's rice land, and plants onions as a cash crop on her land after the rice has been harvested.

Men who are not full-time farmers may not bother to plant a cash crop. They too, however, benefit directly from the rice land farmed by their wives. These men receive some benefit from their labour on the land, because self-sufficiency in rice considerably reduces the financial obligations towards members of their elementary family.

Adat, kinship and marriage, then, are part of the everyday discourse of Minangkabau economic life. Indeed, so important are relations of kinship and marriage that they appear to define a community or network of social relations existing between the individual subsistence cultivator and the land. The pattern of *suku* organisation is of importance to the modern villager because it provides him with both a conscious model of property relations and a model on which claims to rights of cultivation must be based. This is not to say that in this realm of concrete discourse and economic behaviour we can easily isolate what some have chosen to call a lineage mode of production (see Terray, 1972; Rey, 1973; Meillassoux, 1975, among others). The relations of the subsistence economy, the realisation of this community, are not immediately visible, nor are other principles of economic organisation lacking. This problem must be tackled at another level altogether, and it is necessary here to stay with the concrete world of Sungai Puar, in order to evaluate the significance of subsistence production in the reproduction of Minangkabau producers.

4

Agriculture and subsistence: the reproduction of the subsistence community

If an economic structure functions to produce and reproduce the material conditions of social existence, then an economy is not simply a technological phenomenon. Rather the economy serves to combine labour, techniques and means of production in order to reproduce a society's material base. In the previous chapter we saw that Minangkabau peasant society is reproduced, in part, through the subsistence cultivation of rice, and that this depends upon the constitution of a subsistence community through the ideology of *adat*, and through certain specific social structures. In this chapter I want to look in more detail at the degree to which subsistence production fulfils these functions, the ways in which the community serves to organise the techniques of rice cultivation, and the proportion of socially defined subsistence needs met through the cultivation of irrigated rice.

In spite of its declining importance as a mode of subsistence, subsistence agriculture remains an important feature of village life. Blacksmiths, seamstresses, traders and others spend some of their time working the land. Many owe their position to income derived from cash cropping, to a lump sum of cash obtained from pawning or selling land, or to the advantage gained from the fact that a proportion of their subsistence is derived directly from rice cultivation. Land is, in a sense, a mark of social existence. To possess it is to be a member of the village community. Land ownership is a form of insurance. Land may be sold in hard times and its product may mean the difference between a good or a hungry year.

Techniques of rice cultivation

The basic village crop is rice. Because of the lack of any clear-cut

58

wet and dry seasons, it is possible to grow rice at any time in the year. Unlike the practice in other rice-growing areas, here villagers perform the basic tasks of rice cultivation – planting, transplanting and harvesting – individually without regard to others. The sweep of village rice fields reveals rice in all the different stages of maturity at any one time.

There is a variety of local strains of rice, among them *padi kunaing tinggi* and *padi kuniang rendah* (tall and short yellow rice), *padi putiah* (white rice), *padi hitam tabik* and *padi hitam* ('black' rice), and several varieties of glutinous rice (*sapuluik*).

The quality of individual holdings of rice land varies greatly according to access to irrigation water. Some fields in the lower reaches of the village are too wet even without irrigation to grow any rice at all. On these, villagers generally plant a species of reed known locally as *mensiro* and used in mat-making. Other plots do not have sufficient water to grow any rice at all. A few holdings are situated so that they can be irrigated for rice cultivation twice a year.

Irrigation is both by rainwater and by a number of channels that bring water to the fields from springs and streams which have their source higher up the mountain. Inefficient irrigation systems and the irregularity of the land on the mountain slopes mean an over-all insufficiency in water supplies to the *sawah* of Sungai Puar. In the cultivation of rice on irrigated fields it is essential that water flow steadily through the submerged fields (see Geertz, 1963a, 28ff.).

The people of Sungai Puar plant rice in small seed beds, which are usually enriched by natural fertilisers, particularly human and animal excrement. When the seedlings are five or more weeks old they are transplanted into the fields (*sawah*). To prepare a field for transplanting, water is allowed to run into it and the soil is turned with either a broad-bladed hoe (*pangkuah*), a buffalo-drawn plough (*bajak*), or a combination of the two.

When the initial preparation of the soil is complete, water is again allowed to flow into the fields to a depth of several inches. The water is kept at the required level by the earthwork dykes, which are constantly in need of repair. Maturation of local varieties of rice takes about five months.

The main work between transplanting and the harvest consists of weeding and supervision of the water flow. The amount of time spent on these tasks varies considerably from one person to another, depending largely on the amount of time he or she can spare from other economic activities. As the crop begins to ripen it must be guarded against birds, which constantly threaten the ripening grain. Some fields are criss-crossed with cotton thread, from which pieces of cloth are hung to frighten the birds off. There are elaborate mechanisms, hand- or water-powered, which beat pots and pans together. Children are brought in to yell at birds, and scarecrows dot the fields as the farmer prepares to harvest the crop.

When the rice has yellowed and the grain is ripe for harvest, it is cut with a curved sickle (*sabik*). The farmer grasps the sickle in one hand, holding a single rice plant of several stalks in the other. He then draws the serrated blade across the plant about six inches above ground level. The stubble is left in the field, often to be eaten by buffalo and goats.

The cut stalks are gathered into bundles. The farmer typically separates the grain from the stalks by a process known as *mairiak*. He treads with his bare feet on the end of the bundle of rice stalks and then shakes the bundle and the grain falls off onto a mat which is laid out in the field. This process may have to be repeated several times before all the grain has been separated. The separated grain is then winnowed in the fields, stuffed into sacks and carried from field to house.

The Minangkabau language, like Indonesian, has three different words for rice. The separated grain left after winnowing is called *padi. Padi* is milled to yield the husked white seed known as *bareh* (Indonesian: *beras*). Cooked rice is called *nasi*.

In Sungai Puar *padi* is milled either in one of the water-driven rice mills or by hand-pounding with wooden stampers. The mills (*kincia*) all operate with water wheels. The wheel turns a large wooden shaft with pieces of wood attached to it at intervals. These bits of wood function in the way that the cams do in a motor-car engine. The rotary motion of the 'cam' shaft is converted into a vertical force applied by heavy wooden stampers which separate the husks from the seed in larger mortars placed below them. Separated husks are sometimes taken back to the fields to be burned as fertiliser, or are fed to ducks and chickens.

To summarise, the basic tasks necessary for rice cultivation in the village are preparing the seed beds, planting and caring for seedlings, transplanting, preparing fields to receive the seedlings (including repairing earthworks, terracing and irrigation), weeding, guarding the maturing grain, cutting the stalks, separating the *padi* from the stalks, winnowing and milling. The basic tools necessary are the hoe, the buffalo-drawn plough, the sickle, mats and winnowing baskets, bags to collect the harvested *padi*, and milling equipment. While such labour-saving devices as hand- or petrol-powered hullers, machine-driven rice mills and the like are available in Bukit Tinggi, none of these is used in Sungai Puar. Neither did local farmers, at the time of my research, employ chemical fertilisers, weedkillers or pesticides in rice cultivation.

The main input, then, is human labour power, while perhaps the only crucial physical capital consists of irrigation works, dykes and terracing. Labour requirements in rice cultivation vary from farmer to farmer, and task to task. Rice cultivation of this kind demands greatest attention at certain crucial stages in the cycle — in transplanting, preparation of the fields, weeding and harvesting. For long periods of time in the cycle the farmer needs to spend relatively little time in cultivation. Individual farmers may also spend more time than others, and in this way increase yields per hectare. Diligent supervision of the water flow, exhaustive weeding and careful harvesting are all methods by which more intensive labour input can increase per-hectare yields.[1]

Transplanting is the first stage in which a number of people may be required to work together. Up to ten women may cooperate in planting seedlings in the *sawah*. Weeding can be done on an individual basis, since the work can be spread over several weeks. More people may be required to guard against birds, and often children help with this. At least two and often more people co-operate during the harvest: one cuts the plants, a second separates the grain and sometimes a third, usually a woman, winnows in the fields.

In his analysis of the Guro social formation, Emmanuel Terray starts with the productive forces. Basing this approach on the often

1. That increased intensity of labour can greatly boost productivity per unit of land is a commonly recognised aspect of irrigated rice cultivation. For studies which discuss the contribution of labour input to yields cf. Geertz, 1963a for Java and Robert Ho, 1967 for Malaysia. It should, however, be noted that while rice cultivation may, as Geertz suggests, be exceptionally sensitive to increased labour inputs, it too is susceptible to dininishing returns and that therefore the marginal product of labour will rapidly decline at a certain point. This can, however, remain invisible, since labour is not paid, nor are labour costs closely calculated, at least in subsistence cultivation.

quoted passage of Marx, in which Marx argues that 'It is not the articles made, but how they are made, and by what instruments, that enables us to distinguish different economic epochs', as well as Balibar's discussion of the basic elements of the mode of production (see Terray, 1972, pp. 98ff.), Terray proceeds to distinguish modes of production on the basis of the different forms of cooperation within the productive process. It would be possible to make a similar analysis of the concrete labour process in Minangkabau subsistence agriculture. However, this would be an extremely narrow view of the Minangkabau subsistence community. To expect some coincidence between concrete labour processes and the relations of production in subsistence agriculture, it seems to me, is to run the risk both of empiricism, in which the concrete, observable situation is confused with the abstract concept of a mode of production, and of vulgar materialism (see Friedman, 1974) in which we mistakenly read off the social organisation of the economy from the localised processes of production. This is even more true when we realise that concrete forms of cooperation in Minangkabau subsistence agriculture are themselves the result of the interaction of different structures. Hence, for example, the use of extended simple cooperation in transplanting is not directly determined by the technology of rice cultivation, but rather by the kin group community, mediated by the ideology of communal solidarity. The same tasks may be performed in different ways according to the demands made on the producer's labour by other forms of economic endeavour. Because the world of concrete economic behaviour can never be the simple reflection of specific modes of production, it seems to me that it would be a mistake at this level to look for modes of production in each different form of the labour process.

Productivity

Rice in Sungai Puar is grown entirely for consumption. I know of no instance when rice was sold. At the same time, only a very few farmers grow enough rice for their family's annual needs. Almost all families in the village must buy a large proportion of their rice in the market. To estimate the proportion of demand fulfilled by subsistence cultivation it is necessary to estimate total yield, total consumption and the total number of consumers. This can be done in a number of ways.

I carried out a survey of Limo Suku rice land during my field-work. With the help of a lecturer from the local Agricultural Faculty, I measured each separate holding of rice land, and its productivity was visually evaluated. The holdings were then placed in four different categories according to potential yield, given existing techniques of cultivation. The results of this survey are included in Table 4.1.

It must be emphasised that these categories are not precise, the obvious difficulty of a visual assessment being accentuated by the fact that yields vary considerably within categories not only because of slight variations in the quality of different holdings in the same category, but also because, as I have already observed, access to water and soil fertility are not the only determinants of yield: the nature and quality of labour input are also very im-portant. Nonetheless, this rough classification of Limo Suku rice land gives a general picture of total yields.

The estimated yields are averages in each category. There are also annual variations, because of the variations in the effects of animal and insect pests, and in water supply. Too much water in any one year can be just as disastrous as drought. Flooding just after transplanting is dangerous because immature plants are easily damaged. Heavy rains which come when the grain is almost ripe can also damage the crop. In mid-1972 floods hit the west coast of Sumatra, almost completely destroying the *padi* crop there. While the highland areas were unaffected, farmers in the coastal villages were badly hit. The ripening crop was completely washed away in some places. The flood also deposited large quantities of sand, rock and wood on the fields and completely destroyed terracing and irrigation channels, and as a result yields were adversely affected in following years as well. While major disasters of this sort are rare, minor ones are more frequent. For this reason the estimated yields must be taken only as a rough guideline for any particular year.

In the period of my fieldwork, 93.45 hectares of land in Limo Suku were used for wet rice cultivation. My survey covered 86.76 of these, the other 7.7 per cent remaining unsurveyed for a variety of reasons. Table 4.2 summarises the results, applying the average yield estimates from Table 4.1. The 86.76 hectares yielded an estimated total of 178.7 tons of *padi* (unhusked rice). If we assume that the unsurveyed land was of similar quality this gives a total annual yield for Limo Suku of 192.5 tons.

A survey carried out by the Faculty of Agriculture of Andalas University in Padang arrives at an estimated annual consumption of *padi* of 275 kilos per person — an average figure for a family, with adults consuming more than children (cf. Kantor Sensus dan Statistik Propinsi Sumatera Barat, 1970). Taking the population of Limo Suku as 3,376, this means that the residents need a total of 925 tons of *padi* every year for their own consumption, as compared with our estimate that they produce 192.5. If these estimates are roughly correct, then, total production fulfils only about one-fifth of consumption needs. This result is interestingly confirmed by the common estimate among the villagers that on the average each family in Limo Suku grows enough rice for between two and three months' eating.

There are two other ways to estimate the proportion of total subsistence needs fulfilled by subsistence cultivation in Limo Suku. According to official government statistics (see Said, 1970) rice land in Agam gives an average yield of from 2.9 to 3.5 tons per hectare. Even if we take a figure below the annual average of these two estimates, we arrive at a new subsistence ratio of 48.1 per cent, more than double the ratio calculated above. It is also possible to make an estimate based on my own census data in which respondents supplied information on household yields. This gives a much lower subsistence ratio of 16.9 per cent. Because the

Table 4.1 *Categories of rice land in Limo Suku*

Land Class	Estimated yield per crop (in metric tons)	Crops per year	Average annual yield (metric tons)
I	3/hectare	2	6/hectare
II	2/hectare	1	2/hectare
III	¾/hectare	1	¾/hectare
IV	¾/hectare	½ (one every two years)	⅜/hectare

two independent estimates which I have calculated from data I collected myself are in relatively close agreement with one another, while differing widely from the official estimates, I think it is fair to assume that the government statistics are politically biased. Of the two ratios calculated from my own data, I would think that the slightly higher ratio of 20 per cent is the more accurate. Minangkabau villagers are in general extremely reluctant to give out information to anyone on their own private sources of income. I would assume, therefore, that the census data slightly under-estimate yields per household. The summary of data on rice production presented in Table 4.2 is thus based on what I take to be the most reliable evidence.

It is important to note that Limo Suku is not typical of West Sumatra as a whole in this respect. In general, villagers in West Sumatra have more rice land, devote a greater proportion of their time to rice cultivation, and produce a larger proportion of their consumption needs. In Table 4.3 I have attempted to draw out this contrast. The subsistence ratio is based on my own estimates of average yields, and government statistics on availability of rice land and population (see Said, 1970). It is important to keep this in mind in the discussion which follows. These figures show that while all villages in West Sumatra rely on commodity production to meet their needs for a cash income, that reliance is stronger in Limo Suku than elsewhere.

I have no figures on the total production of fruit and vegetables in Limo Suku. Government statistics for the district of Agam show that in 1968 *per-capita* production of maize was 1 kilo; cassava,

Table 4.2   *Rice production in Limo Suku*

Rice land	=	93.45 hectares
Population	=	3,376
Total yield	=	192.5 tons/year
Rice land, *per capita*	=	0.028 hectares
Per-capita consumption	=	275 kilograms/year (unhusked rice)
Subsistence ratio (proportion of annual consumption needs fulfilled by subsistence production)	=	20.8 per cent

Table 4.3   *The subsistence ratio in West Sumatra by 'Kabupaten'*
(district)

Kabupaten	Rice land per capita (hectares)	Subsistence ratio (per cent)
Agam	0.115	85.4
Pasaman	0.148	110.0
50 Kota	0.135	110.3
Tanah Datar	0.124	92.1
Padang/Pariaman	0.082	60.9
Solok	0.109	80.9
Pesisir Selatan	0.113	84.0
Sawah Lunto/Sijunjung	0.100	74.3

6.5 kilos; sweet potatoes, 4.63 kilos; potatoes, 2.96 kilos and chillies, 8.88 kilos. Production of other crops was negligible. The over-all yields of these crops are, however, based on extremely rough estimates.

Economic relations in rice cultivation

While analyses of lineage societies, such as Terray's analysis of the Guro, attempt to demonstrate that different concrete branches of production are organised according to different principles of economic structure, such is clearly not the case for the Minangkabau peasant village. While, for example, access to land is largely dependent on membership in the subsistence community, the economy demonstrates the combined effects of different systems of productive relations. Villagers thus have a number of different forms by which they allocate labour and tools to the subsistence cultivation of irrigated rice in Sungai Puar.

This is, for example, reflected in the unequal distribution of *sawah*. A single holding of rice land consists of a number of small plots or 'plates' (*piriang*). A number of people own land that is scattered in different parts of Limo Suku. In Table 4.4 I have outlined the distribution of rice land in this village section. Individual holdings are very small. Exactly half are between 0.05 and 0.15 hectares. Almost 90 per cent are 0.3 hectare or less. Only one holding is larger than one hectare. Given average yields, only holdings of 6,650 square metres will produce enough rice for a family of five. The number of holdings capable of providing enough rice for subsistence is thus very small.

Rice may be produced by the labour of owners themselves, wage labour, share-cropping and cultivation by communal labour.

Many villagers who own land perform all the necessary tasks themselves. Typically the owner will have the help of her husband and children. If a holding is relatively small, family labour alone is sufficient to perform all transplanting, weeding, preparation of the soil, and harvesting. Some families use their own buffalo to plough the fields, others keep a buffalo for someone else. This allows them both to plough their fields, and to keep one out of every two calves born to the buffalo.

Owner-cultivation may be found in combination with other labour arrangements. While the owner and her family may do most of the work, they may choose to hire labourers to carry out transplanting. In other cases they may decide to call in a group of close kin and affines to help with the harvest.

A large proportion of families in the village hire wage workers for some or all agricultural work. Wage labourers are often specialists. A ploughman (*tukang bajak*) receives a higher wage than a woman who hires out to transplant the seedlings, not only because his job is thought to be more highly skilled, but also because he must supply both buffalo and plough. Payment to labourers is either in cash or in kind. It is most usual to pay ploughmen and transplanters in cash, and to pay those who assist with the harvest in rice. In all cases the owner of the land is expected to provide meals and drinks for the labourers while they are working.

Perhaps the most frequent arrangement in Limo Suku for the cultivation of rice land is share-cropping. A share-cropper supplies all necessary inputs, except for seed, in exchange for half the harvest. The verb 'to share-crop' (*pasiduoan*) means literally to divide in half. If the land is of poor quality the share-cropper can expect a larger proportion of the harvest (usually two-thirds).

The share-cropper may in turn hire labour if necessary. Some share-croppers are full-time farmers, others are not. Some people who have no land of their own become part-time share-croppers in order to supplement their cash income.

Table 4.4   *The distribution of rice land in Limo Suku*

Size of holding (m²)	Number of holdings
1–500	75
501–1,000	185
1,001–1,500	103
1,501–2,000	61
2,001–2,500	53
2,501–3,000	34
3,001–3,500	17
3,501–4,000	11
4,001–5,000	11
5,001–6,000	11
6,001–7,000	4
7,001–8,000	2
8,001–9,000	1
9,001–12,000	3
Not recorded	5
Total 934,522 = 93.45 hectares	576

Communal labour is rarely used today in Limo Suku. Occasion-ally harvesting of the land is done communally. This kind of co-operation is Sungai Puar is called *gotong-royong*, a Javanese term. In other parts of West Sumatra such labour cooperation is called *julo-julo* or *lambiari*. The tradition is that close female kin of the landowner and the in-married men (*urang-sumando*) cooperate in the harvest. I also observed a group of young unmarried men who helped a woman with her harvest. These boys were not related to the owner, but were members of her neighbourhood group.

Today, at least, a communal harvest is more of a social occasion than anything else. The owner must provide a meal in the fields before the work begins. When the workers finish the harvest they return to the owner's house for a second meal. They also receive cooked rice and *sambal* (curry) to take home with them. Because the communal harvest is primarily a social occasion, landowners who are careful with their money prefer to hire wage labour. It is more expensive to feed the communal group, and any available

68

bystanders, than it is to pay a fixed share of the crop to a contract labourer.

While share-cropping arrangements are common, renting of land in Limo Suku is rare. During my fieldwork, no one rented land to plant rice. There were a few cases of land rental in the off-season, when the farmer planted a vegetable cash crop in the *sawah*.

The following cases serve to illustrate the variety of social arrangements for rice cultivation, as well as the variety of tasks going on at any one time. These observations were made in a single day while I was surveying the holdings of Limo Suku.

Plot A. This plot is owned by Lias, a woman about 50 years old. It is worked by a female share-cropper, Aisyah, who assumes full responsibility for cultivation. This particular arrangement calls for a 5:6:1 division of the crop: five parts to Lias, six parts to Aisyah and one part for seed and as payment for work on the field. I observed the process of harvesting. Apart from Aisyah there were three workers, two men and one woman. The two men cut the rice and stamped on the stalks to remove the grain. The woman, with Aisyah's help, was winnowing. The total harvest was expected to be 12 *baban* or sacks of grain (each sack giving about 20 kilos of husked rice). The workers received payment in rice. One sack was divided among the workers in a ratio of 8½:8½:3, the men receiving the larger share. The whole operation was observed by Lias.

Plot B. This piece of land belongs to Ramlah. She is both owner and cultivator. The work I watched was hoeing or turning up the field after the rice harvest in order to plant potatoes. A man did the hoeing, supervised by Ramlah. He was paid Rp. 150 plus two meals per day for the work. He will take six days to do the job.

Plot C. At the time of the survey this plot of land was being ploughed, again in preparation for a potato crop. Taher, a full-time ploughman, is being paid Rp. 600, two meals and a snack per day to complete the job. He estimates that it will take him two days to finish. The buffalo does not belong to him, but he keeps it for a woman who owns it. Apart from the use of the buffalo for ploughing, he keeps half the offspring. This land is not share-cropped. The owner merely pays labourers to do the heavier work.

Plot D. Hadijah owns this piece of land which she received in pawn from Rosna. She does much of the work of rice cultivation herself. The job I watched, transplanting, was being carried out by four women from a neighbouring village. These women will complete the job in a day. They are paid Rp. 200 each for the day's work. They will not receive a meal.

An over-all picture of the arrangements for working rice land is presented in Table 4.5, which is based on material collected in the re-census of the village sample. I have included only those holdings on which I was able to get complete information.

These data do not give the full picture since, as I have pointed out, share-croppers themselves frequently make use of wage labourers. They do, however, show the popularity of share-cropping, at least under economic conditions prevailing in the early 1970s. Villagers seem to prefer to give their land to a share-cropping tenant, rather than to employ labourers to do most of the work, in spite of the fact that the latter arrangement may be more profitable. One farmer told me that the cost of hiring wage labour on a holding which produced 14 sacks of rice was about Rp. 2,500. This includes wages paid for transplanting, ploughing and harvesting. The owner would still be required to weed, guard the crop against birds, and prepare the seed beds. At that time rice sold for Rp. 46 per kilo in the Bukit Tinggi market (see the bi-monthly bulletin of economic figures published by the Provincial Government, *Indikator Ekonomi*, for the months of November and December, 1971). The total wage was then equivalent to 2.7 sacks (*baban*) of *padi*, whereas a share-cropper would expect at least seven sacks. Most people told me that they preferred to give land to a share-cropper if they could afford it. Informants put a great value on the fact that when someone else works your

Table 4.5   *Arrangements for rice cultivation in Limo Suku*

Nature of arrangement	Number of holdings
Worked by owner and her family. Harvest either by owner or communal	26
Main tasks all wage labour	28
Wage labour, harvest communal	10
Share-cropping	90
Worked by owner with some wage labour	6
Total	160

land, you do not need even to think about it. They naturally will try to get the best possible yield, and you get the *padi* delivered to your house. You do not even have to go to the *sawah* to watch if you want to stay away.

It was also my impression that the nature of the arrangements varied according to both the relative wealth of the landowner, and economic conditions in general. It is clear that owners with a relatively stable income from other sources tended to give their land out to share-croppers, while the less well-off, particularly women without husbands, tended more often to work the land themselves. I also suspect that there is a reversion to owner-cultivation in times of economic decline in the commodity sector.

Depending on how one looks at it, the number of people engaged in agriculture varies from about 50 per cent of the working population to a small number of individuals. At one extreme are landless villagers who derive their entire income from other economic activities. At the other are the comparatively few full-time farmers, wage labourers and those who depend for their entire livelihood on agriculture. The majority of people fall somewhere in between – cultivating small plots for subsistence, receiving rice from share-croppers on their land, performing some tasks on their land and hiring labour to do the rest. Of the 499 working men in my census, 61 described themselves as full-time farmers. Of a sample of 40 male farmers, 11 worked as ploughmen, 12 as share-croppers, one as a wage worker, 10 worked their wives' land, and six combined these in one way or another. Of 856 working women, only 21 said that they were full-time farmers. These small numbers, however, give a highly misleading picture of women's participation in subsistence agriculture. More than half of these women had access to at least some ancestral land. Those who described themselves as 'farmer' were those who worked as wage labourers and share-croppers. The rest listed their occupation as *'rumah tangga'*. To translate this as 'housewife' is misleading, since subsistence farming is, according to local conceptions, a form of domestic labour equivalent to cooking, washing and cleaning. A large proportion of these women performed at least some agricultural labour on their own rice land.

While, as we have seen, women have direct access to rice land through their *suku*, men also have access to land and its product through either their mother or their wife. In the discussion of com-

71

modity production which follows, a great deal of stress will be placed on the relation between subsistence and commodity production. For this reason it is important here to present a picture of the distribution of access to rice land among men as well as women. Table 4.6 shows the high proportion of men with some access to land, as well as the proportion of their subsistence needs which could be fulfilled by the rice crop. The data are derived from the re-census of the village sample. The size of the crop refers to the total harvest on the land, whether it goes to the owner or to a share-cropper. This, then, is a potential figure, since many people give out their land to share-croppers, or pay labourers out of the total harvest.

The table includes data on men only (both residents and migrants). Exactly 700, or 59.5 per cent of the total male working population, have access to some land, whether or not they work as farmers. If we recall that an annual harvest of five sacks (*baban*) will supply a family of five with sufficient rice for two months out of every year, the above data show that subsistence rice cultivation makes a potentially significant contribution to the consumption needs of many families. While only a few have potentially a year's supply of rice, a large proportion have enough for at least two months out of each year. 475 working men are completely landless.

The cultivation of rice on ancestral land in the Minangkabau village serves in part to produce and reproduce the material conditions of the social existence of the members of the subsistence community. While, however, relations of kinship and marriage are the dominant economic structure in the community — for they serve largely to determine access to irrigated rice land — the variety of economic forms in rice cultivation testifies to the importance of other principles of economic organisation. It might be argued that to the extent that access to the product of subsistence cultivation is equally spread among the working people of the village, communal relations dominate. The unequal distribution of land, as well as the coexistence of forms of wage labour, share-cropping and renting alongside owner-cultivation and communal labour arrangements, are manifestations of the fact that, to use a term much favoured by Althusserians, concrete economic forms are overdetermined in the Minangkabau economic formation.

Neither is the situation as simple as this. As we shall see, sub-

72

Table 4.6 *Access to rice and rice land in Limo Suku for working men (residents and migrants)*

Harvest (*baban*)	0	1–5	6–10	11–15	16–20	21–30	31–40	41–50	51–60	60+	Total
a. Married men (access through wife)	463	242	144	56	21	20	0	0	5	1	952
b. Unmarried men (access through mother)	12	96	56	34	12	9	0	0	4	0	223
c. Total	475	338	200	90	33	29	0	0	9	1	1,175

sistence cultivation of rice reproduces more than the subsistence community. Subsistence cultivators, and those who have access to their product, are at the same time producers of commodities sold in the market to yield a cash income. The domination of the subsistence community by other economic systems means that subsistence production itself serves to reproduce, in part, other forms of production and distribution, as well as classes only indirectly involved in the village community. For this reason it is significant to note that even in Sungai Puar, where land is scarce relative to the population, about one-fifth of basic consumption needs are produced for subsistence. It is therefore necessary to go beyond this admittedly sketchy view of subsistence production to the sphere of peasant commodity production in Minangkabau villages.

5

Commodity production in the village economy: the case of blacksmithing

Since the people of Limo Suku grow rice exclusively for their own consumption, and only a small proportion of that, they, like other peasants, rely on production of commodities specifically for the market to provide themselves with the rest of the food and the other goods and services they need. Clothing, furniture, building materials, tools, lamps, stoves, bicycles and the like are all considered necessary to life. The result is a national and international division of labour, under which individual Sungai Puar peasants produce a number of commodities. In exchange for their commodities they receive money — all market transactions are conducted via the Indonesian *rupiah* — which in turn they use to purchase other commodities produced in other parts of Sumatra, other Indonesian islands and other parts of the world. Just as some of the goods on sale in the Bukit Tinggi market are locally produced and some are produced in other parts of the world, so some of the commodities produced in West Sumatra are brought and consumed locally and some are aimed at the world market. Rubber, coffee, tea and spices produced by Minangkabau peasants are not just sold within the province, but find their way to markets in Europe, Japan or America. In turn a large proportion of the bicycles, cloth and other manufactured goods bought by villagers come from outside the national boundaries.

There is no village in West Sumatra independent of this international economic system. Sungai Puar, however, relies perhaps more heavily than other villages on the market. For this reason it provides an extremely useful illustration of the growth and organisation of commodity production in Minangkabau.

Minangkabau villagers, as I have pointed out, produce a wide variety of commodities. Even in the village section of Limo Suku, clothing, metal ornaments, mats and baskets, vegetables and fruits are produced for sale. Most villages, however, specialise in the production of one or two basic goods. Limo Suku is known throughout West Sumatra for its blacksmithing industry. For resident men blacksmithing is the main occupation. Of 499 working in the village, 281 are blacksmiths. Migrants from Limo Suku also work as smiths in the other villages and towns of Sumatra. Of 714 working male migrants, 152 work as blacksmiths.

For this reason I chose the Limo Suku smiths as a focus for my research. In later chapters I will show, however, that the organisation of smithing in Limo Suku is in many ways typical of the organisation of peasant commodity production and distribution throughout the province. In this chapter I shall concentrate on the techniques, decision-making and social organisation of the blacksmithing industry in Limo Suku in the years between 1970 and 1972.

Limo Suku smiths turn out the axes, sickles, hoes, ploughs, machetes and other steel implements used in kitchens and fields throughout the province. By and large they sell the finished implements in the Bukit Tinggi market. Pedlars and small merchants in Bukit Tinggi buy Limo Suku steelware and re-sell it either to consumers who come direct to the market or to other small traders, who in turn sell in other parts of the province, and even in other provinces in Sumatra.

Techniques of smithing

The smiths of Limo Suku forge scrap steel in small workshops known as *apa basi*. The smiths themselves are known as *tukang basi* (steel smiths), or *pandai basi* (those who are skilful with steel).

A typical *apa* is a small thatched hut. Sizes vary, but most *apa* are square, with sides about six metres long. The walls are of bamboo slats separated by gaps of several inches, through which light enters. Most *apa* have a solid wooden door fitted with a padlock. The *apa* are not concentrated in one part of Limo Suku, but are scattered evenly in all neighbourhoods. While some stand in other sections of the village, the large majority of *apa* are located in Limo Suku.

The ring of hammer on anvil can be heard during the day throughout the section. To enter an *apa* during forging is to be bombarded by sound and by the heat of the coal fire. The local

76

dialect has several different words for the sounds produced in forging.

While the techniques of smithing vary to some extent according to the particular product, all smiths perform certain basically similar operations. First, all scrap steel is forged, i.e. heated in a coal fire and pounded out on an anvil. Second, all goods require some finishing work after the basic forging. Finishing of steelware is done with files, rough paper and polishing grit.

In the forging process scrap steel is heated on an open hearth, which is raised up on a brick, stone and mortar shelf about 60 centimetres off the dirt floor. An anvil is placed just in front of the hearth. The fire itself is regulated by a pair of hand-operated piston bellows. The bellows operator sits on a platform above and behind the hearth. He holds the pistons, the heads of which are made from feathers or bits of cloth, one in each hand, and moves them up and down alternately.

The smiths make the bellows from galvanised sheet metal. A duct leads from the bottom of the bellows to a point in the hearth either beneath or behind the coal fire. During forging the bellows must be operated at an even pace. If too much air is forced through the duct the steel becomes overheated and loses shape in the fire. Too little air underheats the steel, which is then too brittle for forging. One man removes the bit of steel from the hearth with a pair of tongs, and holds it on the anvil surface. The red hot metal is then beaten with heavy sledgehammers, with a smaller hammer or with a combination of these.

The smith must be careful to keep each bit of steel outside the fire for a short time. Hence at any one time a number of bits of steel will be placed in the fire. These are then forged in rotation, allowing for continuous forging, and at the same time keeping loss of heat in the steel to a minimum. Depending on the implement being forged, each piece of red-hot steel may be placed in the fire five to sixteen times before the process is complete.

After the implements have been roughly forged, they are tempered (*disapuah*) in water. This completes the forging, after which the rough goods are set aside to cool. Forged goods can then be finished, a process that sometimes involves considerable filing and polishing.

As a rule forging is carried out by a number of smiths working together. Each smith in a forging unit is a specialist, and it is rare that he will perform more than one of the tasks involved. A single man, called the *nangkodoh*, controls the pace of the work. The *nangkodoh* handles the tongs, holds the steel on the anvil, wields one of the smaller hammers and directs the heavy sledgework by a unique signalling process. With different hand signals he can call for a variety of sledgehammer blows. It is the *nangkodoh* who decides when to return the steel to the fire. A second man operates the piston bellows, a smith known as the *tukang ambuih*. Because it is less strenuous and requires less skill than the others, this job may be performed by either an old man or a young boy. Finally, one or two sledgers are required in the forging of heavier goods like hoes and axes; these are known as *tukang tapo*.

The amount of filing and finishing of steelware varies. When the forged product requires only minimal finishing work, this is done by either the *nangkodoh* or one of the *tukang tapo*. When more finishing work is required, a single individual may be needed to perform this work only. He is known as the *tukang kikia*.

What follows is an illustration of the process of forging. It describes a single morning's work in the *apa* of Adam. Apart from Adam, the *nangkodoh*, there were two sledgers and an old man to operate the bellows. They started work early, at seven in the morning, outside the *apa*. They cut scrap rail up into pieces, each piece big enough for a single hoe (*pangkuah*) blade. Adam then started a fire, and seven pieces of steel, each weighing about two kilos, were placed on the hearth. It took the rest of the morning, until 12.30, to forge seven hoes from the scrap rail. Each piece of steel was removed from the fire 14 times during the course of the morning. Adam directed the actual forging with hand signals. He signalled the intensity of the blows required from the sledgers and the kind of blow needed (direct, rotating or drawn). In some cases the sledge strikes the steel directly. In other cases the process requires hammer blows in which the head of the sledge is drawn quickly across the face of the hoe blade. This makes an even, bonded surface and prevents cracking. Because the sledgers stand at right angles to each other, if one is required to draw the hammer across the steel, the other must rotate the head of his hammer to give similar direction to the force (see Figure 5.1). These drawing and rotating movements are not immediately obvious to the observer; at first sight it looks simply as though the sledgers were

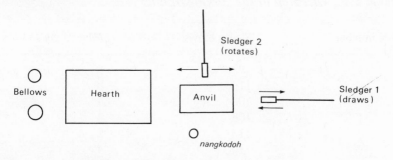

Figure 5.1   Forging hoes (seen from above)

hitting the steel directly. The speed of the blows obscures the difference in kinds of blows struck.

Apart from directing the process and holding the steel firmly on the anvil surface, Adam, the *nangkodoh*, also holds a small hammer in his right hand. When the steel is removed from the fire he strikes it several times to knock off the crust which has formed, and just before returning it to the fire he strikes it again several times, to correct distortion caused by the sledgehammers.

Table 5.1 describes one stage in the work on each of the seven hoes forged. The second column is the total number of hammer blows struck by the two *tukang tapo*. The third column represents the number of blows struck by the *nangkodoh* before returning the steel to the fire. The work being done on this stage required the sledgers to rotate or draw the blows across the surface of the steel, as indicated in Figure 5.1. The sledgers averaged 100 blows per minute between them. In between they rested briefly, and this one step took about 15 minutes altogether. There is no evidence that Adam counted the number of hammer blows. The relative uniformity among the seven hoes simply reflects the fact that for each stage in forging the *nangkodoh* has a clear picture of what is being done to each hoe blade. He then measures at a glance the changing shape of the implement, and directs the forging accordingly.

This single process, then, took about 15 minutes. When it was finished the smiths took a short break, and then continued forging. After the hoes are completed the blades are filed.

Axes, like hoes, require a good deal of heavy sledging work, but

Table 5.1   *One step in the forging of hoes*

Hoe number	Sledge blows	*Nangkodoh*'s blows
1	99	8
2	110	8
3	108	7
4	108	4
5	113	5
6	110	4
7	114	6

considerably more filing in order to produce a sharp cutting edge. The other main steel goods produced – knife blades, sickles and machetes – require less heavy sledging. The forging of knife blades, for example, is usually done by a *nangkodoh* alone, with the help of a bellows operator. The *nangkodoh*'s small hammer provides sufficient force. Sickles similarly can be made by two people, while machetes (*parang*) may require a third person who works alternately as sledger and filer.

Of all these products, knives require the most filing. After the blades have been forged and tempered, the smith files them in order both to give a sharp edge and to give the blade a slightly rounded shape. The shape of the blade varies slightly according to the style of each particular smith.

The production of hoes, axes, sickles and machetes is carried out entirely by single, independent cooperative units. While the composition of these groups varies according to the implement being made, the basic work roles are standard. Almost all *apa* groups specialise in a single product. Very rarely will a single group make more than one type of steel ware.

Table 5.2 gives a picture of the composition of the work groups. The material is taken from a preliminary survey of 50 *apa* which I carried out in February 1971. The distribution of *apa* in the sample is not to be interpreted as representative of the relative proportions in the entire village: as I shall observe more fully below, individual smiths working alone form the vast majority of smithing units.

As these data show, there is a typical cooperative work group

Commodity production in the village economy

Table 5.2 *Composition of work groups according to product*

Product	Number of *apa* in sample	Nangkodoh	Tukang tapo	Tukang ambuih	Tukang kikia
Axe	5	5	9	5	4
Hoe (large)	4	4	7	4	–
Hoe (small)	1	1	1	1	–
Knife (blade)	9	9	2	9	–
Knife (filing)	9	9	–	–	9
Knife (blades and filing)	7	7	3	3	9
Wood plane	1	1	2	1	–
Horseshoe	1	1	1	1	–
Axle	1	1	–	–	–
Nails	2	2	–	1	–
Knife (blade) and nails	1	1	–	1	–
Sickle	4	4	5	4	–
Steel spoon	1	1	–	–	1
Spade	1	1	–	1	–
Machete and sickle	2	2	3	2	4
Cake mould	1	1	1	1	–
Total	50	50	34	34	27

for some of the goods. For hoes, usually four people work together – one *nangkodoh*, two sledgers and one bellows operator. Any filing and finishing can be carried out before or after the day's forging, or even during the day when the *nangkodoh* does not need all the workers for forging. Five people typically cooperate in the production of axes: one *nangkodoh*, two sledgers, a bellows operator and a specialist for finishing the forged axe heads. Sickles, on the other hand, are usually made by three people because their production requires less heavy sledge work than does that of axes and hoes. It is only in the production of knives that there seems to be any variation in the forms of cooperation. All the tasks necessary to the completion of a knife – from forging to finishing – can be carried out usually by one person or at most two people. Forging the blades usually requires a second person to operate the bellows. Finishing can easily be done by a single smith working alone. This flexibility of techniques and forms of cooperation generates a variety of forms in knife production,

81

ranging from the single individual — the most common unit — to larger groups that forge and finish knives within a single enterprise.

The tools employed by the blacksmiths of Limo Suku are both simple and small in number. While they must purchase some of the basic *apa* equipment, they themselves make most of the simpler tools used in forging.

The hammers they use are of two basic kinds. The sledgers use a three-kilogram hammer-head mounted on a flexible wooden shaft. The *nangkodoh* uses a number of smaller hammers, all of which weigh about one kilo. These hammers, as well as the tongs used to handle the red-hot steel, are made as a matter of course by the smiths themselves. The bellows are constructed from purchased alloy sheets. The tempering is performed in an oil drum which the smith converts into an open receptacle by cutting off the top. The oven is built up from an ash and water mixture, covered with brick and stone.

The most costly of the basic tools that the smith must purchase is the anvil. An anvil may cost anywhere between Rp. 25,000 and Rp. 50,000. Since the smiths cannot make their own files either, they must buy them in the Bukit Tinggi market. The files, in fact, are all made outside Indonesia. (Table 5.3 summarises the inventories of tools in several *apa*.)

An estimate of the cash investment in an *apa* need cover only those tools and equipment bought in the market. The price of files in 1970 was between Rp. 650 and Rp. 700 each for a standard size. These are frequently replaced. Vices, used mostly in filing the forged steel, are also foreign made, but are more rarely replaced. The cost of replacement would have been about Rp. 5,000 in 1970. A single vice would last at least ten years, and probably more. As I observed previously, anvils were available for between Rp. 25,000 and Rp. 50,000. These, too, rarely need to be replaced. None of the *apa* I visited was stocked with a new or recently purchased anvil. Most anvils had been purchased second-hand from another smith. A few smiths worked with borrowed anvils, and in one case one that was rented. Many of the anvils in use during my research dated from about 1960, when a local entrepreneur set up a smithing business on a large scale and provided his workers with new tools. Some anvils came from a government cooperative formed in the same period, and some may even date from the Japanese occupation of 1942.

Table 5.3   *Inventory of tools in several 'apa'*

Product	Tools
1. Axe	1 anvil; 2 sledgehammers; 1 vice; 4 files; 1 steel-cutting adze; 2 medium hammers (1 kilogram); 6 assorted small hammers; bellows; oil drum; tongs
2. Knife blades	1 anvil; bellows run with bicycle mechanism; 3 hammers; 3 files; 2 sledgehammers; 1 metal saw; 1 metal plane; oil drum; tongs
3. Hoe	1 anvil; 1 vice; bellows; 2 sledgehammers; 2 files; 4 tongs; oil drum; 12 small hammers
4. Sickle	2 anvils (smaller one not in use); 1 sledge-hammer; 1 vice; 2 small hammers; 1 file; 3 tongs; oil drum
5. Knife (forging blades and finishing)	1 anvil; 4 vices; bellows; 2 sledges; 15 files; 3 saws; metal cutter; 3 small hammers

While the stock of tools in a typical *apa* is both small and relatively inexpensive, the requisite raw materials represent a relatively large investment – an investment, moreover, which is continuous. The basic materials are coal and steel. In addition to these the smith needs periodically to buy files, sandpaper, oil, wood for handles, packaging materials and the metal stamps with which he impresses his personal trademark on the finished goods.

Coal is brought in from the Ombilin mines in Sawah Lunto, a town about 100 kilometres from Sungai Puar. At least in recent years, with the decline in mining operations in Sawah Lunto, this coal has been of very low quality. The coal used by the smiths today comes from the surface, as most of the shafts have fallen into disuse. Because of the low quality of the coal, smiths told me, it has to be pre-burned before it can be used.

The smiths use also a kind of charcoal made from coconut husks. This is a less popular fuel because it generates less heat than coal of an equal cost. It is used primarily in periods when coal is difficult to come by.

Coal is transported to the village by individual traders. In 1971 the most important of these was a retired army officer. He usually rented a lorry in Sawah Lunto, then arranged for purchase and transport to Sungai Puar. In the village he sold the coal to individual smiths. Periodically, obstacles to the trade in both coal and scrap steel led to shortages in the village. The two main obstacles were shortage of available cash, which hampered the merchants, and bureaucratic interference by members of the police and armed forces, who were said in some cases to impound the shipments.

The steel used by the Sungai Puar smith derives from scrap. According to my informants, it is only since the Japanese occupation that scrap has been used to the exclusion of new steel. I was told that previously steel specially made for forging was imported from Holland and sold in Chinese shops in Padang. The Japanese introduced the smiths to scrap steel; ironically a large proportion of the scrap used today is rail from the Padang to Pakan Baru railway, started by the Japanese but left incomplete. In addition to rail, other kinds of scrap are brought from Pakan Baru — usually parts from scrapped cars and lorries, as well as other bits and pieces.

The use of scrap steel sets limits to the quality of the completed steelware. While the primitive techniques employed in the village in any event do not permit effective regulation of carbon content, the smiths are further handicapped from the start by the nature of their materials. An attempt is made to overcome these shortcomings by, in effect, matching the steel to the product. Knifemakers, for example, make blades primarily from *basi per*, i.e. scrap from the springs and suspension of scrapped vehicles, which is tough and elastic. Axes and hoes require larger quantities of scrap, but the smiths can use harder, higher-carbon steel for these goods because elasticity is not so important. The harder steel also allows for a sharper cutting edge. Axes and hoes, then, are usually made from scrap rail.

Rail and *per* both have shortcomings, stemming from the differential effects of carbon content. The problems can be overcome by mixing the steel in forging. Hoes, for example, can be made by inserting a layer of more durable, flexible steel between two layers of harder (higher-carbon) steel. The user can then file the hoe to a sharp edge, and yet not fear cracking. The inner layer offsets the brittleness of the higher-carbon outer layer. This process is rarely used today, unless a customer orders such a hoe directly from the *apa*. It is said that Limo Suku smiths once used

84

a similar but more intricate process of lamination to make *kris*, the long curved ceremonial daggers known throughout Indonesia. These more intricate techniques are rarely used today, however, because of both the poorer quality of the available raw materials and the expense. Consumers who are prepared to pay a higher price prefer to buy imported rather than locally produced steelware.

The forms of cooperation in smithing in Sungai Puar are largely determined by the mix of tools, raw materials, techniques and labour. Together these influence the productivity of labour measured as the ratio of physical output to labour input, and their progressive evolution over time leads to increasing productivity. While it is difficult, for theoretical reasons, to make a statement about the absolute level of development of the productive forces in smithing, it is possible to conclude in general terms that smithing in Limo Suku is relatively unproductive when measured in this way. The relatively large contribution of living labour (in contrast to labour 'congealed' in material inputs) to the value of the final product, the minimal nature of the technology employed and the relative unimportance of material costs in comparison to labour costs are all manifestations of the low level of the productive forces and the relatively low organic composition of capital. It is difficult, in fact, to imagine smithing under more technologically primitive conditions. There are indications, indeed, that the technological level of smithing has actually declined in the last century and a half (see below, Chapter 8).

One would be hard put to it to argue that this situation is attributable largely to ignorance of better techniques. It was recognised, for example, that if oil were used for tempering instead of water, the implements would be of a better quality. Many smiths have worked in machine shops in the North Sumatran city of Medan, and are aware of the advantages of mechanisation. Older smiths often pointed out to me, too, that if only better steel were available at a reasonable price they could turn out higher-quality steelware as well as a greater variety of products. There is, for example, a high demand for spare parts for buses, lorries and motor cars. These can be produced only with power-driven lathes, more precise techniques of measurement and better raw materials. Of this, too, most smiths were aware. In order to understand the low productivity of smithing in Sungai Puar, therefore, we must go beyond a consideration of the available technology and analyse the social organisation of smithing.

There are a variety of ways in which a society could 'organise' smithing, given the techniques described above. In other words, there can be no deterministic relation between the forces and relations of production. To put it this way is, it seems to me, to go against the spirit of some recent attempts to apply Marx's concept of the mode of production to pre-capitalist societies (see Balibar, 1972; Terray, 1972 and Hindess and Hirst, 1975) in which the economic base is visualised as a two-sided combination of technological relations (appropriation) and social relations (property). For while these authors stress the penetration of one by another, they nonetheless appear to separate productive forces analytically from the rest of the social formation and assign to them a determinative function 'in the last instance'. At this stage in my own argument I want to remain agnostic on the question of determination. I shall return to this problem in more detail in Chapter 7. At this point it is necessary merely to point out that in West African castes, the linking of smiths within a non-commodity agricultural unit as described for Swat (Barth, 1959), putting-out systems, and merchant-financed productive units are all different ways of organising the production of steelware, all of them compatible with the techniques described above.

In Sungai Puar in the years 1970 to 1972 smithing was organised into small enterprises, which produced steelware for exchange. The means of production, tools and raw materials, were individually owned as private property, known in Minangkabau as *harto pancarian*. The owner of the means of production was in all cases both entrepreneur and productive labourer. In a sense, then, the term *nangkodoh* has three separate meanings, in that three separate roles often combine in the person of a single smith. Firstly, *nangkodoh* refers to a particular productive role, i.e. the smith who directs forging operations, holds the hot steel with the tongs and uses a small hammer. Secondly, a *nangkodoh* is entrepreneur or manager of the enterprise. He buys materials, decides what is to be done and when, decides what is to be produced and how much, takes the goods to market and, when necessary, arranges for labour. Finally, the *nangkodoh* is the individual owner of the means of production.

The economic organisation of smithing concerns the social relations of production, distribution and consumption. Distribution is the function of the market, and smiths rely almost entirely on the Bukit Tinggi market as an outlet for their goods. The *nangkodoh* typically takes all his completed goods to one of some 25 traders in steel goods in Bukit Tinggi. These merchants, mostly Sungai Puar men as well, range from the roving street pedlar to the owners of small shops with investments in steelware of up to Rp. 2,000,000.

Tusan, for example, is a merchant of about 40 years of age. As a young man he worked as a smith in Sungai Puar, and managed to save enough money to buy a small shop in the Bukit Tinggi market. He buys the whole range of steel goods from the smiths of Limo Suku, and sells to individual consumers in the market who come to shop, or to other traders who buy larger quantities and transport them to other parts of Sumatra. Most of his spare cash he turns into steelware. As a result he is said to have accumulated about Rp. 2,000,000 worth, which he can sell when the price is right. Like the other merchants in Bukit Tinggi, Tusan has long-standing relationships with a number of smiths. He specialises in knives (although he sells all kinds of goods), and seems to trade regularly with perhaps 10 individual Limo Suku knife-makers who bring their wares to his shop on market days, or directly to his house in the village, to which he returns every day. He tries both to buy regularly and to buy a regular amount from these 10 smiths. Like other merchants Tusan occasionally lends small amounts of cash — never, as far as I could gather, large amounts — to producers with whom he has a trading agreement. There are no large-scale involvements of merchants in production, and no large debts of smiths to merchants.

By contrast, there is in effect a relatively continuous advancement of credit in the other direction. A merchant usually receives finished goods from smiths partly on a consignment basis, paying only as he sells them. If the market is good, the merchant will pay each week for about 50 per cent of the received goods. The following week, if sales are good, he will pay the remaining 50 per cent, and for 50 per cent of any new goods given to him. In effect then, when turnover is high, the producer receives the whole value of his goods each week while maintaining a permanent advance of credit to the merchant equal to 50 per cent of average weekly sales. Relations between merchants are similar. They will sell wholesale to roving pedlars, offering up to half the goods on consignment. The outstanding sum will be repaid by the pedlar if and when he is able to sell his goods in his trading area. Because these relationships require some trust on the part of the wholesaler, they tend to be stable over a period of time.

While a merchant may advise smiths about the state of the market, he has no direct say in the running of their operations. He may accept a specific order in Bukit Tinggi, and pass it on to one of his smiths. He may also have to vary the quantity he buys each week according to changing market conditions. According to one of the smiths who sells to Tusan, for example, in the six months leading up to the fasting month the market is relatively good, prices are stable and he can sell almost as much as he can produce. In the other half of the year prices are lower and demand shrinks.

When market conditions are bad, merchants pay less than 50 per cent market value to producers, and take a larger proportion on consignment. This tends to discourage smiths from producing more than the market will bear. By and large smiths of Limo Suku opt for decreasing production rather than stock-piling when demand for their goods is low.

Typically, as pointed out above, blacksmiths themselves take completed goods to Bukit Tinggi on market days. On Wednesdays, and often on Saturdays as well, forges may be shut down for at least a half-day while the *nangkodoh* goes to market. *Nangkodoh* are quite willing to sacrifice the time in order to reinforce the personal tie with the merchant in this way, as well as to pick up information on prices and conditions. At the same time they treat the excursion to Bukit Tinggi as a social outing, as well as an opportunity to shop for other household requirements.

Relations of distribution, then, serve to link entrepreneurs of similar standing. A small merchant is in many ways similar to a *nangkodoh*. Both act as independent decision-makers who rely on steady turnover to provide them with the cash needed for subsistence. While there are some merchants with a relatively large amount of capital, most, like the smiths, have little long-term investment. Merchants, like *nangkodoh*, are usually self-employed, and typically rely on labour other than their own perhaps even less than do the smiths. Transactions between two or more people, or tasks requiring the labour of two or more workers, such as the distribution of steel goods to areas outside the district of Agam, tend to be carried out by independent entrepreneurs, rather than by salaried representatives of a single entrepreneur. Relationships among small producers and distributors are thus between equals, in the sense that there is no direct economic control of one by the other. Just as no merchants own *apa*, so no smiths own shops. Relatively fluent operation of this system is ensured through this very independence, competition and the consignment system, which runs from producer to primary and thence to secondary distributors.

Much the same holds true of economic relations among people involved in the production process itself. During the period of my research a variety of productive forms existed side by side, although the individually owned enterprise was the predominant one. Under this typical arrangement a single producer owns his means of production, buys raw materials and sells his goods freely in Bukit Tinggi. Relations among such producers are analogous to the relationships between smiths and merchants – an economic equality among economically independent entrepreneurs. This is not to say that all producers and merchants are equally wealthy – on the contrary. They are economically equal, however, in the sense that no one is tied by relations of property to another. An individual owns the *apa*, the tools, the raw materials and the stock of completed products.

All this, however, is not to say that producers and pedlars are autonomous economic beings set down in the anarchy of an unstructured setting. Just as Marx showed that the apparent freedom of the labourer under capitalism masked a division between owners of the means of production and those who had only their labour power to sell, so he showed that behind the apparently natural constitution of a commodity economy lay a social as well as a technological division of labour. The social relations in the commodity economy appear, in fetishised form, as relations between the commodities themselves expressed as exchange value. Producers and merchants appear all to be linked by the material flows between them. However, as Marx shows in the opening chapters of *Capital*: 'This fetishism of commodities has its origin . . . in the peculiar social character of the labour that produces them' (1971, vol. 1, p. 72). Exchange value is itself a product of a social system which converts concrete to abstract human labour, and labour time to socially necessary labour time. This in turn rests on a technical division of labour whereby individuals are required to produce goods which have for them no direct use value, and, more importantly, on a social division of labour under which producers of goods are the owners of their products. The social division of labour in a commodity economy refers, therefore, to a particular kind of property relation, which gives to producers the control of their product. It is therefore necessary, then, when discussing an economy of seemingly autonomous producers such as this one, to recognise that behind the fetishised relations between commodities stands a social relation among producers, and between producers and merchants.

While the independently owned productive unit is the predominant economic form in the Limo Suku blacksmithing industry, there are others. In some *apa*, *nangkodoh* hire labourers for a wage. In others, close kin ties — particularly the father—son relationship — are used to recruit labour. In the former case, payment for labour takes the form of a division of revenue, in the latter, methods were less formal.

In *apa* with wage labourers there prevails, despite the employer—employee relationship, an ideology of equality. This is reflected in the way the smiths conceptualise payment to labour. Work is paid for on a sort of piece-work basis. The piece-work rate is calculated on the basis of the cost of raw materials, or the market price. It is commonly assumed that the total cost of raw materials should equal the total payment to labour. Total cost of production is, then, reckoned to equal $2x$ where x is the cost of raw materials. If, for example, the steel goods turned out by a single *apa* in one week can be sold for Rp. 10,000, then the *nangkodoh* calculates his 'wages bill' — which interestingly includes his own return as well, as we shall see — by dividing this in half. One half should cover the cost of coal, steel and other cash outlays, the other half paying for labourers[1] — including the *nangkodoh* himself. Assume, for example, that there are four workers: one *nangkodoh*, two sledgers and one bellows operator. The *nangkodoh* sets aside half the money, i.e. Rp. 5,000, to buy coal, steel and other necessary inputs. The other half is divided into five equal parts (the number

1. This is the general rule. In some cases, due to price changes, the cost of raw materials exceeds half the total (see below for examples). Here the additional money comes out of the share for the *apa*.

of workers plus one). Each of the four workers receives one share, Rp. 1,000 each in this example. According to the general conception, the *nangkodoh* receives a share exactly equal to that of all the other productive workers. But there remains the fifth share: this is said to be 'for the *apa*'. When I asked how this share was used, since raw materials and other inputs had already been accounted for, and since most tools were produced by the work group itself, the answer was that it was for general upkeep of the *apa* — what we might call depreciation and maintenance. As I shall show, under normal conditions this fifth share goes almost entirely to the *nangkodoh*. In spite of an ideology of equality, which extends to an egalitarian conception of the distribution of income within the *apa*, there is it seems, a kind of hidden profit accruing to the owner of the *apa* — the *nangkodoh*.[1] In some cases this fifth share does not go entirely to the *nangkodoh*, as I shall also show. Nonetheless, Table 5.4 demonstrates how average returns to *nangkodoh* are higher than returns to wage workers in the *apa*.

These data are taken from a survey of earnings in 11 *apa* (see below). Because the figures have been calculated after the deduction of expenses to be taken out of the share 'for the *apa*', they show that the *nangkodoh* can extract a slight surplus from his labourers — a surplus which an independent producer has no means of generating.

It is unusual for a single entrepreneur to hire more than two or three labourers, although some employ up to four. Thus the total number of workers in a single *apa* ranges from one, for an independent producer, to five for some *apa* (I always include the *nangkodoh* himself as one of the productive labourers). Only outside the village do smiths work in larger enterprises, outstanding examples of which are the machine shops in Medan in North Sumatra, and the railway and mining workshops in West Sumatra.

Where labour is recruited on the basis of a kinship tie, it is unlikely that earnings will be distributed in the manner just described. When a father has persuaded his son to work in his *apa*, he will

---

1. It is interesting to note in passing the history of the profit concept in Britain in the nineteenth century. Meek (1973) attempts to show that a developed theory of profit came only with the break-up of small-scale handicraft production and the advent of the factory system. It was at this time that the classical economists, particularly Smith and Ricardo, began to look for a separate form of income, different from wages and rent, which was to be called 'profit'.

Table 5.4   *Average earnings of smiths*

Worker	Average net return per hour (Rp.)
Nangkodoh	62.6
Independent producer	51.0
Sledger (wage worker)	32.1

probably not pay him a wage. One such father explained to me that he supported his son, and therefore did not need to pay him a share of earnings. The boy agreed that his father was generous with pocket money, and he did not expect to earn a wage. Similar informal compensation arrangements frequently apply when a man hires a young male kinsman to operate the bellows, or an older man – for example, his own father or father-in-law. When, however, the *nangkodoh* works with a close kinsman of about the same age, such as a brother, then payment is closely calculated. As it happens, the use of kinsmen in an *apa* is neither popular nor frequent. Many smiths expressed a disinclination to employ kinsmen. There was general agreement that ties of kinship and business do not mix. The instances of reliance on kin seem to have been cases of less successful smiths who had trouble scraping together sufficient cash to start an *apa*.

Table 5.5 illustrates the variety of economic forms in smithing by presenting material on the class position of all the smiths in my sample census, including residents and migrants. The data are largely self-explanatory. They show the preponderance of the individually owned enterprise in 1972. Of 512 blacksmiths who live and work in Limo Suku or elsewhere, only 117, or 22.9 per cent, work for a wage within a traditional *apa* group. An additional 4.1 per cent work for a larger enterprise outside the village, and 9 per cent, mostly young men, work for a close kinsman; 61.6 per cent of all smiths own their means of production. Indeed, the tendency towards individual enterprises is even stronger, since the appearance of class differentiation is partly the result of age, a fact illustrated if we compare the categories of married and unmarried smiths.

Decision-making and economic behaviour

A survey I carried out during my fieldwork provides us with a

Table 5.5 *Economic relations in blacksmithing – breakdown by class of total population of working smiths (residents and migrants)*

Productive role	Married smiths			Unmarried smiths			Total	
	Number	Row percentage	Column percentage	Number	Row percentage	Column percentage	Number	Column percentage
Nangkodoh (4–5 labourers)	23	96	6.5	1	4	0.6	24	4.7
Nangkodoh (2–3 labourers)	100	90	28.4	11	10	6.9	111	21.7
Independent producer	115	64	32.7	65	36	40.6	180	35.2
Wage worker	72	62	20.5	45	38	28.1	117	22.9
Worker with close kinsman	8	17	2.3	38	83	23.8	46	9.0
Wage worker with large enterprise	21	100	6.0	0	0	0	21	4.1
Other	13	100	3.7	0	0	0	13	2.5
Total	352			160			512	

statistical picture of the operations – the micro-economics – of these entrepreneurs. Data were recorded for each of 11 *apa* over a period of one month on the number of hours worked, the quantity of goods produced and sold, the number and earnings of the workers, consumption of raw materials and other costs. Data from six *apa* were collected during the month of June 1972 and from the remaining five in the following month. At the same time consumption surveys of 11 families were also carried out. One smith from each *apa* was selected, and data were recorded in his home on daily purchases of food, clothing and other consumption goods.

The data on production are presented in Table 5.6. Costs were calculated on the basis of information supplied by the individual *nangkodoh* and from other sources. The cost of producing a small axe known as *kapak tukang* can serve as an illustration of the methods employed in the survey. In order to produce one *kodi* (20) of these small axes, a *nangkodoh* must spend Rp. 1,690 on materials alone, in the following proportions:

Scrap steel (rail)	= 1½ kilos/axe	@ Rp. 30/kg	= Rp. 900/*kodi*
Coal	= 2½ kilos/axe	@ Rp. 10/kg	= Rp. 500/*kodi*
Files	= 2/7 *kodi*	@ Rp. 650 ea.	= Rp. 186/*kodi*
Polishing grit	= ½ kilo/*kodi*		= Rp. 15/*kodi*
Sandpaper			= Rp. 90/*kodi*
Total cost of materials			= Rp. 1,690/*kodi*

The list excludes depreciation on or replacement of the stock of tools, anvil and *apa*. Since tools and the building are produced free by the workers, however, their cost in money terms is minimal. The anvil, too, represents a very small cost per unit of product because it lasts for a long time.

The other major expense is the payment to labour. The price of *kapak tukang* in 1972 was Rp. 3,000 for a *kodi*. Labour costs are thus reckoned to be Rp. 1,500 per *kodi*. Wages are in this way related directly to productivity. As I have already pointed out, if there are four workers in the *apa*, the wage is divided into five equal parts, one share of Rp. 300 going to each worker, and the fifth kept back 'for the *apa*'. The *nangkodoh* must pay wages to the others out of his own pocket, regardless of whether the goods produced have been sold and paid for. Wages are usually paid every Thursday and Sunday. There is a difference, therefore, between what the *nangkodoh* actually receives in any one week, and his potential earnings which are not always immediately realised. To summarise for the case of the production of *kapak tukang*:

Cost of materials	= Rp. 1,690/*kodi*
Labour	= Rp. 1,500/*kodi*
to other workers	= Rp. 300/*kodi* each
to *nangkodoh* (includes share for the *apa*)	= Rp. 600/*kodi*
'Profit' (price less costs)	= Rp. 110/*kodi*
Potential earnings of *nangkodoh*	= Rp. 410/*kodi*

Given the market price at the time of the survey, raw material costs for small axes exceeded expectations. The extra Rp. 190 needed to cover the cost (the difference between total material costs and half the revenue) came out of the share for the *apa*. Under normal circumstances, then, assuming that the *nangkodoh* makes no other cash outlays (as is normally the case) the profit over and above the *nangkodoh*'s wage share would have been Rp. 300/*kodi*. The relatively low profit in this case is, then, exceptional. Nonetheless the *nangkodoh*'s potential earnings are a little over 30 per cent greater than those of any other worker, because of the surplus hidden in the share for the *apa*.

The data presented in Table 5.6 bear out some of the points made earlier. Raw material costs greatly exceed initial levels of investment. Average estimated raw material costs per month for all *apa* are Rp. 13,629, for those *apa* in which steel is actually forged, Rp. 16,013 and for *apa* which forge the heavier goods, axes and hoes, Rp. 21,499.

Unlike other peasant activities, smithing is almost a full-time specialisation. The average number of hours spent in forging in a month is 132.8. This excludes extra hours spent, such as the time a *nangkodoh* spends in managerial tasks like marketing. It also excludes the twelfth smith in the sample, who missed more than a month's work because of illness. It was not unusual, moreover, for some *nangkodoh* to stop smithing for periods of at least several weeks. What the figures show is simply that, when working, Limo Suku smiths tend to work full time.

Table 5.6 *Production survey of 11 'apa' for one-month period*

Apa number	Number of workers	Days	Hours	Product (1)	(2)	Coal* (Rp.)	Steel* (Rp.)	Other* (Rp.)	Material* costs (total) (Rp.)	Wages (Rp.) Total	Nang-kodoh	Sledger
1	4	17½	135	kapak tukang		6,250	25,000	750	27,885	24,750	9,900	4,950
2	4	22	179	kapak (2½ pound)		7,475	13,000	1,900	20,680	23,375	9,350	4,675
3	4	4	48	kapak (2½ pound)		–	–	–	7,520	8,500	3,400	1,700
4	5	25½	222	kapak tukang		10,000	–	2,350	49,885	44,250	14,750	7,375
5	3–4	11	112	sickles		900	–	–	7,650	13,125	5,425	3,281
6	3	15	119	knife blades		1,550	–	–	3,520	3,275	–	–
7	4	8	54	hoes	machetes	2,100	–	–	12,195	7,650	–	–
8	1	23	148	knives (files)		–	(blades) 3,000	220	3,500	–	–	–
9	1	14½	107	knives (files)		–	(blades) 2,000	–	2,300	–	–	–
10	3–4	21	179½	knives (files and forges)		1,150	980	400	4,000	10,300	5,000	–
11	2–3	20½	157	kapak tukang	machetes	2,500	–	300	10,790	7,400	–	–

* The data on the cost of materials refer (for coal, steel and other) to materials actually purchased during the time of the survey. The material costs figure is based on the cost at the time of materials used up in production. There is a discrepancy between the two because in any one month smiths may be drawing from their stocks, or they may be laying in stocks.

Table 5.6 continued

Apa number	Total amount produced (1)	(2)	Value of goods (Rp.)	Amount received (Rp.)	Profit (potential) (Rp.)	Total to nangkodoh (wage plus profit) (Rp.)
1	16½ kodi†		49,500	49,500	-3,135	6,765
2	11 kodi		46,750	34,175	2,695	12,045
3	4 kodi		17,000	17,000	880	4,280
4	20½ kodi		88,500	55,300	-5,635	9,115
5	15 kodi		26,250	22,500	5,475	7,150
6	44 dozen		11,000	8,500	4,205	4,205
7	126 hoes	30 machetes	43,750	26,250	23,905	23,905
8	13 dozen		9,750	5,250	6,250	6,250
9	2 dozen small	7 dozen large	8,700	8,700	6,400	6,400
10	26 kodi small	4 kodi large	20,600	15,100	5,800	10,800
11	axe – 2 kodi	machete – 9½ kodi	25,000	4,000	6,810	6,810

† 1 kodi = 20

The data also show the higher potential earnings of *nangkodoh*, as owners of the means of production, as well as the greater risk that they must take, as evidenced by the fact that potential earnings were rarely realised in the short run.

Smithing is a strenuous occupation: it involves hard physical labour in difficult conditions. It can also be dangerous, as those who have had to submit to an operation to remove bits of metal which splintered off in forging can testify. For their efforts the smiths are poorly rewarded. Total output per worker is low. Time is lost because the *nangkodoh* or independent producer takes off at least one half-day per week to go to Bukit Tinggi to sell, or, often, because coal and steel are in short supply. Because smiths operate on the proverbial shoe-string they cannot stockpile their basic raw materials in sufficient quantity to ride out these periods of shortage. In some periods of the year demand for their goods is slack, and there is no point in overproducing. Cash, on the other hand, is a daily necessity for most. Even if the smith has enough rice to provide for his family for a proportion of the year, families need vegetables, fish and other food. The level of savings is low; any interruption of the cycle of production and marketing can therefore cause hardship.

But even apart from these vicissitudes – even when most forges are operating at full capacity – smithing does not provide a comfortable living. Even when demand for his products is sufficient to permit him to work a full five days a week, a *nangkodoh* may earn only a little over the equivalent of £2 a week.

Why should this be so? Why should it be that labour in this part of the world yields such meagre rewards? Why is it that the technological level of smithing is so low? Frequently the answers provided by anthropologists and other social scientists to questions like these lay most emphasis on the processes of individual decision-making. It is often argued that the peasant producer is held back by traditional attitudes which lead him to make less than economically optimal arrangements and decisions. Is the Limo Suku smith failing to grasp the opportunities offered to him? Is he behaving in a way which a western 'economic man' would consider irrational? Can the structure and technology of blacksmithing in Limo Suku be explained in terms of the attitudes and decisions of individual smiths, or must we turn elsewhere for answers to these questions?

The data presented in Table 5.6 make it possible to examine critically one important aspect of the micro-economics of black-smithing typically involved in this kind of argument – the question of scale.[1] Many anthropologists concerned with the problem of underdevelopment focus their explanations on the small scale of peasant enterprise. For example, Peter Lloyd, in summarising a number of studies of peasant society, concludes that these societies are characterised by the 'social isolation of the individual family and the intensity of competition between families. Cooperation is minimal' (1971; p. 40). Foster (1960) and Rubel *et al.* (1968) have termed this phenomenon 'atomism'. The assumption behind many of these studies is that it is the small scale of peasant enterprise that prevents development, and hence it is the obstacles to cooperation stemming from social organisation that are, at the same time, the major obstacles to economic (i.e. capitalist) development. These obstacles have usually been thought to be cultural – e.g. amoral familism (Banfield and Banfield, 1958); fatalism, child-rearing techniques (Swift, 1965) and the like.

The data presented in this chapter allow us to counter these suggestions and to show that the micro-economic behaviour of Limo Suku blacksmiths represents a 'rational' adaptation to certain existing economic structures. The facts that cultural explanations prove inadequate, and that micro-economic analysis, as we shall see, fails to explain these economic structures, mean that an answer to our questions must be found elsewhere.

Let us consider the hypothetical case of a *nangkodoh* who, having read Foster, decides to expand his production by expanding the size of the *apa* work group, thereby overcoming the problems of small-scale organisation. It is doubtful whether simply expanding the work group alone would increase his profits. While adding more workers might increase total output, by allowing workers to 'spell' each other and thus work marginally faster, it is highly unlikely that marginal productivity would exceed marginal costs. Although the data in Table 5.6 are not statistically significant, they do illustrate this point. If the production schedules of *apa* numbers 1 and 4 are compared, it will be seen that both produce the same goods – *kapak tukang*. The only difference in internal organisation is that number 1 has only four workers while number 4 has five. Number 4 produces 79 per cent more goods in only

1. I have dealt with this problem in more detail elsewhere (Kahn, 1975).

64 per cent more total time spent by the *apa* group in forging. The larger group, then, appears to be more productive. Nevertheless, because of the added cost of employing a fifth worker, the *nangkodoh* in number 4 earns 24 per cent less than the *nangkodoh* in number 1. In fact, of course, productivity per man-hour is lower in number 4. Increased production, therefore comes at greater expense, unit costs are greater, and the *nangkodoh* earns less. This merely illustrates – obviously such a simple, single comparison could not prove – my general impression that the size of work groups reflected the most 'economic' combination of factors of production under existing circumstances.[1]

A second way to enlarge the scale of production would be for *nangkodoh* to finance additional work groups. Some of the tools might be shared, but most tools and all raw materials would have to be duplicated. Because he could not work in both groups at the same time, the entrepreneur would have to find a second man to work as *nangkodoh* in a second *apa*. This kind of amalgamation of *apa* units under individual ownership took place at least once between 1958 and 1965 (see below, Chapter 7). It is possible that such expansion would result in very slightly increased production. One of the *nangkodohs* – or quasi-*nangkodohs* – would not be forced to close down the forge once a week to go to market. However, the increase in output would be minimal, and the only advantage to be gained is that the entrepreneur might increase his profit, without the absolute amount of surplus in the economy being increased unless this profit were used to increase productivity. Given conditions in the early 1970s, however, this kind of expansion remains an unlikely possibility for several related reasons. First, there are few, if any, entrepreneurs with sufficient capital to finance more than one *apa*. Cash outlays are quite high when the extension of credit to the merchants, the need for at least some stockpiling of raw materials and the need to pay workers promptly are taken into account. Related to this is the relatively low price of steelware. Given the price structure, there is relatively little room for profits. As I shall argue later, it was rising prices in the late 1950s and early 1960s which partly accounted for the increased scale of entrepreneurial units. Finally,

1. A similar conclusion was reached by Schultz, an agricultural economist, in a survey of anthropological studies of peasant agriculture. Schultz concluded that: 'There are comparatively few significant inefficiencies in the allocation of factors of production in traditional agriculture' (1964).

it would be very difficult for our expansion-minded entrepreneur to find anyone willing to act as *nangkodoh* in the second *apa* at a wage equal to that of any other wage labourer. It was said, for example, that only those few *nangkodoh* in some financial trouble, due to emergency expenditure, would work for the government project in 1971 (Chapter 7). Low rates of capital accumulation within smithing, low profits, relatively low prices and the wage structure are the main factors which militate against increased scale of economic enterprise in Sungai Puar. These factors are all reflections of more basic aspects of economic structure, particularly the structure of an economy dominated by individual enterprises.

It is clear that the *nangkodoh*'s options are constrained by a number of givens. The combined effect of market prices, costs and wage levels serves to set very rigid limits to the form of black-smithing enterprises. The crucial limiting factors in the decision-making model must be taken as given. They themselves are not subject to analysis, and therefore remain external to it. It will be my contention that these factors are external only in that they appear so to any theory based on individual decision-making. When the scope of the analysis is broadened — spatially, temporally and theoretically — it will be seen that the apparent limits to decision are merely manifestations of basic economic relations in the social formation. In subsequent chapters I shall attempt to show that when this is recognised the specificity of peasant production in concrete cases can be more adequately understood.

This discussion of a concrete case of peasant economic activity demonstrates both the advantages and the disadvantages of dealing solely with a concrete object of study. As I have shown for the case of subsistence agriculture, this case illustrates the dangers of applying abstract models too directly. While Terray, for example, finds that economic forms in particular branches of the Guro economy are almost direct realisations of two different modes of production, such a conclusion would be vastly to oversimplify the concrete world of the Limo Suku smith. In this branch of the economy, as in subsistence agriculture, a variety of forms exist side-by-side. Capitalist labour arrangements are found alongside petty commodity production. Even the capitalist-like enterprises are permeated by other relations. The small scale of enterprises employing wage labour is partly a result of the alternative of individual production. The ideology of equality and profit-sharing which covers up the *nangkodoh*'s surplus is, moreover, determined in part by the predominant economic form. To attempt to root the abstract in the concrete, to localise a mode of production, or to expect some neat coincidence of particular technologies and specific productive relations is to degrade both levels of analysis.

While, therefore, a concrete analysis points up the difficulties in direct application of abstract models, it also has severe disadvantages. The most obvious is the one made manifest in the paradox of local social and economic forms. I have argued, and in this illustrated a point made by others, that on the one hand Limo Suku smiths are largely following certain principles of economic rationality which arise from the givens of their economic existence, while on the other hand, all that micro-analysis can show is the internal rationality of behaviour within externally imposed limits. Rational adaptation does not lead to the kind of economic growth which planners, and the smiths themselves, actively pursue. If anything is irrational, then, it is these barriers to growth set by economic structure. It is not because they produce certain kinds of goods that smiths organise themselves in this way. Neither does the technology of smithing determine these forms. Rather, as I shall try to show, it is because peasant producers stand in a particular social relation to other classes in the social formation that smithing takes on the specific social forms described in this chapter. To illustrate this point further I shall present a discussion of other kinds of economic activity in the village. It will be seen that smithing is, in the main, typical of commodity production and distribution.

6
Occupation, class and the peasant economy

While rice cultivation and blacksmithing are the most common occupations of the people of Limo Suku, they are not necessarily the most preferred. Farming throughout the province and smithing in the village are truly the work of peasants (*urang kampuang*), work which is difficult, hot and uninteresting. All villagers, the young in particular, show greater interest in other possibilities. Many aspire to a job in government service. However lowly, a government clerk (*pegawai*) has a steady income, lives in an urban environment and avoids dirtying his hands by heavy labour. Almost on a par are those who manage to enter the armed forces. The high value placed on jobs of this sort at the same time leads to an emphasis on the value of education for those who can afford its inevitable costs.

While government service is attractive to some, many aspire to the life of a merchant or trader, the preferred occupation of Minangkabau migrants for centuries. Commercial work combines the practical with the romantic — it provides both an income and a chance to escape what are seen to be the narrow confines of village life.

Within the village, too, it is possible to earn money in other ways, although the alternatives are not nearly so attractive. There are a limited number of entrepreneurial niches. At the same time, local men and women make mats, produce a species of light metal goods known as *progol*, run small shops and cafés and teach in village schools. Neither does this exhaust the list of possibilities, as Tables 6.1 and 6.2 show. The tables themselves do not indicate the presence of a number of villagers whose major source of income is the pension which accrues to retired government employees and armed service personnel, nor of the *adat* chiefs and religious officials, who hold positions which, although they are

Minangkabau social formations

Table 6.1   *Occupations of working residents*

A. Men (married and unmarried)

Occupation	Number
Blacksmith	281
Carpenter	15
Progol-maker	12
Craftsman (other goods)	11
Tailor	2
Merchant	58
Student	49
Serviceman in armed forces	1
Labourer	1
Driver	7
Farmer	49
Civil servant	6
Missing data	7
	499

B. Women (married and unmarried)

Occupation	Number
Rumah tangga	663
Craftswoman	3
Farmer	30
Mat-maker	13
Seamstress	61
Farmer + mat-maker/seamstress	5
Merchant	32
Student	44
Teacher	5
	856

Table 6.2   *Occupations of working migrants*

A. Men (married and unmarried)

Occupation	Number
Smith	152
Carpenter	9
Progol-maker	1
Craftsman (other goods)	24
Tailor	7
Merchant	321
Student	60
Serviceman in armed forces	16
Labourer	10
Dos (horsecart) driver	7
Barber	1
Driver	25
Farmer	11
Civil servant	46
Unemployed	7
Missing data	17
	714

B. Women (married and unmarried)

Occupation	Number
Rumah tangga	413
Craftswoman	1
Farmer	7
Mat-maker	1
Seamstress	3
Merchant	17
Student	42
Civil servant	15
	499

not full-time occupational specialisations, nonetheless have economic implications.

Broadly speaking, the economic activities of the people of Limo Suku might be divided into three main categories, which are at least implicitly recognised by the people themselves. These categories are: domestic labour, peasant commodity production and distribution, and wage and salaried work. The categories depend on two important distinctions. The first of these is between what is in some sense really work as opposed to what is not, a distinction which refers partly to the expenditure of physical effort (*bagarak*), but perhaps more to earning money. Most people, therefore, do work which is in some sense not considered real, but which nonetheless involves both time and effort. Clearly women, more than men, are involved in this sphere – something which I have already pointed out with regard to the census data. When asked their occupation women most frequently answered '*rumah tanggo*', a term which could most simply be translated by 'housewife'. It inevitably implies, however, at least something, and often a good deal, besides household chores. Most 'housewives' cultivate rice, raise animals and do other agricultural or gardening work. Men who are not full-time farmers also do not directly equate agricultural work with 'real work', i.e. work which earns a cash income.

There is a second distinction between work which does produce a cash income through either the production or the distribution of commodities on a small scale in what might be called the peasant sector of the economy, and wage or salaried work in which income is paid by the government or a large private firm. A strong distinction is made, for example, between a peasant producer and an urban worker, a distinction which recognises the uniqueness of the wage form.

Having briefly discussed the three sorts of occupation pursued by the villagers, I shall turn to the peasant sector, for my aim is to uncover the basic similarity which links all such economic activities and distinguishes them from both the subsistence and the non-peasant sector of the Indonesian economy.

Commodity production and distribution: residents

Peasant production in the village and outside is carried out by both women and men. There is a rough division of labour between female and male crafts, although women are also engaged in some primarily male activities like petty trading. There are some rather important differences between the organisation of female and male crafts.

The main occupations in the village peasant sector for men, apart from smithing, are carpentry, *progol*-making, selling and trading, and farming. Carpenters in Limo Suku can be roughly divided into house-builders and furniture-makers.

House-builders contract either for a daily wage or, more often, for an over-all payment for their labour. Few house-builders work alone. Instead most prefer to hire at least one assistant who shares in the payment. Some specialise in woodwork and carpentry, while some are experts also in stonework and masonry. The demand for new houses in Sungai Puar is relatively high. There is also a large demand for household repairs and renovations. In between jobs house-builders often work as furniture-makers, smiths, agricultural labourers and the like.

Some carpenters specialise in making furniture — beds, chairs, tables and cabinets. Most of them work alone, although again some hire labourers. Both house-builders and furniture-makers work either alone or in very small productive units with at most two or three employees. There are no large-scale entrepreneurial units, nor is there any use of mechanised methods of production. All those involved in carpentry are productive labourers, there are no cases of a non-working entrepreneur who finances a carpentry workshop. Most furniture-makers work in either their own homes or small sheds or out-houses built in the compound. They usually work to order from local customers and rarely sell to people outside the village.

After blacksmithing, the making of metal goods called *progol* is the largest men's craft in Limo Suku. *Progol* refers to a range of functional and decorative items made most often from thin metal sheet. This sheet metal is not forged, but rather pressed into wooden moulds. *Progol*-makers produce decorative hangers for mosquito netting and lamp holders; during the election, they did a busy trade in campaign buttons.

Other *progol*-makers work in a heavier metal alloy which is shaped with hammers and pliers. The most common product of this heavier work is beard clippers, which are still often used instead of razors.

Most *progol*-makers work either alone or with members of their own elementary families. Fathers and sons frequently work together – and there is no strict division of earnings. The largest *progol* enterprise is owned by a man with three small workshops in the compound of his wife's house. All his employees are close kin, most of them his sons-in-law, who live in the house.

The statistics on village occupations show a surprisingly large number of merchants living in Limo Suku. Many of these are traders who work outside the village, but spend some days in the village with their families. Some of these engage in a form of trade known as *manggaleh babelok* of 'trading around'. These men and women base themselves in Limo Suku and go away regularly on temporary trading trips. Some of the resident traders live in the village and work in Bukit Tinggi or other market towns. In most districts of West Sumatra there is a kind of satellite market system of weekly local markets, which supplement the market days in the market centre. Small traders bring goods to these local markets from either their home villages or market centres like Bukit Tinggi. Some Limo Suku merchants buy agricultural produce or the products of local craftsmen to sell in these local markets. Some own or rent stalls or small shops in one or several nearby market towns, to which they travel – on foot, by bicycle or by *oplet* – on market days. A number of resident traders and merchants also own land in Limo Suku, which they may farm part time.

There is another group of merchants and traders living in the village who buy goods outside in order to sell them within the village. The steel and coal merchants mentioned in the previous chapter fall into this category. They may sell direct to blacksmiths or, in some cases, to yet smaller local traders, who in turn sell to the smiths.

Finally, there is a relatively small group of people who own or rent shops and stalls in the small Sungai Puar market known as the *Balai Panjang*. This is a small market area with about 10 small shops and a covered area where agricultural produce – rice, potatoes, tomatoes, chillies, sweet potatoes and the like – is sold to local housewives. These shops sell a variety of things such as dishes, kitchen utensils, cigarettes and stationery. Apart from the local market there are a number of small shops known as *lapau* which sell soap, cigarettes, small amounts of food and spices, dried fish, eggs, sweets and cakes, and the paraffin used by all villagers for cooking and lighting. Some of these *lapau* double as coffee shops, where the owners and their families serve coffee, tea, cakes, and some cooked snacks like *bubua* (a rice porridge) and occasionally *ampiang badadiah*, a local delicacy made from molasses, stamped rice flakes and a kind of buffalo-milk cheese. At night some village men gather in the *lapau* to drink coffee, gossip and play cards or dominoes.

There are a large number of *lapau* in Sungai Puar. It seems as though every second or third house has a small window in which the occupants hang a few bunches of bananas or a couple of packets of cigarettes for sale. Of the larger *lapau* which serve coffee, there were eight during my stay. The owners of these coffee shops were all ex-migrants who had worked as traders before returning to the village. All these local shops are individually owned and run either by the owner alone or with help from members of his or her family. They buy supplies in one of the local markets, from local producers or in Bukit Tinggi, and sell them to villagers at a minimal mark-up.

The level of investment in local trading enterprises is very small, with the possible exception of the coal and steel merchants. There is a general tendency for trade goods to pass through several hands before they actually reach the consumer — with each participant in the chain receiving a small fraction of the mark-up. In contrast, a large enterprise would control the whole trade, both wholesale and retail. The coal trade provides a good example of this process. One villager, when he gets some cash together, finds a lorry owner—driver and contracts with him to bring coal in from Sawah Lunto. When it comes to Limo Suku the shipment is immediately broken down and sold to a number of small traders and *lapau*-owners, some of whom buy no more than a single sack. These people pre-burn the coal and break it up into smaller lots, which they deliver and sell to individual smiths. Almost all the actors in this chain are independent, trading on minute amounts of merchant capital. The lorry driver, the wholesale merchant and the local traders may be linked through temporary debts, as some goods are given on consignment. But all are independent actors. Indeed the actual trade chain may be different each time. This is in direct contrast with what a vertically integrated commercial firm might look like, with its own transportation, wholesale and retail outlets.

While women are involved in some of the above-mentioned crafts, they are outnumbered by men. Women more often engage in sewing and mat-making to earn a cash income. Many young women starting at the age of about 14 sew clothes for sale in the Bukit Tinggi market. The main commodity they sew on machines is children's clothes, for which there is a large demand both in the village and throughout the highland area. They also sew some adults' clothes, but children's clothes are far more important. The designs are relatively standardised. The cloth is cut and sewn by women on foot-powered machines in their homes. The finished products are sold mostly in Bukit Tinggi by street pedlars, many of whom are also women. Most seamstresses work part time.

As for the other crafts, the cooperative group in sewing is small. Most frequently women work alone in their houses. In some cases a mother works with her daughter or daughters, or women work with their sisters. Some buy their own machines, while others rent them. Here, however, the similarity with men's crafts ends. While productive groups in smithing and carpentry coincide with the entrepreneurial unit, and while the productive worker is an economically independent actor, many seamstresses are tied into larger enterprises. While some of them own their own machines, most women produce for a larger entrepreneur who supplies them with cloth, patterns and orders, and takes the finished goods to sell in Bukit Tinggi. Over-all control of the sewing industry rests largely in the hands of a small number of merchants, mostly men. These men earn a profit which is entirely independent of wages.

Because villagers were extremely reluctant to admit that they worked for an outsider − often known as an *induak samang* or *tokai* − and since rich merchants absolutely refuse to discuss their arrangements, I was not able to get detailed data on the scope and size of these operations. One such entrepreneur, perhaps the richest man in Limo Suku, refused even to allow me to do a census of his household. My impression was that there were at least two men who 'put out' cloth to up to 50 women each. Others, men and women, run smaller enterprises of this type, with ties in each case to perhaps 10 women who do the actual sewing. In the case of these smaller enterprises, run by women, the entrepreneur does some of the sewing herself and takes the clothes to sell them herself in the market.

Finally, a number of women sew alone, without outside control. They may work with daughters or other close kin and share the earnings.

While sewing involves mostly younger women, many older women make mats from a reed (*mensiro*) which grows in the village. The reed must be dried in the sun and flattened before it can be woven into mats. Older women told me that they preferred to make mats both because when they were young there was no machine-sewing (a comparatively recent occupation), and because sewing required more strength and stamina. The women, particularly those over the age of 50, typically have very bad eyesight. They said that they could not cope with the hand—eye coordination so important to using a sewing machine. Mat-making on the other hand, is less strenuous and can be done almost entirely by touch. Women up to 90 years of age continue to make mats.

All locally produced mats are of the large, floor-mat type used as a basic floor covering. Finer mats laid down for eating and praying are usually machine made and brought into the village from elsewhere.

As with sewing, mat-making is not often a full-time occupation. Like the seamstresses, the women who make mats often do so on a putting-out basis, with local entrepreneurs providing the raw materials, paying a piecework wage, and selling the mats in Bukit Tinggi or in one of the satellite markets in the area. Other women grow their own reeds, dry them and stamp them flat before weaving the mats and selling them directly. Others buy the reeds and then sell to a merchant. Both sewing and mat-making are characterised by a larger proportion of large-scale entrepreneurial units than the other occupations in Limo Suku, although, as for the other crafts, there are independent producers as well.

Commodity production and distribution: migrants

The main occupation of migrants — apart from those who work in the government or capitalist sectors — are smithing, other craft work and trading. Trading (*manggaleh*) is the migrant Minangkabau occupation *par excellence*. Trading and farming, for the village residents, are considered the main work of the Minangkabau, although the two are usually conceived of as polar opposites. Most merchants and petty traders become so, they say, because they do not have the patience for farming, the epitome of village work. Traders are in general envied by other villagers, who see the life as easier and more interesting than the dull life of the villages. Traders and travelling men feature prominently in Minangkabau myths and stories.

Minangkabau traders buy and sell amost everything — the Chinese in West Sumatra have no monopolies as they do in other parts of Indonesia. In a market place in any West Sumatra town can be found the usual range of home-grown foodstuffs — chillies, rice, tomatoes, cabbage, potatoes, sugar, fish, meat, oranges, bananas, pineapples, papayas, mangoes and spices — as well as imported tinned foods; dishes, pots, pans, and a variety of tools both local and imported; books, stationery and school supplies; lamps, stoves, sewing machines and bicycles; mirrors, soap, tooth-paste, scent and small items of clothing (all called *kolontong*); batik and imported cloth, shoes and clothing; and so on. A single area of the Bukit Tinggi market place is informally set aside for each particular branch of the retail trade. Here a large number of merchants, small and large, display their wares side by side. Shoppers, then, have a vast choice, although the types of individual product are relatively limited.

There is very little overt competition among merchants for customers, in the sense of open efforts to bid customers away from one another. On the other hand all transactions require bargaining, a long-drawn-out process. While the competition appears always to be between individual customer and merchant, if the customer is unhappy with the merchant's final price, he or she will simply move on to the next stall; and while a second merchant will begin to bargain only when the customer moves to his particular stall, the fact that bargaining does take place and seems to be genuine suggests that the ability of customers to move from one stall to another, bargaining, reflects some implicit competition among the merchants. On the other hand, in spite of a total lack of open collusion, the prices for any particular good seem to end up relatively uniform.

Customers do not cooperate with each other either in any direct way. A person who feels that he is being unfairly treated by a shopkeeper never turns for support to a bystander. He or she simply moves on to another place. It seems that when someone is cheated — either customer or merchant — there is no pity for the victim. Rather there is a kind of admiration for the more clever bargainer, and what amounts to scorn for the victim.

Peasants have frequently been described as standing in fear of shopping — fear of the superior intelligence, skills and power of the merchant. In Minangkabau there is no such fear. All Minangkabau are expected to be commercially competent, and commercial astuteness is highly admired.

A villager who plans to buy anything in the market usually inquires among friends as to the price he or she would expect to pay. In fact, whenever anyone returns from the market carrying a new purchase, he is constantly greeted with the question '*Bara bali?*' — 'How much did you pay?' In this way villagers keep a constant eye on prices, as well as on the bargaining skills of their fellow villagers.

There is a fairly well established hierarchy of merchants in any market. At the top are the owners of shops known as *toko*, which are either rented or owned. A *toko* is a relatively large, glass-fronted shop, frequently located outside the main market area. The next step down is a smaller, temporary-looking wooden structure known as *kedai*. These small stalls may have wooden shutters, display shelves, and enough room for the shopkeeper or keepers to sit down inside. Some *kedai* sell prepared food and coffee, for which purpose the keepers erect a canvas covering, tables and chairs. There are slightly smaller shops known, from the Dutch, as *kios*. *Kios*, like *kedai*, are small wooden structures with a temporary look, with just enough room for the keeper to display his wares and perhaps a very small space for him to sit. While customers enter a shop, they must always stand outside a *kedai* or *kios*. Shopkeepers with slighly less capital will usually rent an umbrella in the market place, and display their wares either on low wooden platforms or on cloths laid out on the pavement, a style of selling known as *kaki limo*. Merchants own or rent *kedai*. *Kaki limo* pedlars either pay a small daily fee to set up in the market, or sell without licence on street corners or outside bigger shops. Similar to the *kaki limo* style of trade is the use of push-carts. Even small pedlars carry their goods around the market place, selling to anyone who stops them.

In Bukit Tinggi the larger shops are usually open six or seven days a week, while many of the smaller traders come only on Wednesdays and Saturdays. The proportion of larger shops, both

113

Minangkabau- and Chinese-owned, seems to increase in the larger urban areas. While all towns and cities have at least one market area (*pasar*), the shops outside the market are small in number in Bukit Tinggi. In Padang there are many more shops, and in Jakarta an even larger proportion. In the smaller market towns around Bukit Tinggi, which are active only one day out of each week — although all have some shops opened permanently — most of the *kedai* and *kios* are rented. One such market frequented by the people of Limo Suku is held on Sundays in a neighbouring village. The Sunday market has about 15 wooden stalls opened on market day, while only two or three of the small shops stay open on other days of the week.

The structure of the distributive network has already been described to some extent. To set up as an independent trader, capital is needed. With small amounts of ready cash, a trader can buy goods in one part of the market and sell them in another or, more frequently, buy things in one market and transport them to sell in a second. Amri is a case in point. He goes most days to the market in Bukit Tinggi from his home in Limo Suku. With only about Rp. 5,000 trading capital he buys a whole roll of white cloth in one shop and then hawks the cloth throughout the market. He has no fixed place of business, and sells in the middle of the crowd of shoppers. His only investment, apart from the cloth, is in a pair of scissors and a ruler. His profit comes from the fact that he can sell small amounts of cloth at a slightly higher unit price than he pays for the whole roll.

Most trading profits are based on either of two similar principles. The first, illustrated by Amri, is that buying in bulk — even in what would seem to us as a small amount — is cheaper than buying small amounts. The second is that goods bought in one place can often be sold at a slightly higher price in another place — either because the product is not locally produced, or because the market is difficult to get to. These two principles may also be combined, as for *kedai* owners in the village who buy in 'bulk' in Bukit Tinggi and sell the goods in Limo Suku.

The basic principle of organisation in most markets, at least in West Sumatra, is that if more than one person is involved in any transaction, then they should be financially independent of each other. Only in a few cases — as for example with the owners of *toko* — do merchants have paid workers in their enterprises. Even in the case of a shop, the shop owner will often treat his employee as an independent entrepreneur, who takes the goods on consignment and sells them for a small percentage of the earnings.

Thus the only definite thing that can be said about merchants is that they buy something, usually with their own money (or a proportion of it), in one place and sell it in another. They may or may not be involved in productive activities as well, i.e. processes which add Value to the final produce (see below, pp. 120f. for a discussion of the nature of merchant's profit); they may or may not sell directly to consumers and they may or may not sell goods on consignment.[1]

Only small amounts of capital are necessary to begin work outside the village. Apart from capital, a potential trader needs access to the market and information. Small-scale trading of the type described as *kaki limo* and *manggaleh babelok* is thought to be a stepping-stone to better things. There is no indication, however, that there is any great mobility of petty traders to shop owners. Mobility seems rather to be a product of economic conditions; in certain periods it increases, in others decreases — a fact of some significance to which I shall return (see below, Chapter 8). In normal times profit margins are extremely low, competition strong. There is no guarantee that a trader will be able to sell at a profit at all. There seem to be more cases of small trading capital being wiped out by a single bad deal, or by fires, which are frequent in the market areas of towns. Over a period of several months the main markets of Padang, Bukit Tinggi and Pakan Baru were destroyed by fire. Most trading capital — in the form of goods stored in the market stalls — was destroyed. In short, the villagers' aspirations after the life of the merchant are often unrealistically focused on the few stories of success, of pedlars who became shop owners. The life of the petty traders, who dominate the distributive network, is hard and full of risk; and while the majority of village migrants never progress beyond petty trade, it is the socially mobile traders whom people keep in mind when comparing the advantages of migration to residence in the village.

The term *pegawai* is used by the villagers to refer to all kinds of employees such as clerks, teachers, labourers and government administrators. Most of these jobs call for a level of education

1. For discussion of very similar principles of market organisation in Indonesia see Dewey (1962) and Geertz (1963b) for Java, and Siegel (1969) for North Sumatra.

higher than can be attained in the schools of Sungai Puar. Most government employees, except unskilled labourers, hold at least a secondary school certificate. Apart from the armed forces training centres, all secondary and tertiary institutions are expensive, both because fees for entrance and study are high and because the student needs money on which to live outside the village.

Indonesian civil servants earn a monthly salary and receive, as well, some kind of allocation to buy rice. The higher administrators at district and provincial level are also housed at government expense, or at least in subsidised housing, and some are provided with government cars or jeeps. While the salary of the average government clerk may be low, the job is coveted because of the fringe benefits, and possible opportunities to receive bribes. In addition many government clerks have free time and the inside knowledge to take part in business outside office hours. School-teachers also have a good deal of prestige. During my research, however, salaries were abysmally low, and most teachers had to do other part-time work when they were not teaching.

A number of migrants work for a wage either as clerks or as labourers in the private sector. By and large, villagers frown on the idea of a labouring job. They express a cultural preference for independent work. Nonetheless many consider a labourer with a relatively secure job quite lucky.

Many migrants, particularly young men, work on buses and lorries, the main form of transport in Sumatra. These young men work as either drivers or conductors. Usually a bus or lorry crew works as a team. They often pay a set rate or a percentage of their earnings to the owner, and share equally in the rest of the proceeds. It is therefore in their interest to see that as many people and as much freight as possible are transported on each journey.

Because of the concentration of blacksmiths in Limo Suku, it is not surprising that a large number of emigrants also work as smiths. Today the large majority of migrant smiths live in Padang, in villages in the Pariaman district (especially along the Padang–Bukit Tinggi road), in Bukit Tinggi and in the city of Medan in North Sumatra.

In the Purus section of Padang there are from 10 to 15 *apa* in operation at any one time. Most of these are owned and run by *nangkodoh* from Sungai Puar. The Padang smiths produce the same range of goods as do the villagers. In Padang, however, smiths produce relatively greater numbers of horseshoes, because there and in other towns in West Sumatra the *dos* or horsecart is still an important means of transport. Wherever *dos* are in use there is a demand for blacksmiths, who in Purus as well as elsewhere both make and fit horseshoes while the *dos* drivers wait.

The Purus *apa* make a range of tools — particularly hoes and machetes, as well. But the market for these goods is local only and the demand correspondingly low. Bukit Tinggi and Medan are more important regional markets than Padang for rural agricultural areas.

In Purus *nangkodoh* as well as labourers in the *apa* are migrants from Sungai Puar. It is said, on the other hand, that Sungai Puar blacksmiths in the Pariaman district prefer to hire local labour. Informants told me that the relatively large number of landless labourers in the district had served to depress the level of wages that *nangkodoh* have to pay.

Perhaps the largest concentration of migrant Limo Suku smiths is to be found in the city of Medan, the largest city in Sumatra. Medan is the commercial centre and port both for the Deli plantations and for a large oil field, as well as being an important marketing centre for much of north and central Sumatra. My information about these workers comes almost entirely from returned migrants. In addition a large proportion of steelware produced in Sungai Puar finds its way to the Medan market.

Some migrant smiths work in Medan for small steel industries and machine shops. The largest number, however, work alone or in small groups and produce knives and kitchen utensils of forged steel and aluminium. These are sold in the Medan markets, mostly to individual customers.

A considerable number of migrants work in crafts and small industries, some of which are related to smithing, others not. Carpenters and furniture-makers from Limo Suku are found scattered throughout West Sumatra. Many of them rent small shops or stalls where they make and sell their wares. Other migrants repair metal goods in market towns, with tiny investments in soldering materials. Migrants make containers and other objects from thin steel, alloy sheet and scrapped tins. Still others with a smithing background work as bicycle or motor mechanics (*muntir*).

117

From this brief discussion of the other economic activities of Sungai Puar peasants, it will be seen that the organisation of peasant production and distribution in general is remarkably close to the organisation of smithing. In all cases the technological level of the various small industries is low. Carpenters, smiths, seamstresses and merchants rely heavily on their own capacities rather than on the use of labour-saving devices.

The economic organisation in most cases is also similar. Most frequently craftsmen and merchants work alone, owners of their basic means of production and distribution. The use of wage labour is almost completely absent. Even when wage labour exists, it does so in a disguised way, with non-owners usually preserving a semblance of economic independence and the proceeds being shared among workers. The entrepreneur in all cases receives an extra share because of his relationship to property, and yet workers are almost never paid a straight wage. The only exception to this is the case of women's crafts. Apart from migrants who work entirely outside the peasant sector of the economy, it is in women's crafts alone that the predominant economic form is the large-scale entrepreneurial unit.

Because I focused on blacksmithing and on male economic activities, I have some difficulty in accounting for this extremely important phenomenon. Why it should be that large entrepreneurial units grew up preponderantly around women's economic activities I cannot say satisfactorily. It is, of course, possible that the fact that they are women is incidental, and that it is because of the small amounts of equipment, and the purely part-time basis of the work, that there is greater need and opportunity for an entrepreneur. This, however, seems to me unlikely, if only because the same could be said about some male activities as well. The answer seems more likely to be linked to the social or class position of women, and would seem to belie Tanner's argument about the relatively high status of women (Tanner, 1974) in Minangkabau. At least in the commodity sector of the economy it seems that women are more easily proletarianised than men. This is an extremely important problem and calls for more research.

The similarity in organisation of peasant productive and distributive trades in the commodity sector can be illustrated by comparing the data presented in Table 6.3 with similar data on black-

Table 6.3   *Breakdown by class of six major occupations (men:*
residents and migrants)

Class	Married men		Unmarried men		Total number	Total percentage
	number	percentage	number	percentage		
Wage worker	129	18.3	69	34.2	198	21.8
Works alone	365	51.8	107	53.0	472	52.0
Employer of labour	199	28.2	14	6.9	213	23.5
Wage worker with kinsman	12	1.7	12	5.9	24	2.6
Missing data	91		17		108	
Total for which data are available	705		202		907	

smithing presented in the previous chapter (see Table 5.5, p. 93).
Table 6.3 represents a description of the class breakdown of
workers in the commodity sector. Workers in six main occupational specialities – of both residents and migrants from Limo
Suku – have here been characterised according to whether they
are individual owner–workers, whether they work for a wage in
some form or another or whether they are employers of wage
labour. Employers of wage labour, as we have seen, most commonly employ at most one or two other workers. 'Employer'
here does not, therefore, refer to employers of a large labour force.
In this calculation merchants are included. The breakdown of
merchants shows a structure similar to that of producers. I have
assumed that merchants who own shops (*toko*) are employers of
labour. If anything, the data for merchants overestimate the
number of employers, since not all shop owners do in fact have
wage workers.

Of these workers, then, 52 per cent, the largest group, are
individual, independent producers or traders. 75.5 per cent of the
total are self-employed – i.e. they either work alone or hire wage
labour. Only 21.8 per cent work for a wage with a non-kinsman.
Finally, the table shows that younger men more often than older
men work for a wage. Hence the group of wage workers is composed partly of young unmarried men, many of whom, given the

domestic cycle, are likely to become self-employed when they get older.

Unfortunately I did not have the time or the resources to collect detailed material on costs, prices and individual decision-making for Limo Suku occupations other than blacksmithing. Similar calculations were, however, made for the Bungus fishing industry. The similarities in economic organisation and technical level of all the small-scale enterprises in Bungus and Limo Suku suggest that, as in the case of smithing it would be possible to show that they represent in some sense an optimal combination of productive factors given existing market conditions, the over-all lack of capital and the economic structure. As for smithing, the main problem is to explain the constraints on decision-making. This kind of explanation cannot be sought at this level of analysis. It will be my aim in the next chapters to broaden the base of the analysis in order to produce a more fundamental explanation of peasant economic organisation in Minangkabau.

While in later chapters I shall examine the nature of individual production and distribution at a more abstract level, it is necessary at this stage to draw the reader's attention to a final basic similarity which links the varied forms of economic endeavour which I have discussed in this chapter. It will be noted that in the case of enterprises employing wage labour it is possible to speak of a profit in the narrow and precise sense of the term given to it by Marx's discussion of capitalist relations of production. Here, profit is at one level a form of income accruing to the owner of the means of production, and at another it derives from the production of surplus value by the direct producers. Surplus value in any particular case represents the difference between the cost (in Value terms) of reproduction of the producer's labour power and the total Value produced in the process of production. While the rate of exploitation of surplus value may differ from one branch of the economy to another, the free flow of capital results in a tendency for the rate of profit to equalise throughout the economy.

In a capitalist economy it is, however, impossible to equate in any direct way the profit made by a merchant and the profit made on productive capital. The latter stems from labour value added to the value of constant capital in the productive process, while the former can only derive from surplus value. A merchant's profit, then, in a sense comes out of society's total productive surplus.

This is, of course, to oversimplify, since at this stage no account is taken of the relation between price and value.

In an economy of individual producers and traders, however, we cannot speak of surplus value or profit. The cost of any commodity is dependent entirely on the value of constant capital used up in production and the value of the producer's labour power. Here we have neither profit in the narrow sense, nor a free flow of capital, since capital is defined in the narrow sense as a relation between owner of the means of production and labourer. We can, however, assume a mobility of labour itself. Although in any concrete peasant economy there are clearly blocks to the free flow of labour from one branch of the economy to another, it seems necessary first to assume mobility and then to examine the effects of obstacles to it. If we do assume perfect labour mobility, it is then possible to see that there should be, in the long run, an equalisation of return to economic activities. If return is higher in one branch than another, mobility would eventually wipe out this differential. Furthermore, if we assume labour mobility, then we must assume free movement not only from one branch of production to another, but from production to distribution and vice versa. Thus as long as no monopolies exist on particular trades in this idealised peasant economy, producers and traders will enter into economic activity in any branch when that branch returns to the individual the socially average cost of reproducing his own labour power. Here, whether an individual works as producer or trader, the principle is the same. Mercantile and productive activities are more closely analogous, in the absence of surplus value, than they are within the capitalist mode of production.

This, however, leads us to a final point about concrete economic organisation in Limo Suku. Local economic organisation, as I have argued, falls into two main sectors, a subsistence sector and a commodity sector. In the former I include both domestic labour and labour on the irrigated rice fields. Property here is subject to certain restrictions stemming from lineage control of land, and from a marriage system which regulates male access to the product of subsistence cultivation – in short it is subject to restriction by the social relations which constitute what I have called the subsistence community.

Blacksmiths, carpenters, and merchants, in contrast, are entirely market-oriented. They depend on the national and international

121

division of labour in order to sell and distribute their products, as well as to provide them with most of their basic necessities.

However, what is most significant about this is that the two sectors are intimately linked. In other words most families are at the same time subsistence cultivators *and* commodity producers. Subsistence production makes varying degrees of contribution to a family's total consumption needs. There is considerable variation throughout the province; the subsistence sector is less important in Limo Suku, for example, than elsewhere. At the same time there are differences among the people of Limo Suku. Some have access to more land and hence can satisfy a greater proportion of their rice needs than can others. Does this have any consequences for commodity production?

In looking at the organisation of subsistence agriculture I suggested that access to land and to its product is extremely important to the individual entrepreneur. A supply of rice to the household might significantly affect the degree to which an entrepreneur is able to cover costs. A constant supply of rice makes it relatively easy for an entrepreneur to keep the financing of his enterprise separate from the consumption demands of his own family. Finally, land can act as a form of insurance. Pawning and selling land can provide capital for a new enterprise, or keep an old enterprise going in periods of temporary slump.

Tables 6.4 and 6.5 allow the reader to evaluate the importance of access to land. Table 6.4 presents the data on the amount of subsistence rice available to a family cross-tabulated according to place of residence. It is often assumed that migrants come largely from the landless class. For Limo Suku this does not seem to be the case. This may be because of the large commodity sector within the village based not on access to land.

Table 6.5 represents an attempt to correlate class in the commodity sector with access to subsistence rice land. While these data are not conclusive, they seem to show that regardless of whether a man chooses to become a smith, a carpenter or a merchant or works at another craft, and regardless of where he chooses to carry out his work, his class position seems to be affected by the amount of land to which he has access through either his wife or his own family of origin. In general, wage workers on average have access to less of the rice they need to have provided by subsistence cultivation than do independent traders and

Table 6.4   *Cross-tabulation of harvest by place of residence*

Count row percentage
Column percentage

Size of harvest (baban)	(1) 0	(2) 1–5	(3) 6–10	(4) 11–15	(5) 16–20	(6) 21–30	(7) 31–40	(8) 41–50	(9) 51–60	(10) 61+	Row total
Residents	1,063	685	403	194	57	42	0	0	15	2	2,461
	43.2	27.8	16.4	7.9	2.3	1.7	0	0	0.6	0.1	50.5
	45.5	55.1	55.4	62.0	55.3	38.9	0	0	48.4	28.6	
Migrants	1,268	558	323	118	45	66	3	0	16	5	2,402
	52.8	23.2	13.4	4.9	1.9	2.7	0.1	0	0.7	0.2	49.3
	54.3	44.9	44.4	37.7	43.7	61.1	100	0	51.6	71.4	
Data missing or unavailable	3	0	2	1	1	0	0	0	0	0	7
	42.9	0	28.6	14.3	14.3	0	0	0	0	0	0.1
	0.1	0	0.3	0.3	0.1	0	0	0	0	0	
Column total	2,334	1,243	728	313	103	108	3	0	31	7	4,870
	47.9	25.5	14.9	6.4	2.1	2.2	0.1	0	0.6	0.1	

123

Table 6.5a   *Cross-tabulation of class by harvest (excluding farmers). Married men, harvest in wife's home*

Count row percentage
Column percentage

Size of harvest (baban) Class:	(1) 0	(2) 1–5	(3) 6–10	(4) 11–15	(5) 16–20	(6) 21–30	(7) 31–40	(8) 41–50	(9) 51–60	(10) 61+	Row total
Craftsman or merchant, working alone	148	112	49	20	3	2	0	0	0	0	334
	44.4	33.5	14.7	6.0	0.9	0.6	0	0	0	0	45.8
	44.7	53.8	40.5	50.0	18.8	15.4	0	0	0	0	
Small-scale employer	76	43	44	13	9	7	0	0	0	0	197
	38.6	24.4	22.3	6.6	4.6	3.6	0	0	0	0	27.0
	23.0	23.1	36.4	32.5	56.2	53.8	0	0	0	0	
Worker in craft or trade (wage)	60	28	13	3	2	1	0	0	0	1	108
	55.6	25.9	12.0	2.8	1.9	0.9	0	0	0	0.9	14.8
	18.1	13.5	10.7	7.5	12.5	7.7	0	0	0	100.0	
Worker in craft or trade, with kinsman	7	4	3	1	1	2	0	0	0	0	18
	38.9	22.2	16.7	5.6	5.6	11.1	0	0	0	0	2.5
	2.1	1.9	2.5	2.5	6.2	15.4	0	0	0	0	
White collar (includes teacher and doctor)	18	8	8	3	1	1	0	0	0	0	39
	46.2	20.5	20.5	7.7	2.6	2.6	0	0	0	0	5.3
	5.4	3.8	6.6	7.5	6.2	7.7	0	0	0	0	
Manual with large enterprise	22	8	4	0	0	0	0	0	0	0	34
	64.7	23.5	11.8	0	0	0	0	0	0	0	4.7
	6.6	3.8	3.3	0	0	0	0	0	0	0	
Column total	331	208	121	40	16	13	0	0	0	1	730
	45.3	28.5	16.6	5.5	2.2	1.8	0	0	0		

124

Table 6.5b *Unmarried men, harvest in home of origin*

Count row percentage
Column percentage

Size of harvest (baban)	(1) 0	(2) 1–5	(3) 6–10	(4) 11–15	(5) 16–20	(6) 21–30	(7) 31–40	(8) 41–50	(9) 51–60	(10) 61+	Row total
Class:											
Craftsman or merchant, working alone	42	40	13	9	2	2	0	0	0	0	108
	38.9	37.0	12.0	8.3	1.9	1.9	0	0	0	0	40.6
	32.6	57.1	34.2	47.4	50.0	66.7	0	0	0	0	
Small-scale employer	5	1	6	2	0	0	0	0	0	0	14
	35.7	7.1	42.9	14.3	0	0	0	0	0	0	5.3
	3.9	1.4	15.8	10.5	0	0	0	0	0	0	
Wage worker in craft or trade	51	19	8	1	1	0	0	0	0	0	80
	63.8	23.8	10.0	1.2	1.2	0	0	0	0	0	30.1
	39.5	27.1	21.1	5.3	25.0	0	0	0	0	0	
Worker in craft or trade, with kinsman	24	8	9	5	1	1	0	0	0	3	51
	47.1	15.7	17.6	9.8	2.0	2.0	0	0	0	5.7	19.2
	18.6	11.4	23.7	26.3	25.0	33.3	0	0	0	100.0	
White collar	4	0	0	2	0	0	0	0	0	0	6
	66.7	0	0	33.3	0	0	0	0	0	0	2.3
	3.1	0	0	10.5	0	0	0	0	0	0	
Manual, with large enterprise	3	2	2	0	0	0	0	0	0	0	7
	42.9	28.6	28.6	0	0	0	0	0	0	0.0	2.6
	2.3	2.9	5.3	0	0	0	0	0	0	0	
Column total	129	70	38	19	4	3	0	0	0	3	266
	48.5	26.3	14.3	7.1	1.5	1.1	0	0	0	1.1	

producers, who in turn have less, on average, than employers of wage labour. These correlations confirm the importance of access to subsistence rice land, as well as to domestic labour to work the land. They suggest an important relationship between the subsistence and commodity sectors of the village economy.

While, again, I propose to develop this theme in later chapters, it should be clear why these correlations exist. If it is remembered that costs of commodity production and of distribution are determined by the cost of the labour power of individual producers and merchants, and if it is further noted that, given perfect labour mobility, individuals will choose those branches of the economy in which at least the social average return is guaranteed, then clearly access to subsistence land will have an important effect on the individual's ability to enter certain branches of production or distribution. For access to subsistence land guarantees that a proportion of the cost of reproducing the peasant's labour power will be borne outside the commodity sector of the economy altogether.[1] When some inequality in access to subsistence production is an added factor, then it is highly likely that this inequality will affect not necessarily the choice of occupation *per se*, but rather the ability to enter one of the more lucrative productive or distributive roles.

In this and the previous chapter I have discussed in some detail the commodity economy of a single village in the Minangkabau highlands, and attempted to establish the predominance of a specific form of economic organisation – the individual enterprise.

This appears to contradict a number of studies in the region and in other peripheral areas which have experienced capitalist penetration. In particular it seems to conflict with a basic tenet of much imperialism theory, particularly of the Leninist variety, which maintains that the penetration of capitalism inevitably brings with it a differentiation of the peasantry and hence the development of capitalist relations in agriculture.

While in his work on the history of the Javanese peasantry Geertz (1963a) maintains that involution rather than class differentiation has been a dominant process, recently others have maintained the opposite, i.e. that rural society in Indonesia under the pressure of colonialism has experienced a division into classes on

1. This is a theme which I have developed elsewhere in relation to the problem of unequal exchange (Kahn, 1974b).

the basis of access to agricultural land. Stoler, for example, in taking issue with Geertz, argues: '. . . "shared poverty" and the levelling mechanisms inherent in closed, corporate communities represent only a *temporary* adaptation to external pressures. Although colonial rule enhanced horizontal ties, I suggest that in the long run vertical structures were strengthened, gained dominance, and thus systematically undermined the basis for "shared poverty" ' (Stoler, 1977). On the basis of material she collected in a Javanese village, Stoler attempts to dispute Geertz's contention that communal labour practices serve to share out wealth, arguing that the ideology of sharing actually serves to cover up inequalities. Similarly Gerdin (MS.) argues against the involution hypothesis for Lombok.

Similar arguments have been put forward to suggest that rural Malaysia has also experienced a concentration of land holdings in the hands of the few. Swift, for example, writes: 'I maintain that every important field of economic activity shows a change from a fairly equal distribution of wealth to one where a small number of peasants are set off from their fellow villagers by substantially greater income and possessions' (1967; 241). And Ali, while taking issue with the cultural explanation for concentration put forward by Swift, nonetheless maintains the dominant influence of class differentiation in a comparison of four Malaysian villages. He points to a clear inequality between the 3.2 to 8.8 per cent of villagers who control between 24.3 and 56.2 per cent of the land in these villages (Ali, 1972).

The argument is not, of course, a new one. Perhaps the best-known instance of it is the substantial disagreement between Lenin and Chayanov on the nature of the Russian peasantry. While the latter maintained the predominance of the so-called 'family labour farm', Lenin, in *The Development of Capitalism in Russia*, argued that capitalist development in the Russian economy in the late nineteenth century had led to the transformation of the rural economy and hence a process of rural differentiation – the dispossession of some peasants and the conversion of others into rural, if small-scale, capitalists. A perusal of the articles in the *Journal of Peasant Studies* would lead one to conclude that such differentiation is a dominant process on the peripheries of world capitalism, and hence that the material I have presented here on the predominance of the small-scale, individual enterprise is

127

atypical for an area which has had a long history of contact with the capitalist West.

In opposition to those who maintain the inevitability of differentiation I would make several points: firstly, that the situation I have described for the village of Sungai Puar is in fact quite typical for the province as a whole; secondly, that while differentiation does indeed take place in peasant agriculture, it may be relatively insignificant in relation to the more important class differences which have evolved in peripheral regions outside the peasant economy altogether; thirdly, that the data provided by the proponents of differentiation nonetheless frequently demonstrate the predominance of the individual enterprise; and finally, that differentiation is the product of a specific set of historical circumstances, not just the penetration of capitalism, and that even in a single area like West Sumatra it may take place in some periods and actually be reversed in others.

As I pointed out in the Introduction, the limited statistical material available on farm size in West Sumatra confirms the view that the majority of peasant farms are under one hectare. The predominance of the individual enterprise is also confirmed by my study of the coastal fishing village of Bungus. While a number of villagers owned nets (*pukek*) and hired local men on a daily basis to operate them, the largest number of fishermen in 1972 went night fishing in individually owned small boats. I also collected some information on rubber-tapping in the region around Silungkang, and found again that owner-tapping and small-scale share-tapping seemed to be the main form of organisation, while large owners of rubber land were almost non-existent. Finally the material on the organisation of the retail trade collected from Sungai Puar migrants, indicating the great preponderance of small-scale individual trade, appears to be typical of the organisation of trading in the major towns of West Sumatra.

All this is not, of course, to argue that Indonesia is a classless society. On the contrary, there are vast class differentials between peasant producers and the upper reaches of the bureaucracy, armed forces, owners of plantations and those involved in the largely foreign-controlled capitalist sector. It would therefore be misleading to dwell on what are, in comparison to these, relatively minor differences among peasant producers in attempting to make a case for the development of capitalist agriculture from within the peasant economy itself.

Indeed while the data provided by the proponents of differentiation for the region certainly indicate that there are *some* large landowners in certain parts of the country, the data can also be read in different ways. Also, as we have seen, Ali concludes from his figures that between 3.2 and 8.8 per cent of Malay villagers own between 24.3 and 56.2 per cent of the land, nonetheless the figures also show that in three of the five villages 34, 41 and 44 per cent of the people own between one-third and three acres, and are in all likelihood individual rubber owner-tappers, fishermen and coconut farmers, just as the largest group of Sungai Puar peasants are self-employed. In spite of the evidence of differentiation, therefore, it remains that the largest number of peasants are neither capitalist landlords nor wage labourers. The predominant form of economic organisation remains petty commodity production.

Finally, as I have shown elsewhere (Kahn, 1975), differentiation, while it does occur in rural West Sumatra, is the product of a specific set of historical conditions. It may take place in certain periods, as it did in Minangkabau from the late 1950s to the mid-1960s. In this period there is no doubt that the process of differentiation in the rural areas was the dominant trend. That trend was, however, reversed, and by the late 1960s the owner-operated peasant enterprise was again the main form.

It is, then, misleading in a number of ways to suggest that incorporation of a peasantry into a capitalist system results inevitably in the class differentiation of rural producers and the evolution of rural capitalism.

As we shall see, there are no theoretical grounds for assuming its inevitability. Indeed, the opposite case, the predominance of small-scale productive organisation, appears to be equally important, and for Minangkabau in the early 1970s was clearly a much more frequent occurrence. It is that predominance which I wish now to attempt to explain.

7

The structure of petty commodity production

In the previous six chapters I have presented material on the peasant economy of Minangkabau, as well as attempting to place the peasant economy in its social and economic setting in the modern Minangkabau village. I have been concerned to show that an understanding of peasant economy rests on an understanding of the operation of small-scale commodity production and distribution. I have taken some care to keep this description in historical context, assuming both that this form of economy is particular and that it is historically specific. As we shall see in later chapters, Minangkabau economic organisation in the past has been quite different. In other words, this form of peasant economy has a *pre*history as well as a history, to use Marx's term. This being the case it becomes necessary, in order to understand the economic conditions in modern Minangkabau to understand both its own laws of operation and the historical conditions under which such an economic system was born in the specific history of the Indonesian social formation.

There are, therefore, two major questions which need to be answered. First, the (in a sense) more anthropological question — given what I have called petty commodity production, what are its implications? Secondly, how was the petty commodity economy formed — what are its conditions of existence, reproduction and future transformation? Only in this way can we claim to have located the peasant economy in space and time.

The way in which I have chosen to ask these questions clearly derives from certain theoretical premises which will only be stated here. A major assumption is that different economic systems have different laws of functioning, an approach quite different from the formalist assumption of a universal economic rationality which transcends social and historical context. This assumption derives partly from Marx's critique of political economy in which he attempted to demonstrate the historical specificity of the categories of bourgeois economy. Discussing the different case of capitalism, Marx wrote:

One thing is clear — Nature does not produce on the one side owners of money or commodities, and on the other men possessing nothing but their own labour-power. This relation has no natural basis, neither is its social basis one that is common to all historical periods. It is clearly the result of past historical development, the product of many revolutions, of the extinction of a whole series of older forms of social production (*Capital*, vol. 1, p. 169).

This view, encompassing as it does a concept of the social determination of economic organisation, is, of course, not unique to Marx. In one form or another it is shared by numerous anthropologists.

The other major assumption in what follows is perhaps more tendentious, and derives again from an analogy with Marx's analyses of capitalism. I will maintain here, but not at this stage defend, the position against recent critiques of the structural interpretation of Marx, that Marx's analysis of capitalism is both historical and structural. It is structural in the sense that much of the critique of political economy is taken to be an abstract analysis of a structure, the Capitalist Mode of Production, which has certain law-like effects at the level of concrete social formations. It is historical in the sense that the emergence of the structure in history is said to be dependent upon the development of certain necessary *preconditions* (or presuppositions) (*Voraussetzungen*). It is well known that for Marx there were two for capitalism: the development of the labourer as 'free labourer, as objectiveless, purely subjective labour power' on the one hand, and the existence of value as 'someone else's property . . . as capital' confronting the free labourer on the other (*Grundrisse*, pp. 397f.). These preconditions, it is maintained here, are derived precisely from the analysis of the Capitalist Mode of Production as a structure.

To understand the history of any specific capitalist formation is, therefore, to grasp the historical conditions (*historische Bedingungen*) under which these preconditions are fulfilled. In the section in *Capital* on primitive accumulation Marx wrote that the 'history of this expropriation [the primitive accumulation of capital], in different countries, assumes different aspects, and runs through its various phases in different orders of succession and different periods' (*Capital*, vol. 1, p. 716).

There is a further assumption in the analysis which should be mentioned briefly here, namely, that in spite of the fact that petty commodity production appears today within a world capitalist system or, as others would have it, within a social formation in which the Capitalist Mode of Production is dominant, it remains in some sense outside it as well. This is again a premise which has come under criticism, particularly from those who maintain the concept of a world capitalist totality which embraces all corners of the world involved within the system of capitalist distribution. We shall return to this point in the discussion of the concept of social formation.

In this chapter I shall examine the structure of petty commodity production, while in later chapters I shall use the knowledge of this structure to examine the conditions of its emergence, reproduction and transformation in Indonesian society. It will be argued that in developing the concept of petty commodity production I have ignored the usefulness of certain superficially similar concepts, specifically Chayanov's Family Labour Farm (1966) and Sahlins's so-called Domestic Mode of Production (1974). These two concepts, however, differ from the concept of petty commodity production employed here, because unlike it they begin and end the analysis with the productive unit, narrowly defined, rather than deriving the productive unit from the social structure which produces it. Such a path allows Chayanov, for example, to explain the structure of the family labour farm from a specific rationality, i.e. the desire to avoid self-exploitation. As will become clear below, the concept of petty commodity production allows us to argue in the opposite direction, that is, from the structure to the rationality.

In the analysis which follows, finally, I shall not use the concept of a petty commodity mode of production, in the sense of political and ideological structure. I am concerned only to construct the concept of an economic structure – a combination of forces and relations of production. No assumption will be made about a determined or necessary superstructure, built up on this economic base in order to reproduce it. Such an assumption would amount to tautology. The question of what constitutes the conditions of existence of petty commodity production in a determinant social formation, to use the terms employed by Hindess and Hirst (1976), must be a subject for concrete analysis.

Petty commodity production: the economic base

In the Althusserian tradition, carried on in slightly modified form in the recent work of Hindess and Hirst (1975, 1977a, 1977b), the economic base of a mode of production is a two-sided system — a distinctive combination of forces and relations of production. Hindess and Hirst stress the distinctive nature of this set of relations in arguing that in order to define a mode of production we must have a single form of productive relations corresponding to a single kind of productive force. 'Productive relations' means the social relations which serve to link labourers, non-labourers and means of production — a link called the property connection after Balibar (1970). In referring to 'forces of production' the Althusserians seem to mean not the term in its widest sense, but rather the forms of cooperation in the productive process. It seems to me that this is to read too much into Marx's passing definitions of a mode of production, and his changing use of the concept of productive forces. It has, for example, led Hindess and Hirst to reject the possibility of an Asiatic mode of production, a rejection for which Taylor (1975–6) has taken them to task. Again, however, the debate has been at cross-purposes, since Taylor is looking for the Asiatic mode of production in concrete societies in which different labour processes may exist side by side, while Hindess and Hirst explicitly reject empirical verification in favour of logical consistency.

Even within the strictures of the Hindess and Hirst approach, however, it is possible to specify the petty commodity economy. Using Balibar's terms, that economy is characterised by individual ownership *and* appropriation by the direct producers. There are, therefore, no non-labourers with economic control of the means of production.

For Balibar and Hindess and Hirst appropriation refers to an aspect of the productive forces, i.e. to the technical relationship among producers. Petty commodity producers appropriate the means of production individually because they have the economic

133

power to set production in motion through direct access to productive property.

Ownership is an aspect of the social relations of production, that is, it refers to the economic relations of property. Petty commodity producers own their means of production individually.

On the basis of these distinctions, petty commodity production can be contrasted with capitalism and feudalism. Unlike feudalism, the direct producer in petty commodity production owns the means of production as well as appropriating them. Unlike capitalism, the owner of the means of production in petty commodity production is also a direct producer. Finally, the producers own the means of production separately, i.e. there are communal rights neither of appropriation nor of ownership within the petty commodity mode of production.[1]

To say that within petty commodity production the means of production are individually owned and appropriated is not to say that there are not economic relations among producers. On the contrary, I will maintain that the separation and equality of producers is itself a social relation. This relationship gives rise to a specific kind of fetishism, a one-to-one relationship between people and things, and people therefore appear to stand in isolation from one another in a kind of natural anarchy. The conception of property as a relation between people and things, rather than as a social relation, would blind us to the kind of social relation implied by separate access to individual means of production.

This preliminary discussion of the nature of petty commodity production allows us to deduce some of the conditions necessary for its evolution. The emergence of petty commodity production depends firstly on a process of separation, i.e. a separation of producers from any class of non-labourers with property rights in the means of production. If petty commodity production is to appear, it can do so only when economic ties of servitude to a state or a class of lords have been broken. For this reason petty commodity production often marks a period of transition, for example when feudal or Asiatic property relations are in the process of breaking down. It is also evident that petty commodity producers may exist when a group of people have managed to

1. This casts some doubts on the usefulness of Balibar's attempt to look for three unvarying elements in production: labourer, non-labourer and means of production. The concept of the absence of a non-labourer becomes rather meaningless.

break the general ties of servitude linking the mass of the population to the State or to a class of feudal lords. Within the European social formation during the height of feudalism large numbers of producers existed outside the manorial system as owners of their own property.

The evolution of petty commodity production also depends on a second form of separation. While the birth of capitalism depended on the separation of the mass of producers from the means of production, the emergence of petty commodity production requires the separation of the mass of producers *from each other*. In other words, for petty commodity producers to become individual owners of their means of production, all forms of communal appropriation must be dissolved. Historically, petty commodity production has often been associated with the breakdown of tribal society and the dissolution of communal rights in property which accompanies such a breakdown. A similar process may occur with the introduction of new economic activities within tribal societies such that, while older economic communal forms are retained, individuals engage in new activities outside the tribal property system.

Finally, petty commodity production depends on technical division of labour, the creation of markets and mobility of the factors of production — a crucial precondition for the emergence of petty commodity production, as well as a basic condition of its reproduction, a point to which we shall return. The division of labour and markets is often created by the expansion of other modes of production. By opening up parts of the world to the world market, and by exporting goods which destroy certain branches of indigenous production, capitalism has often served the function of creating the basic conditions for the emergence of petty commodity production at its periphery.

These three processes — the dissolution of property rights of non-producers, the separation of producers from each other and the creation of a division of labour — are all part of the prehistory of the petty commodity mode of production in its pure state. In other words, if petty commodity production is to come into existence these three processes must occur in some way or other within a social formation.

As Marx constantly pointed out for capitalism, the prehistory of a mode of production is not to be confused with its own laws of operation. Whatever historical events have contributed to the rise of petty commodity production, once established, the relations of production must be reproduced. It is the way petty commodity production reproduces its own conditions of existence which concerns me here. It should be borne in mind that an analysis of the processes of reproduction implies the same level of abstraction, and a concern with the processes of structural causation within the mode of production. Historical causation is specific to concrete cases of the emergence of a mode of production in a specific place in a particular period of time. Moreover, within concrete societies, the structures of reproduction may change or become distorted. It is possible to conceive of remnants of feudalism, for example, being reproduced in a social formation dominated by capitalism, not through the intervention of the political instance, but rather through the market. This corresponds to the role of the landowning class in nineteenth-century England discussed by Marx in his analysis of ground rent (*Capital*, vol. 3, part 6).

It might be assumed that petty commodity relations of production can exist without a structure of reproduction. This would be to fall into the trap of assuming that because producers are both separate and equal, in the sense that they do not exploit each other in the process of production, they are actually independent of each other. I would maintain that the opposite is the case, i.e. that egalitarian relations such as those existing among petty commodity producers are social relations and hence must be reproduced. They are not a natural, equilibrium state of human existence, but rather a product of social existence.

Like capitalism, petty commodity production is reproduced through the economic instance. In other words, the specific conditions necessary for the preservation of productive relations — separation and equality — must be maintained through the processes of production and distribution.

This process of reproduction can be illustrated by a formula for the cost of reproduction derived from Marx's formula for the reproduction of capitalism. In its most simple form, the cost of reproduction (CR) is expressed in the following way:

$$CR = C + V \qquad\qquad (i)$$

where C represents the cost of reproduction of constant capital consumed in the productive process, and V is the cost of reproduction of labour power, both expressed as Values (socially necessary, homogeneous, abstract labour time). Formula (i) is a general expression of the cost of simple reproduction of all modes of production. It describes the objective labour costs of reproducing the total material base of a society up to previous levels, although the formula itself might not be particularly pertinent to a non-commodity economy.

Using the cost of reproduction formula, it is possible to express the price of production (PP) for any particular good, or for society's total material needs, by converting value to exchange value:

$$PP = C + V \qquad \text{(ii)}$$

In formula (ii) C and V are expressed not as values, but in terms of exchange values, an expression of money value. Exchange value and the price of production must not be interpreted as referring to price. In his discussion of the reproduction of capitalism Marx was careful to point out the difference between exchange value based directly on the cost of production and price which was influenced by supply and demand. V in formula (ii) is not equivalent to the exchange value of variable capital in any particular branch of production. As we shall see, the exchange value in formula (ii) refers to a social average.

Formula (i) is general to all modes of production. Formula (ii), however, would serve to distinguish petty commodity production from capitalism, and indeed from all systems of commodity production based on the extraction of surplus from the direct producer. To see that this is so and to understand the basic assumption built into formula (ii), it is necessary to return to the cost of reproduction for capitalism. Formula (i), as I have pointed out, is an expression of the cost of simple reproduction for a mode of production, i.e. the cost of replacing the total stock of tools, capital investments in land and the like, as well as reproducing society's total labour power. Capitalism, however, is based on the extraction of surplus value (S) which is used both to reproduce a class of non-labourers and to expand the capital stock. The ability of capitalism to reproduce itself on an expanded scale derives from this form of surplus extraction. The general formula for the cost of reproduction of capitalism is, then, expressed in the following way:

$$CR = C + V + S \qquad \text{(iii)}$$

where S represents the surplus value. To calculate the price of

137

production for a commodity produced under capitalism requires an assumption, i.e. that there is mobility of capital. This means that there is a general tendency for the equalisation of the rate of profit in all branches of production. The equivalent of formula (ii) for capitalist production is, then:

$$PP = C + V + Pr \qquad \qquad \text{(iv)}$$

The additional factor (Pr) refers to the exchange value of the profit, calculated on the basis of the average rate of profit throughout the system. If profit is calculated on the basis of the total capital used up in production, then the average rate of profit (R) is equal to

$$\frac{S}{C + V} + \ldots \quad \frac{Sn}{C_n + V_n} \Big/ n,$$

where n is the number of branches of production in the economy. To calculate Pr for any branch, we must multiply R by the exchange value of (C + V) in that branch.

The difference in the formulae for the capitalist mode of production and petty commodity production is the absence of surplus value in the latter. The total value of goods, of course, is not different. This point can be illustrated with respect to the mode of extraction of surplus value under capitalism. The Value (as opposed to use value or exchange value) of any commodity produced is equivalent to the total abstract, socially necessary labour time embodied in that product. That Value has two sources: 'Living' labour and 'dead' labour. The former is labour expended in production of the commodity. The latter is labour 'congealed' in the constant capital — tools, machines, raw materials, etc. — used up in the process of production.

The extraction of surplus value under capitalism depends on the difference between labour as a measure of value, and labour power which is the capacity of the labourer to create value. In order for a labourer to produce value, he or she must be replenished, as it were. His or her capacity to labour must be generated before the productive process. The levels of consumption, education and family organisation required to produce and reproduce labour power vary historically as well as socially. Nonetheless, labour power itself has Value, a value equivalent to the value of all those material goods and services thought necessary to keep a labourer alive, healthy and a social individual. Wages, then, represent a payment for labour power.

138

The cost of reproduction of labour power is, however, not necessarily equal to the Value generated by that same labour power. It is the difference between this cost of reproduction and the Value generated by labour power which is the basis for the surplus value extracted by the capitalist. This can be illustrated using some arbitrary figures. Let us say that to produce 100 axes, a factory owner uses up machines and raw materials which embody four hours of congealed labour, i.e. the production of this constant capital which is used up in the production of 100 axes took a total of four hours of socially necessary labour time. Let us say further that the labourer who produces these axes in a single day requires on average a total of four hours' worth of goods, services, family care and vocational education to reproduce his or her own labour power, for an average working day of eight hours. If the labourer works for eight hours to produce 100 axes, then the value of the 100 axes is 12, i.e. the total socially necessary labour time expended in production plus the value of constant capital used up in the production of the 100 axes. While the Value of the 100 axes is equal to 12, the cost to the owner of the means of production is less. The capitalist, when calculating his costs, reckons to pay for the constant capital plus the labour power used up in the production of 100 axes. This cost to the capitalist is only eight, because the labourer must sell his or her labour power. The cost is eight because four hours' worth of constant capital is used plus eight hours of labour time which costs four hours to reproduce. The surplus value of four is, then, drawn off by the capitalist. This is summarised in formulae (v) and (vi).

$$\text{Value of 100 axes} = \quad\quad\quad\quad (v)$$
$$12 = 4C + 8L = 4C + 4V + 4S$$

where L is the number of hours taken to produce 100 axes. The cost of production of the 100 axes is less.

$$\text{CP} = 4C + 4V \quad\quad\quad\quad (vi)$$

The difference between the total cost of production to the capitalist and the value of the completed commodities is the surplus value extracted in the productive process – a consequence of the capital relationship which forces the direct producer to sell his or her labour power as a commodity.

This explains the difference between the formulae for petty commodity production and those for capitalism. A petty commodity producer who turns out 100 axes, let us say, must labour for 16 hours and use constant capital valued at four hours. The value of the 100 axes is, then, 20, a value generated by 4C and 16L. The labourer works alone and extracts no surplus value from anyone else.

It will now be noted that in writing the formulae for the cost of reproduction and prices of production under petty commodity production, I have built in a basic assumption, i.e. that the cost of reproducing the labour power of the producer is equal to the difference between the value of the commodities produced and the value of constant capital. In other words, I have assumed that value added in the productive process by the labourer is equal to the cost of reproducing his or her labour power. I have demonstrated that within the capitalist mode of production it is the difference between these two factors (V and L) which allows the capitalist to extract a surplus.

The assumption that the cost of reproduction of labour power is equal to the value added to the value of constant capital in the production process is basic to an analysis of the petty commodity mode of production. The capitalist who wishes to maximise returns on his investment naturally seeks a branch of production with the highest rate of profit. Complete mobility of capital results, however, as Marx has shown, in an equalisation of this profit rate — a result of constant movements by individual capitalists to invest in the most profitable sectors of production. It is this very process which brings with it the equalisation of profit rates (cf. *Capital*, vol. 3, pp. 142ff.). While the capitalist can do this simply by 'sending' his capital to the more profitable branch of production, according to the nature of petty commodity production, producers can maximise return only by actually taking up a new trade, i.e. by producing those commodities for which the return is higher. While higher return to the capitalist is measured in return on money investment, higher return to the petty commodity producer is measured in terms of return on labour input. The over-all tendency in petty commodity production, then, is firstly for any possible surplus to diminish, and secondly for the rate of return to labour to equalise throughout all branches of production. Surplus cannot be extracted by the producer, if that surplus is distinct from the goods and services he or she actually consumes. Movement of producers away from less well-paid and towards more well-paid branches of production results in an adjustment of prices such that return to labour inputs becomes equalised. For this reason the V in formula (ii), as I have pointed out, is equivalent to the social average return to labour.

For these reasons I think that it is legitimate to use formulae (i) and (ii), and to use a law of value to represent an initial state of petty commodity production. The assumptions upon which the formulae are based, particularly the lack of surplus and profit, are compatible with the nature of the social relations of production which I have set out. An analysis of the reproduction of the petty commodity mode of production must show, among other things, how the basic conditions of separation and equality as manifest in formulae (i) and (ii) are maintained. These conditions may be fulfilled by the relations of production and distribution themselves, as is the case for capitalism.

Any disturbance of the balance among producers which tended to favour some at the expense of others would eventually destroy the relations of production by allowing one group an advantage. Under normal circumstances, however, imbalances of this sort are prevented through pressures exerted by the economy. This can be illustrated with the case of a single producer who seeks to earn a 'profit' through investing in new techniques of production. If a producer were to invest in more productive technology he would soon be able to increase his own returns by selling at the market price, which would then exceed his own cost of production. Assuming at the outset that all producers are equal, we must assume that the value and exchange value of V are equal throughout the economy. A change in productive techniques by a single producer or group of producers would immediately upset the balance, by changing the initial state illustrated in the formulae.

Those who were able to adopt the new techniques would lower their costs of production and hence earn a profit — the difference between the price and the new, lowered, cost of production. If this were to continue it would change the situation by allowing certain producers to extract a surplus through the market at the expense of other producers, eventually impoverishing the others and giving rise to a class without its own means of production.

Under normal circumstances, however, such a development can be prevented by the operation of the economy, and in particular by the relations of distribution. A petty commodity producer, in order to earn a profit, must charge prices which are in fact higher than his costs of production. If there were a mobility of factors of production guaranteed by the market, such a situation would be only temporary. The profit would eventually attract producers from other branches of the economy, leading to a reduction of the artificially inflated price, and a return to conditions of equality. As long as the temporarily more wealthy producers have no form of monopoly, they cannot prevent the reorientation of the economy which serves to restore equilibrium. In particular, of course, the reproduction of petty commodity production depends on absolute labour mobility, i.e. producers must be free to move into any branch of production or distribution.

Increased productivity does not, therefore, bring with it any basic changes in the relations of producers to each other, at least in the initial stages, although, as I shall argue below, the development of the productive forces eventually comes into conflict with the relations of production. Initially, increased productivity results only in an increase in the actual volume of goods in circulation. A proportion of this increased wealth may go towards increasing living standards by increasing the absolute material make-up of 'V'. This increased standard of living brought by the development of the productive forces would then be shared equally throughout the community of producers – to all branches of production – through the process of distribution. It should of course be borne in mind that the *value* of a given volume of goods actually decreases with increased productivity, since development of this sort results in a lower labour input for a given volume of output.

In effect this means that, regardless of the commodity, the price of production will be determined by the exchange value of constant capital consumed in the process of production plus the average rate of return to labour. From the point of view of the individual producer, this means that he will produce a commodity only if, given the existing price structure, he can earn at least enough to live at a standard equal to the social average (the price of reproduction of labour power is socially determined, in that the volume of goods considered necessary is socially determined). If his return were to prove greater than the social average, competition would force the prices down. Competition in this case would result in a mobility of labour, or of the actual techniques of production, brought by increased profitability in any branch of production. If the return were to be less than the social average, the opposite process would allow producers to raise prices.

In this discussion, it should again be emphasised, I am deducing from the initial assumptions which concern the operation of the petty commodity mode of production in its pure state. In concrete peasant societies these conditions do not usually hold. There is rarely perfect labour mobility, it is not easy for producers with area specialisation to shift to new branches of production and prices cannot be perfectly flexible.

By allowing prices to adjust in order to allow for an equalisation of return to the labour of petty commodity producers, the market in the petty commodity mode of production serves a function analogous to the role of the 'free' market under capitalism. With capitalism the equalisation of the rate of profit operates through the capital market and the price structure. Similarly, the free flow of either labourers or techniques, as well as the flexibility of the price structures in petty commodity production would serve the function of reproducing both the initial state of individual access to the means of production and equality among individual producers. Just as the system of rewarding labour power, of calculating the prices of production and of extracting a surplus from the labourer reproduces capitalist relations of production through the productive process itself, so the lack of surplus and the method of rewarding the labour of the direct producer serves to reproduce the social basis of petty commodity relations of production.

The basic contradiction

Having discussed the nature of petty commodity relations of production and the way in which these relations can be reproduced, I want now to turn to the dynamic aspect of the mode of production. The strength of a Marxist analysis lies not in its use of a particular terminology to label various aspects of the concrete world, but in the way the concepts uncover the underlying laws of development of particular modes of production. Defining or constructing a mode of production is the beginning, not the end of the analysis. For this reason it is now necessary to show how the above discussion of petty commodity production and reproduction allows us to understand the specific dynamic of petty commodity production, although still at the level of relations of production in their pure state.

I have tried to show how changes such as increasing productivity can be absorbed by the system and the separation and equality of producers maintained. Higher returns, for instance may eventually be shared out equally among producers through the market — an example of the structural dominance of the economy.

At this same time, however, the concept of petty commodity production does not describe a static, or perfectly functioning, system. In this sense, the role of the structures of reproduction is not equivalent to the role of institutions within the functionalist model of society. Just as petty commodity production has a prehistory, so it has a specific dynamic of development which gives rise to contradictions — contradictions which threaten the very basis of the productive relations.

I have pointed out that the definition of petty commodity production does not rule out the possibility of accumulation and of increases in productivity through the development of the productive forces. Under certain conditions petty commodity relations of production are conducive to increases in productivity. I shall also argue, however, that the development of the productive forces eventually comes into contradiction with the relations of production, and threatens to burst their constraining bonds. This is the contradiction basic to petty commodity production.

This contradiction is analogous to the falling rate of profit, a manifestation of the contradiction between forces and relations of production which Marx found to lie at the base of the capitalist mode of production. It seems likely that this kind of contradiction is not restricted to capitalism, but may be shared in one form or another by all forms of commodity production. Just as petty commodity production has a different expression of equalisation of return, so does the falling rate of profit become something quite different, given the qualitative difference between petty commodity and capitalist relations of production.

The contradiction can be illustrated with the aid of the formula for the reproduction of petty commodity relations of production, with the use of some arbitrary numbers. The figures in Table 7.1 have been selected in order to illustrate the effects of the changing organic composition of capital (represented by the ratio C/V) on the reproduction of society's material base. This is presented as a

Table 7.1   *The changing organic composition of capital:*
community of producers

Time period	C	V	CR
T1	40	60	100
T2	50	50	100
T3	60	40	100

quantum increase through time from period 1 to time period 3.
It will be remembered here that C refers to the value of constant
capital (tools, machines, raw materials, etc.) used up in the productive process, i.e. the value contribution to the final product of
'dead' labour time. V is the value of variable capital (the value of
goods and services which are necessary to reproduce the producers'
labour power). The change illustrated in Table 7.1, between T1
and T3, is in the organic composition of capital used up in the
production of a mass of goods with a value of 100. Organic composition, measured here as a value ratio of constant and variable
capital (C/V) changes from 4:6 to 5:5 to 6:4. In all three time
periods, then, 100 units of value are produced. The only difference is that with the passing of time the relative contributions
of living and dead labour power changes. The actual numbers have
otherwise been chosen arbitrarily to illustrate this effect.

In order to illustrate the effects of the development of the
productive forces it is necessary that the reader understand the
basic assumption which lies behind all such uses of the organic
composition ratio. On this assumption most of the arguments on
the falling rate of profit under capitalism stand. The assumption
is that the development of the productive forces brings with it an
increasing organic composition. Put another way, it is assumed
that increasing productivity means that, for a given amount of
value produced, the relative contribution of constant capital to
the value of the final product increases. As far as I know, this
assumption is never set out clearly by Marx, although it is crucial
to many of his arguments. It must be remembered that we are
dealing with values here. In other words, while the value of the
product is held constant from time 1 to time 3, the actual material
volume of goods is not. Indeed, it is to be expected that the

development of the productive forces actually decreases the value of any given volume of goods. The *volume* of goods produced in time 3 is thus greater than the volume of goods produced in time 1, although the *value* of these goods remains the same.

It is illuminating to turn to the cost of reproduction formula for a single producer, or a single branch of production, within the community of producers. Table 7.2 sets out the effect of the changing organic composition over time on the cost of production of a single producer.

Table 7.2   *The changing composition of capital: single producer*

Time period	C	V	CR
T1	5	10	15
T2	10	10	20
T3	15	10	25

In this table the technical and value composition of capital changes from 1/2 to 1/1 to 3/2 from time 1 to time 3. The value of goods turned out by the individual producer increases. I have also assumed here that the absolute material standard of living of the producer increases at the same rate as does the productivity of this branch of production. For this reason the value of V in each time period remains a constant 10, since with increasing productivity the volume of goods with such a value will increase. This assumption is not crucial to the argument, but does not seem illogical given the built-in assumptions of mobility of labour.

I have suggested that the increasing organic composition which accompanies a development of the productive forces comes into contradiction with the separation and equality of producers. The effects of this contradiction are most evident when we look at the effect of this change on the price of production. In order to do this I shall simply assume that the exchange value of one unit of value is a constant 10 Indonesian *rupiah* (Rp. 10). This means that the price of labour power, i.e. the exchange value of the goods and services necessary to reproduce the labour power of a single person over a single period of time, is Rp. 100. Table 7.3 is based on formula (ii) above for the price of production.

Table 7.3 *Prices of production: single producer*

Time period	C	V	PP
T1	Rp. 50	Rp. 100	Rp. 150
T2	Rp. 100	Rp. 100	Rp. 200
T3	Rp. 150	Rp. 100	Rp. 250

The change in organic composition here (expressed as a ratio of exchange values) is the same change as that expressed in the value composition in Table 7.2. I have temporarily assumed a determinative relation between value and price, such that all changes in the value of a product are immediately manifested as a similar change in exchange value. A complete analysis of increasing productivity would have to take into account the more complex relation between price and value. Again I must stress that the numbers have been arbitrarily selected, and that the magnitudes of change may be misleading. Nonetheless, the figures illustrate the direction of change, which is of concern here.

Table 7.3 shows that in each time period the producer earns enough to reproduce himself, i.e. Rp. 100. If, however, we look at the ratio C/V or price ratio of organic composition, it will be evident that with the increasing organic composition of capital, the producer must at the beginning of the productive process lay out more money in the later periods than he needs to do in the earlier periods. In other words, given the assumptions built into these illustrations, as productivity increases the 'return on investment' decreases. In T1 a producer must be able to pay out, or set aside from previous earnings, a total of Rp. 150 in order to start production. This allows him at the end of the period to reproduce depleted stocks of raw materials, tools and the like, as well as to pay himself the Rp. 100 necessary to reproduce his own labour power. When he sells his goods at the end of the period he will have a further Rp. 150 for the next period of production. In T2, however, when productivity has increased throughout the economy, or at least in the particular branch of production, the amount of money necessary increases to Rp. 200 and in T3 to Rp. 250. In each case the producer realises his investment through the market, and in each case he earns the same amount, i.e. Rp. 100, to reproduce his own labour power.

While in the capitalist mode of production a similar process causes the rate of profit to decline, in petty commodity production increasing organic composition means that larger amounts of money will be needed by the producer in order to get the same amount of money back. Of course this increased amount of money is obtained or realised through selling the completed goods, but the money in circulation is increased. While the amount of money accruing to the producer remains the same, it can only do so because he lays out larger and larger sums on constant capital. Something similar to the return on investment, here measured as a ratio between money laid out by the producer and return to labour, actually decreases over time.

It is equally possible to see that anyone with a sum of cash wishing to set up as a producer will be more likely to choose a branch of production in which the organic composition of capital, and hence productivity, remains low. This intersectoral problem exists because, according to an earlier assumption, the return to labour is equalised throughout the economy. In actual cases there may be a slight monopoly effect due to greater amounts of cash outlay necessary in those branches of production with a higher organic composition. The tendency even in these cases would be for a general equalisation. The monopoly effect of the different levels of cash outlay would probably be less than the analogous effect of larger-than-average enterprises in a capitalist economy.

While it is true that producers eventually recover their increased expenses, the greater risk involved would clearly have the effect of generating what the Minangkabau call bankruptcies, i.e. the forcing-out of small producers who, finding themselves without funds through emergency expenditure, leave independent production to seek work as wage labourers. When considering the case of the petty commodity mode of production in isolation, the effect of the development of the productive forces would be that an increasing number of small producers would lose access to their own means of production, and thus have no way of earning a living.

Even more dramatic would be the effects of increasing productivity at the time of the increases. Suddenly producers who needed small amounts of cash to set production in motion would need larger amounts. The increased level of money in circulation would demand that each time productivity went up, so would the need for cash from outside. While those who adopt the technique first may derive financial advantage, because prices temporarily do not change, freedom of competition, which results in very quick price adjustments, would soon force prices down. Those who had not yet adopted new techniques would thus face a drop in their own living standards.

It should be clear from this discussion that economic crises would be provoked by comparatively small increases in productivity under petty commodity production. In other words, while capitalism in its initial stages actually thrived on increasing productivity, any revolutionary increase in the organic composition of capital in petty commodity production would quickly serve to throw producers out of the system, and increase inequality by giving short-term advantage to those who kept pace with the changes. Individual access to the means of production, and the equality of direct producers, would be quickly undermined, and a form of class differentiation would soon occur. Whether this would lead to conflict or simply a new mode of production in which impoverished producers would become wage workers depends, of course, on concrete conditions.

The above discussion of petty commodity production has focused on the economy, the structural preconditions of its reproduction and the specific form of the contradiction between forces and relations of production. The definition of the economy proceeds from basic principles of the Althusserian interpretation of Marx and moves towards a specification of the economic base — forces and relations of production, and the structures of reproduction. While certain aspects of ideology, in particular the forms of commodity fetishism, have been referred to, I have not attempted a definition of political and ideological instances. At this level of abstraction it would be possible only to indicate the kinds of political and ideological formations which would be compatible with the economic base.

My main aim in this structural analysis of petty commodity

production, as I pointed out at the beginning of the chapter, has been to delineate the preconditions necessary for its emergence, as well as the conditions of existence necessary to its reproduction. I have also tried to show how, even given these preconditions in a determinant social formation, petty commodity production is subject to an internal contradiction which tends to undermine the nature of the productive relations. The basic preconditions outlined here are: the economic separation of producers from any class of non-producers, the separation of producers from each other and the guarantee of a market and a mobility either of labour or of techniques of production.

I have, therefore, introduced certain structural concepts which are necessary before we can account for the existence and reproduction of petty commodity production within a concrete social formation. In other words I have argued that while there may be numerous paths to the evolution of a system of petty commodity production, history must produce these preconditions before it can come into existence. It is now necessary to return to the case of Minangkabau society to see how these preconditions were fulfilled historically, and what kind of economic system gave rise to the modern one.

8
Mercantilism and the evolution of 'traditional' society

The literature on Minangkabau is, with respect to the question of the development of a commercial peasant economy, very similar to the writings of many modernisation theorists. The contemporary situation is usually envisaged as the result of the disintegration of a traditional society subject to the influence in this century of a Western market economy.[1] Gough, in a survey of the impact of Western contact on 'traditional' matrilineal societies including Minangkabau, argues that 'economic changes brought about by contact with Western industrial nations' result in the disintegration of matrilineal groups: 'In their place, the elementary family emerges as the key kinship group. . .' (in Schneider and Gough, 1962, p. 631). Schrieke (1955), Josselin de Jong (1957) and Maretin (1961) all take up a similar position, i.e. that the commercial pressures of Western contact have served to dissolve traditional matrilineal bonds, led to the emergence of the nuclear family and promoted the development of an indigenous market economy. These commercial pressures were, it is maintained, experienced in Minangkabau at the beginning of this century, 'the time of radical changes in the traditional way of life' (Maretin, 1961, p. 173).

Implied in this approach is not only an inaccurate conception of pre-twentieth-century Minangkabau history, but also a misleading continuist view of social change and the development of capitalism. Western contact, primarily through the impact of the market, leads to a dissolution of tribal society producing a commercialised peasantry, a development which is in itself only a transitional step in the development of capitalism. It is clear that Schrieke, the main source for this discussion of social change in Minangkabau,

1. Something implied in some of the writings on social change in West Sumatra. See my more detailed discussion of this problem in Kahn, 1976.

implies that the development of markets in the first few decades of this century would inevitably lead to the development of wage labour and a market in land.

We shall have occasion to take issue with this approach to social change at a theoretical level in a later chapter. Here my aim is different — it is to show that the picture presented above is inaccurate with respect to Minangkabau itself, that the periodisation of Minangkabau history based on a tradition/modernity distinction is oversimplified, and that the historical baseline for the development of petty commodity production is not a 'traditional' tribal society, but a society which had long been shaped by contact with the West, and an economy which had for centuries been drawn into the world market economy. Contact with the West and with a market are therefore inadequate explanations for the emergence of the peasant economy described in previous chapters.

I have chosen in this chapter to focus my attention on the impact of European, primarily Dutch, contact with Minangkabau. This is not to argue that Minangkabau villages were isolated from extra-local influence before the coming of the Dutch merchants in the seventeenth century, nor that the forms of local organisation can be understood in isolation even prior to the sixteenth century. Clearly, for example, Sumatran villages of the interior were influenced by the immensely important trade with China and the Indian Ocean for centuries before the first Portuguese ships entered the East Indies in search of spices. Moreover, it might be argued that trade with the Europeans was not, at least at the outset, very different from trade with Chinese, Indian and Arab merchants which rested on similar principles. Unlike the earlier traders, however, the Dutch eventually revolutionised the world economic system in general, and the societies of the East Indies in particular because, in seeking to maintain favourable trading conditions, they eventually turned towards territorial control and direct administration of the local populations with whom they traded. In a later period of course it was in Europe that industrial capitalism developed, a change which was to have considerable repercussions for the societies of the periphery.

I have elsewhere (Kahn, forthcoming) attempted to analyse Sumatran economic and social organisation prior to the coming of the Dutch. I have argued that Minangkabau society developed in some sense as an off-shoot of the declining empire of Srivijaya (cf. Wolters, 1970, pp. 42ff.) and that a system of dual descent operated in the Minangkabau highlands after the formation of the kingdom in the fourteenth century. Trade and royal power were controlled in the patriline, while local power and the control of land passed through the matriline.

In any case, by the early sixteenth century the power of the royal lineage began steadily to diminish. By the end of the century large parts of West Sumatra were independent of royal rule. Internally both traders and local rulers were able to challenge the power of the king. Externally, first the Acehnese and then the Europeans encroached on the royal domain. The Acehnese, as well as the Dutch, in the seventeenth century made inroads on the western coast of Sumatra. Control of this area of the Rantau, outside the cultural heartland of Minangkabau, was an important means of gaining access to the commercial wealth upon which the kingdom relied. By the end of the sixteenth century the Acehnese succeeded in establishing hegemony over the coast as far south as Pariaman. In the same period the states of Indrapura, Indragiri and Jambi, previously vassals of the Minangkabau kings, became independent (see Kroeskamp, 1931, p. 12).

When the first European merchants came to West Sumatra in the early seventeenth century they were faced with an already changing society. The Minangkabau royal lineage had lost power. Tributary relations were, in all likelihood, being replaced by an increasing autonomy of local communities or village alliances ruled by what have usually been called petty aristocrats (Kroeskamp, 1931; Leeuw, 1926). Whatever the structure of these small communities, it seems that they were based primarily on some form of communal control of irrigated rice land. At the same time, petty traders and peasant producers formed an important part of the local commercial economy. By the late seventeenth century, and probably much earlier, there were large numbers of small merchants and 'businessmen' in most Minangkabau villages.[1]

The beginnings of European mercantile domination

It is clearly impossible in the space of a brief introductory dis-

---

1. This comes from Dias' account of his travels in Sumatra in 1684. His account contains descriptions of villages and the main occupations of villagers in the places he visited. He cites gold-miners, farmers and small entrepreneurs (*negotiaten*) – giving relative numbers for several villages (in de Haan, 1897, pp. 355ff.).

cussion of Dutch colonial rule in Indonesia to do justice to the large amount of historical material which spans a period of almost three centuries from the coming of the Dutch merchants in the first years of the seventeenth century to the dismantling of the Culture System, the culmination of mercantile policy in the East Indies, at the end of the nineteenth century. My main aim here is to present material which allows us to contrast the period of mercantile expansion to the situation which followed the emergence of industrial capitalism in the Dutch colony. At the same time I want to attempt to demonstrate that the effects of local social and economic organisation of mercantile domination were historically specific, that the forms of local organisation which developed in the three centuries of mercantilist policies were different both from those in the period before Dutch contact and from those in the period of capitalist domination. In other words, in order to demonstrate the determinant effect of capitalist domination on the Minangkabau peasant economy in the twentieth century, it becomes necessary, by way of introduction, to illustrate the very different effect of European mercantilism. Elsewhere (Kahn, forthcoming) I have tried to show more closely how what many authors take to be the structure of traditional Minangkabau society was a product of mercantile domination in the nineteenth century, and that the most commonly taken baseline for social change in West Sumatra was not what scholars have throught it to be. The seemingly tradition-bound Minangkabau society of the turn of this century which crumbled under the commercial impact of Western capitalism was not, as many writers have assumed, a carry-over from the pre-colonial past, but a creation of the specific forms of European domination which evolved from the seventeenth century onward (see Kahn, 1976).

It is not feasible for me to provide here an extended theoretical discussion of the nature of merchant capital in general, and the historical conditions which gave specific form to Dutch mercantile interests in particular, topics which I have also developed more fully elsewhere (Kahn, forthcoming). Suffice it to say that the Europeans were not the first to extract profits on merchant capital from the Indonesian archipelago, that the trade monopoly which the Dutch developed to preserve mercantile profits was of necessity also the basis for profits extracted by Indian, Arab and Malay merchants before the seventeenth century and that any

154

formal definition of merchant capital which rests on the concept of trading profits alone is bound to be insufficient to explain the concrete case of the policies of the Dutch East India Company and the colonial government in the period before the expansion of private capitalism in the colony.

If any over-all generalisations could be made about the period of Dutch mercantile domination in the East Indies, they would concern the ways in which first the company and then the colonial government resolved the basic contradiction of merchant capital, i.e. the diminishing profits which free trade inevitably brings. This was accomplished in the first instance through a trade monopoly which, in preventing free trade, ensured that rates of exchange would maintain profits. When, however, historical circumstances gradually undermined the effectiveness of merchant monopoly, a trend developed from trade to tribute and then to direct control of production itself. The reasons for this are, at this point, perhaps too complicated to uncover. However, it is possible to suggest that the various obstacles to the export of money in the Netherlands, the fact that merchants had very little else in the home country which was in demand in the East Indies, the difficulties involved in guaranteed profits being realised on the home market and the competition of both Asian and, more importantly, other European merchants were all developments which militated against pure mercantilism in the East Indies. Coupled with the fact that the monopoly itself required increasing territorial control and political manipulation in the East Indies, these factors led to attempts to extract a surplus in more direct ways, initially through demanding tribute from local allies of the Company, and then, when the Dutch government had taken over the colony, by a system of direct European control of production, and the extraction of surplus through a systematised use of forced labour.[1] While these policies may not at first appear compatible with the interests of merchant capital, they are all, I would argue, logical extensions of it, under certain specific conditions.

1. The argument that Dutch mercantile policy shifted from a concern with profits through trade to profits through tribute is made in a very clear and convincing way by Furnivall (1949). One alternative, that the Dutch should concentrate on the Asia trade, was proposed early on by Coen. The envisaged cloth–spice circuit is described by Sen (1962). Glamann (1958) also takes up the question of the Asia trade. However, it seems that it was the movement towards tribute and forced labour which eventually predominated.

This development of mercantilism had, of course, drastic consequences for the Indonesian economy. It led to a 'feudalisation' process under which political extraction of a surplus, first through local allies of the Dutch and then directly by the colonial government itself, took place. The apparently autonomous, self-sufficient communities of the nineteenth century were merely the end result of an extended period of decline in the peasant commercial economy, a result of increasing extra-village control of village land, and the subsumption of the peasant economy under the requirements of merchant capital. It was in this manner that the Dutch, to use Frank's term, underdeveloped the Indonesian economy (Frank, 1969).

Dutch merchants in Sumatra

Attracted by the Portuguese success in the East Indies spice trade, and excluded from Lisbon, the spice capital of Europe in the sixteenth century, the Dutch and the British undertook their own voyages to the archipelago around the turn of the seventeenth century. The first Dutch ships left the Netherlands for the Indies in 1595, and in the following five years 10 separate companies were formed. While Dutch merchants initially formed separate companies, in 1602, partly to prevent too much competition, the United East India Company (the V.O.C.) was formed. Attracted by the lure of Sumatran gold, the need for fresh supplies of pepper and the fact that Sumatra's west coast lay outside the sphere of Portuguese influence, the first British and French ships visited Sumatran ports in the early seventeenth century.[1] An initial period of conflict between the Dutch and the British, as well as between the Europeans and the Acehnese, was followed by Dutch control of the local trade outlets. This trade monopoly was secured through a series of contracts made by the V.O.C. with local rulers, often in exchange for support against rival chiefs and the Acehnese.

The early Dutch merchants in Sumatra had little interest in political or territorial control for its own sake. Their interest was in the establishment of a trade monopoly which gave them ex-

1. This discussion of mercantilism and West Sumatra relies for its historical material largely on Kroeskamp's interesting study (1931). See also Leeuw (1926) for some additional material on the contracts, and Furnivall (1949) and Hall (1968) for a broader overview of early European relations with the East Indies.

clusive rights, vis-à-vis both European and Asian traders, to all commerce. The contracts, of which the so-called Painan contract is the best known (see Kroeskamp, 1931 and Leeuw, 1926), ensured these trading rights in exchange for Dutch support for the local ruler.

While gold from the Minangkabau highlands may have been the more attractive commodity, it was pepper in these early years of mercantile domination which came to be the mainstay of Company profits in the western archipelago. Ideally, this was to be obtained in exchange for Indian cloth (Sen, 1962), although very often cash was paid. The system therefore rested on fixed rates of exchange for pepper and gold, which in turn was ensured through a politically enforced monopoly. By keeping all other merchants away from the main points of trade along the coast, the Dutch could set the rates of exchange at will. They were particularly worried by the presence of Asian traders, Indians and Malays, who would readily undercut the fixed prices. Profits were realised in different ways, one of which was through the Asian trade itself. Pepper and spices could, for example, be sold in India to yield sufficient cloth to buy more pepper and spices. The surplus could then be sold in the Netherlands for cash, which represented pure profit (see Sen, *op. cit.*).

It was soon found, however, that preserving such a system through trade monopoly had many drawbacks. It became more and more important, in order to reproduce the advantageous trading conditions, for the V.O.C. to take control of territory. To drive out the British and the Portuguese, for example, a military foothold was necessary. In order to protect their European trade, the Dutch established strongholds in Batavia, and in Malacca by capturing it from the Portuguese, thus gaining control of the two main routes to the West — the Straits of Malacca and the Sunda Straits between Sumatra and Java. Meanwhile interference in the internal organisation of the trade areas also became necessary. This meant, for example, careful control of the production of spices in the east, and of pepper in the west. It also meant interference in other branches of peasant production. When, for example, Sumatran villagers in the Batang Kapas and Indrapura in Sumatra turned towards the cultivation of cotton, which was then woven in Padang and Koto Tengah for domestic consumption, in the 1660s there was a concerted effort on the part of the V.O.C. to stop it, for this kind of 'import substitution' threatened the cloth—pepper exchange upon which profits were based. Groenwegen, then a regional head (Opperhoofd) of the V.O.C. on the west coast, recommended that all locally produced cloth be thrown into the sea. He was eventually able to achieve his aims in a more subtle fashion through pressure on local rulers (see Kroeskamp, 1931, pp. 48f.).

The monopoly rates of exchange were actually written into the treaties signed by local rulers. When these treaties were broken the Dutch did not hesitate to take bloody reprisals. Most notable were the 'expeditions' led by Verspreet in the 1660s. Verspreet followed up his conquests by regularising local administration to reinforce the monopoly trade. At the same time, however, even by the second half of the seventeenth century territorial control and taxation had become significant features of mercantile policy. Verspreet's actions may have been directed towards protecting the trade monopoly. However, he also chose to involve the Company in the administration of the west coast, to collect taxes (which favoured subsistence cultivators), and to make an agreement with the king of Minangkabau whereby Verspreet himself became the king's representative (*stadhouder*). This agreement forced the king to recognise all contracts made by the V.O.C. as if they were his own, and to relinquish his rights of taxation over the coastal population. Verspreet's military victories were sealed through a series of 'fines' on local rulers, who were thereby bound to hand over as tribute to the Company fixed amounts of pepper and gold.

In general, then, it is possible to see very early on in the history of European mercantile domination that trade monopolies themselves were gradually superseded by tribute. Furnivall, for example, in discussing other parts of the East Indies refers to a system of tax farms (1949). Whole villages were let out to Company employees or to Chinese entrepreneurs in exchange for an annual payment of rent. Company employees frequently fulfilled their quotas not through trade but through direct demands for tribute on their Indonesian allies.

This tendency was carried further by the British who had, by the end of the seventeenth century, also made treaties with local rulers on Sumatra's west coast. They established a toehold on the coast by building Fort Marlborough near Benkulu (Bencoolen), south of Padang. Like the Dutch, the British were interested at first in the pepper trade, and they too established through political interference an exclusive right to the pepper trade and a favourable monopoly price structure.

By the end of the eighteenth century, however, the British also had experienced considerable difficulties in operating a pure merchant monopoly. Variations in the pepper supply meant that it was increasingly difficult to persuade local producers to plant pepper. Rapid fluctuations in the prices fetched in European markets were in part a result of the competition among the different European countries.

In the eighteenth century both the British and the Dutch therefore moved to a more direct control of production.[1] While tribute and tax farming were one way around these difficulties, forced cultivation was another. At first local quotas for spice production were imposed on those district chiefs who had made contracts with the merchants, but this system was gradually replaced by forced cultivation. Indigenous peasant cultivators were required either to supply corvée labour on land owned by company officials and local chiefs, or to cultivate on their own land a fixed number of pepper vines.

Eventually, of course, the British exchanged their possession on the coast for Malacca on the Malay peninsula. This exchange was enacted by the Anglo-Dutch treaty of 1824 which followed the Napoleonic Wars. By this time the system of forced cultivation had become predominant, in spite of attempts by Raffles, who assumed authority over the possessions of the British East India Company in Sumatra in 1818, to abolish it and replace it by a tax. Raffles's liberal economic policies were overturned at that time. And while similar proposals had been made in Holland by van Hogendorp, the time for such policies in Sumatra was still almost 100 years away. Instead the system of forced cultivation was to become the dominant means of extracting a surplus from Indonesian peasant cultivators in Java and in West Sumatra under the cultivation system instituted by the Dutch Governor General van Bosch in the nineteenth century.

While this summary of the early period of European mercantile domination has of necessity been brief, it is sufficient to show that both British and Dutch merchants relied not just on trade mon-

---

1. The discussion on the British role in the mercantile exploitation of West Sumatra is derived largely from Bastin (1965).

opoly but also on tribute and direct control of production itself as a means of deriving their profits. While a considerable body of historical material is available concerning the European side of mercantile policy, the overall lack of information on Minangkabau socio-economic organisation in this period makes it difficult to evaluate the effects of mercantilism on the local economy. It is clear that villagers, especially in the coastal areas, underwent a great deal of hardship. Before the coming of the Dutch, prices for spices, gold and jungle produce were higher than those paid by the Europeans. Asian traders — Arabs, Indians and Minangkabau — were largely driven out of the overseas trade. We know that large numbers of Minangkabau were dependent for their livelihood, at least in part, on the market. Apart from the producers of the commodities required by the Europeans, there were clearly large numbers of traders and producers involved in a largely localised commercial sector. It seems likely that, at least in the coastal areas, and probably in parts of the highlands as well, rice itself was in short supply. Dias' account of Minangkabau occupational specialisation (in de Haan, 1897) describes the importance of the commercial sector in the late seventeenth century. Marsden's history of Sumatra (1811) also provides information on Minang-kabau commercial activity. His description of gold-mining suggests the existence of entrepreneurial units similar to those which I have described for this century (1811, pp. 168f.). He also discusses independent production of iron tools; wooden objects; silk and cotton cloth; gunpowder; earthenware; gold and silver filigree; krises, cannon and other weapons and iron ore mined near Padang Luar in the highlands (Marsden, 1811, pp. 181ff., 347).

It is possible only to speculate about the effect of mercantile monopoly on the commercial development of the indigenous economy. By reducing prices of certain commodities the monopoly probably also reduced the over-all circulation of commodities and money within West Sumatra. This kind of depression would have encouraged small-scale and individual productive and distributive organisation. While wage labour existed at the time, it is likely that the development of large-scale entrepreneurial organisation was checked by the monopoly on the coastal trade. At the same time, devolution in the commodity sector of the economy may well have led to an intensification of subsistence cultivation.

Perhaps European monopoly caused the greatest overt hardship through demand fluctuation. Peasant cultivators were encouraged to produce pepper for the European market, and yet, being entirely dependent on that market, suffered most when demand fell. However, more significant in terms of the long-term evolution of the Minangkabau economy was the 'feudalisation' process which I have mentioned earlier. In those areas where the European companies relied on tribute and then forced cultivation it is clear that independent entrepreneurial units would not survive for long. Through their superior military strength, and through their support for a local elite, the Dutch introduced new socio-economic forms to Sumatra. What appears as feudalisation is simply the use of the political apparatus to enforce the extraction of a surplus from previously independent peasant producers. Under the pepper-quota system, for example, local chiefs were required to see that all peasants under their jurisdiction planted pepper. This was then turned over to the chiefs, who passed a proportion on to the Europeans in the form of tribute. At the same time the position of these local chiefs also changed. Previously dependent on internal relations for their power, they were now dependent largely on the role allotted to them by the Dutch and the British. This increased political power was itself necessary to the flow of tribute. That this class was able to exercise control through land ownership is evidenced by Marsden's description of gold-miners in the early nineteenth century who were forced to turn over a proportion of their profits to local landowners in the form of rent (Marsden, 1811, p. 167). Hence, while commercial gold-mining may have developed more freely with the decline of the royal lineage and the loosening of the royal monopoly on mining, it seems that after a century of mercantile domination, a new class of landowners was similarly able to derive rent from local entrepreneurs. It is likely, therefore, that the local *adat* hierarchy, including the *panghulu* and others who exercised control over village land, found themselves in a better position than they had before the coming of the Europeans. This is clearly the case in the coastal district, but also seems to have extended into the highlands where, before the nineteenth century, the Dutch did not exercise direct control.

It is not therefore surprising that a Muslim movement known as the Padris began agitating against *adat* authorities and the royal lineage. The Padri movement took the form of a struggle against the corruption of Islamic beliefs and practices by local customs or *adat*.[1] Nor is it surprising that the Dutch chose to intervene on the side of the *adat* authorities as an excuse to move into the Minangkabau highlands.

As I have pointed out, we can only guess at the precise effects of the early mercantile policies on Minangkabau social structure in the two centuries preceding the Culture System. It is clear, however, that the nature of the peasant economy was radically affected by the new forms of external domination of Minangkabau brought largely by the Dutch. By tying some peasants more directly in to the European market considerable hardship was caused. Any possible decline in prices paid to producers, a result of the elimination of competition, itself must have affected other sectors of the local economy which were not so directly reliant on the overseas market. The European shift from trade monopoly to tribute and finally to forced cultivation, at least in those areas subject to direct Dutch control through the contract system, contributed towards a process of feudalisation whereby new systems of land tenure and political domination reduced the scope of the commercial economy and led to different forms of surplus extraction from the peasant producers.

At the same time, partly because of uncertain demand for pepper and spices, competition among different European mercantile powers and the decline in the commercial economy in the East Indies, the V.O.C. in particular experienced considerable financial constraints in the eighteenth century. By 1789 a committee sent from the Netherlands to investigate the state of defence found in the accounts a deficit of 74 million guilders, a deficit which rose to 96 million guilders by 1791. While the Company had originally hidden the losses from its European creditors by borrowing money at higher rates of interest in the East Indies, by the early 1780s it was no longer able to raise loans on the open market (see Hall, 1968, ch. 17). This is not to say that nobody was getting rich, for alongside the official dealings and commerce there was a huge volume of illicit commerce. Officials of the Company were able to make vast fortunes in relatively short

1. For a discussion of the so-called Padri Wars see Cuisinier (1959), Dobbins (1977), and Radjab (1964). That the Padris were an important force before the outbreak of direct war with the Dutch is clear from Kroeskamp (1951) and also from Raffles's memoirs which contain an account of a journey to the Minangkabau highlands (Raffles, 1830).

periods of service in spite of their comparatively low salaries (Furnivall, 1949). Clearly, this was related to the tendency of the Company to substitute tribute for profits on trade alone, and the huge discrepancy between official Company earnings and the unofficial revenues accruing to Company officials must have been a manifestation of the hidden sources of profit brought by tribute flows.

The situation was so bad that in 1800 the Batavian Republic in the Netherlands disbanded the Company and took over its possessions and debts. In 1801 a committee was appointed to report on the colonial situation. While the main force in this investigation was a certain Dirk van Hogendorp, who proposed an end to forced cultivation and the development of a free peasantry in the colony, mercantile interests again prevailed. The committee in the end decided to accept the proposals not of van Hogendorp, but of its President, Nederburgh, who represented mercantile interests by opposing free trade and the flow of private investment to the Indies. In the colony these early decisions resulted in the systematisation of forced cultivation under the so-called Culture System.

The Culture System in West Sumatra

Mercantilism, as we have seen, had certain specific consequences for the socio-economic organisation of the peasantry in West Sumatra. In particular the process of feudalisation contributed towards a decline in indigenous commerce and an increase in the importance of monopoly. While at the beginning of the nineteenth century a variety of local forms of organisation grew up to meet the demands of the Dutch and their local allies for tax and tribute, in the course of the century large parts of Java and the area of West Sumatra were subjected to a uniform system of mercantile extraction known as the Culture System. Based on state control of land and forced cultivation of export crops, the Culture System served to reinforce the process of feudalisation and stagnation in the indigenous commercial economy and to solidify certain aspects of local social organisation. The result, in West Sumatra, was a static system of corporate lineage organisation, an increased autonomy of village communities (or apparent autonomy, since villages were always directly linked to the production of export crops) and hence what I have called the development of a traditional society (Kahn, 1976).

The main Sumatran export crop in the nineteenth century was coffee. Brought to the Indies as a trade good from Arabia, coffee was first planted in Java. By the late eighteenth century coffee was being planted in West Sumatra by Buginese immigrants (cf. Bastin, 1965). In 1820 17,000 piculs of coffee were exported from Sumatra's west coast to the United States (one picul is equal to 133 pounds). By 1833 cultivation had increased so that 60,000 piculs were exported to the Netherlands.

Coffee, like pepper, was grown by Minangkabau peasants in the coastal areas in these early years. Low prices and the Dutch monopoly, however, meant that, again like pepper cultivation, coffee planting was not very popular. Its cultivation spread, however, when the Dutch colonial government took direct administrative control of the Minangkabau highlands on the pretence of supporting the *adat* officialdom against the challenge of the Padris (see above, pp. 161f.). The first centres of Dutch control in the highlands were the forts built in the Padri War: Fort de Kock (now Bukit Tinggi) and Fort van der Capellan (now Batu Sangkar). The defeat of the Padris was soon followed by the institutionalisation of forced coffee deliveries through a systematised, Dutch-controlled *nagari* administrative structure.

Forced cultivation was introduced because of a stagnation in coffee exports from the highland districts of Minangkabau.[1] Under the new colonial government, Minangkabau villagers were required to plant coffee to be sold at fixed prices. Government warehouses were built in Padang Panjang and Payakumbuh, where the coffee was exchanged for either cash or trade goods. Local officials were appointed to oversee coffee production, their compliance being assured by promising them a fixed proportion of the profits made on the coffee trade in their respective areas.

Forced cultivation initially resulted in an increase in output. Exports from West Sumatra rose from 58,000 piculs in 1847 to 122,000 in 1852, reaching a high point of 191,000 piculs in 1857. While the Culture System originally succeeded in increasing colonial profits, by the 1870s this success waned. The most

---

1. Material on coffee cultivation in Minangkabau in the nineteenth century is found in Ples (1878), Huitema (1935), Parels (1944) and Geertz (1960). Geertz makes some attempt to compare the operation of the Culture System in Java and Sumatra.

obvious reason for the decline was the prevalence of a disease which affected the leaves of the coffee bush. *Robusta*, a disease-resistant strain, did not replace the more susceptible *Arabica* coffee in West Sumatra until 1910. There were, however, also social reasons for the failure of forced cultivation.

By the end of the nineteenth century, for example, it seems that the colonial government was beginning to lose interest in the export of consumption goods to Europe, and instead turned to searching for sources of means of production required by Western industry – oil, rubber and minerals (see Wertheim, 1956). At the same time, the 'liberal' cause which had long opposed the policies of mercantilism gained adherents because of the search in the Netherlands for outlets for private, capitalist investment. Until the passing of the Agrarian Land Law in Java in 1870, private Dutch investment in the colony was severely restricted by the colonial government. Such obstacles to free investment were not lifted in West Sumatra until the early twentieth century. The pressure for free trade, free capital investment and the creation of a commercial peasantry was stepped up with the support of new economic interests in the Netherlands.

While by the end of the nineteenth century the policy of forced cultivation had been largely abandoned in most parts of the colony, it was not until 1908 that the system was overturned in West Sumatra and replaced by a tax. This delay is at least partly explained by the resistance of the Minangkabau bureaucracy, which benefited directly from the Culture System. One of the provisions of the so-called Plakaat Panjang – the treaty with the Dutch signed by Minangkabau leaders at the end of the Padri Wars – was that taxes would never be instituted by the colonial government.

The Culture System was based on a dualistic economic policy. The colonial government in the nineteenth century sought to increase coffee production in West Sumatra while, at the same time, preventing the emergence of a commercial peasantry. Since profits came for mercantile interests only through buying cheap and selling dear, there was no attempt to create a market in Indonesia for Dutch manufacture or Dutch capital. Combined with the colonial desire to prevent political turbulence, the main aim was to extract a surplus from villages in the form of cheap coffee or sugar, while at the same time preserving the illusion of

165

self-sufficient village communities. The result was what appeared to be two separate social spheres — a European sector run by Dutch officials and Chinese entrepreneurs and a 'traditional' village sector run on non-economic lines, producing for subsistence and governed by 'traditional' leaders on the basis of *adat* law.

In order to make villages self-sufficient — to prevent any economic flow other than the surplus taken out through forced cultivation — it was considered essential to preserve the subsistence cultivation of rice. In Java the combination of sugar-growing and the cultivation of rice was intended to preserve a separate subsistence sphere (see Geertz, 1963a). Village lands, in effect owned by the colonial government, were divided up regardless of the local structure of land ownership. A proportion of these lands was set aside for the cultivation of sugar cane. Javanese peasants were required to supply the labour force, while at the same time cultivating rice on the remaining village land. While over-all ownership of land then passed to the colonial government, there seems at the same time to have been an intensification of the communal nature of local rights of possession. The author of a well-known book on Dutch colonial policy writes:

Needing large areas of land, [the Culture System] paid no regard to the limits of the small fields nor even to those of the villages. In order to obtain agreement with Adat conceptions of equality, the disposition of more people for its cultivation and other services, the population seems to have parcelled out here and there the available village land into as many small portions as possible, and to have decided to have periodical redistribution in order to allocate collective rights and collective burdens as equitably as possible (Kat Angelino, 1931, p. 436).

While coffee cultivation in Sumatra was organised along slightly different lines, the over-all pattern of ownership was very close to that of Javanese sugar cultivation. Coffee, it is true, was not cultivated in estate fashion, but rather by individual coffee-planters. Nonetheless over-all ownership of land throughout the East Indies lay with the government, for it was on this basis that they could claim rights to the labour of the peasantry.

While forcing Minangkabau villagers to cultivate coffee, the colonial government also sought to encourage communal access to rice land. In this way all villagers would have enough land to fulfil their own subsistence needs, and rice would not become a commodity. Local officials were therefore encouraged to administer carefully the allocation of land on the basis of *adat*. The government at the same time did all in its power to prevent the production of rice for the market, for if rice were to be bought and sold, people in rice deficient areas would turn to other forms of commerce, and landless villagers would pose a political threat to the stability of the Culture System. Kat Angelino's analysis of the effects of the Culture System on land tenure in Java suggests that the redistribution of land, often thought to be a product of an earlier, communal system of land tenure, was in fact a consequence of the Culture System itself, which made access to subsistence land more important than ever.

The almost ludicrous lengths to which the government went to ensure the preservation of a subsistance sector in West Sumatra are described in Schrieke's report on Minangkabau. Discussing the period before the lifting of commercial restrictions, he writes:

In this way the natural development of a district whose latent possibilities had long before pointed to the evolution of an exchange economy was impeded by an administration whose sincere aim − at least in its rice policy − was to maintain law and order. Care had to be taken to see that in every *nagari* as much paddy as possible was stored and as little as possible exported and sold. For a population amply supplied with food meant a contented and peaceful population. A former Padang Highlands commissioner . . . was even of the opinion that the *kinchirs*, those ingenious native rice hulling mills driven by a water wheel, were harmful, since they made it easy for the paddy to be processed into granular rice, for which the export demand was greatest. This civil servant thought that if the population were forced to stamp rice by hand, it would be more inclined to limit stamping required for its own consumption (Schrieke, 1955, pp. 97f.).

To carry out their economic policies − to provide forced deliveries of coffee and universal subsistence cultivation of rice − the colonial government systematised *nagari* administration by creating three new 'native' administrators: the *Laras* (Minangkabau: *Lareh*), the *Nagarihoofd* or *Panghulu Kapalo* and the *Panghulu Suku Rodi* (see Westenenk, 1912−13, pp. 68ff.). The first two were heads of specific territorial units, the first of the district and the second of the village. Their main tasks were to carry out all government directives which affected their territories, to police their districts and ensure law and order and to oversee both coffee and rice cultivation. It was the special task of the hated *Panghulu*

Suku Rodi to enforce the cultivation and delivery of the coffee crop.

In spite of suggestions to the contrary (see Abdullah, 1971, pp. 6f.), it is not at all certain that other village leaders, particularly the heads of kin groups, actually lost power under the Culture System. In his report of 1827, for example, Governor de Steurs wrote: 'Domestic matters should be left to the *panghulu*s to settle according to previous *adat* regulations. The Government officials should be concerned only with general matters' (in Westenenk, *op. cit*, author's translation). Much of Minangkabau property and inheritance law was also preserved (see Willinck, 1909, p. 78). Even criminal law remained the province of these 'traditional' leaders until the 1870s (Abdullah, 1971, p. 6). To encourage the periodic redistribution of subsistence rice land meant at the same time to maintain, or even to increase, the power of the *panghulu* to administer ancestral property.

Indeed, *panghulu* were able to obtain even more direct benefits. While the custom is on the way out in modern Minangkabau *nagari*, it seems that in the past *panghulu* in highland villages were able to demand that a proportion of *suku* land be set aside for their own use. This land is known as *sawah panggadangan gala*. In the coastal village of Bungus even today much *suku* rice land is treated as though it were the property of lineage elders, who receive a proportion of the harvest from *kamanakan* who work the land. In addition to such sources of revenue, most writers on Minangkabau in this period describe a series of payments made to *panghulu* and known as the *isi adat* (see Willinck, 1909, pp. 195, 314ff.; Westenenk, 1912–13, pp. 66ff.).

The obvious effect of the role allocated to the *panghulu* would have been to create, or at least intensify, the process of development of corporate kin groups with communal rights in lineage property vested in the lineage chief. By seeking also to register and then limit the number of *panghulu*, the Dutch further regulated the forms of local kinship organisation in order to fulfil the needs of the colonial government.

While the Culture System had, therefore, a determinant effect on local forms of social organisation, it clearly also had great implications for the peasant economy as well. The rice policy must have served to intensify subsistence cultivation. It is not clear to what extent the government was successful in implementing this policy, but by blocking the development of a market in rice, such a policy would have speeded up the devolution of commodity production in Minangkabau which began much earlier. By subjecting all Minangkabau men to the cultivation of coffee, the Culture System would also have contributed towards this devolution. Moreover, the price of coffee was so low that producers often let it rot on the trees rather than bear the cost of transport to the government warehouses. It is therefore reasonable to assume that, as in the earlier period, the monopoly price system created hardship and a decline in indigenous commercial activity.

Finally, by bolstering up a class dependent on the existing state of colonial exploitation, and by leaving room for *panghulu* whose power was based largely on the preservation of ancestral property, the Culture System also served to undermine the political position of local commercial classes.

By underdeveloping the Minangkabau economy in this particular way the colonial government of course was undercutting its own aims. While increased cash-cropping was necessary to increased profits, commercial backwardness was the inevitable result of the very policy designed to produce those profits in the first place. By creating economic stagnation, declining productivity was ensured, a decline which took place in spite of the increasing costs of colonial administration and demands for higher profits. A Dutch economy which was primarily capitalist and hence expanding could not benefit from a stagnant colonial system. For this reason the dismantling of the Culture System was bound to come from within the capitalist economy itself.

I have been concerned to develop in this chapter a rough picture of the organisation of Minangkabau society in the period before the widespread development of the commercialised peasantry in the first decades of this century. While the discussion has been rather a sketchy one, based as it is on secondary sources, it serves the purpose of shedding a good deal of light on the particular problem which is the central concern of this book. What does the analysis of the period of mercantile domination of West Sumatra tell us about the emergence of petty commodity production as the predominant form of economic organisation in this century?

Firstly, the analysis shows that the nature of Dutch colonial domination in the period 1600–1900 had certain specific consequences for Indonesia in general and West Sumatra in particular. It can be argued, for example, that the specific conditions of reproduction of merchant capital in colonial Indonesia led to a system of colonial exploitation which prevented the differentiation of the peasantry with respect to land on the one hand, and the emergence of private property in land on the other. At the local level, firstly the operation of trade monopoly and later State-enforced deliveries and/or production of valuable export crops were severe obstacles to the emergence of an independent com-mercialised peasantry. Indeed these forms of domination seem to have increased the tendency for land to be periodically redis-tributed within peasant villages. The indigenous elites, composed in West Sumatra of the *Tuanku Laras* and the *Panghulu Suku Rodi*, achieved their position through association with a State com-mercial monopoly and not with respect to ownership of land. Land remained in the hands of small peasant producers, its allocation subjected to 'tradition'. Such stratification as there was, therefore, developed entirely in terms of the circulation of com-modities produced for export and rarely in terms of access either to land or to the means of production.

When, therefore, towards the end of the nineteenth century the Culture System was eventually dismantled and private enterprise was allowed to develop in the colony, it is not surprising that the initiative came from potential European investors, rather than any indigenous commercial bourgeoisie. Nor, as we shall see, is it surprising that most indigenous commercial activity took place in the interstices of the capitalist economy, and that petty commodity relations, rather than capitalist ones, became the predominant form of economic organisation in the colony. It is clear, moreover, that indigenous commercial activity would be most profitable in the sphere of circulation, and therefore from petty traders to Indonesian bureaucrats and Chinese entrepreneurs, a class of merchants rather than a class of landowners would form the basis of the Indonesian bourgeoisie in the decades before Independence.

At a more general level the empirical analysis in this chapter shows that contact with a Western-style market is an inadequate explanation of the way in which peripheral social formations become transformed by incorporation within the world-economy. It is clear that 'the market' on its own does not generate a capitalist economy in which labour power and the means of production automatically become commodities. On the contrary, integration in the world market created by the Dutch had just the opposite effect in Indonesia up to the end of the nineteenth century. Similarly the analysis shows that the market is, on its own, no explanation for the emergence of a commercialised peasantry, nor for the predominance of petty commodity production and, therefore, of the modern form of the Minangkabau economy.

Finally, a study of Sumatran history shows that the developments in the twentieth century cannot be viewed simply as part of a gradual transition to capitalist forms of organisation, but rather that, as in the nineteenth century, the structure of the peasant economy is a specific response to a particular historical conjuncture, a point to which we shall return in the next chapter.

It is now necessary to examine this new historical conjuncture and the nature of the transformation of the Minangkabau social formation in the early decades of the twentieth century.

9

The emergence of petty commodity production

It is possible to trace the origins of the modern Minangkabau peasant economy to the period in which the commercial restrictions imposed under the Culture System were lifted and the economy of Indonesia as a whole was opened up to private capitalism. The main features of the peasant economy, which I have examined in previous chapters, must therefore be explained in terms of the transformation in the nature of Dutch colonial domination in the late nineteenth and early twentieth centuries on the one hand, and the existing social formation on the other. Specifically the predominance of petty commodity production must be explained with respect to the development of colonial capitalism and the existing social formation within which that development took place. The main features of that existing social formation have already been outlined. In the previous chapter I have shown that mercantile domination of the East Indies, first by the V.O.C. and then by the colonial government, generated processes of 'traditionalisation' and feudalisation within the Minangkabau social formation. These terms describe colonial encroachment on existing production processes and the preservation of apparently traditional forms of indigenous land tenure in an effort to prevent the emergence of a commercial peasantry. Rather than resulting in a rapid differentiation of the peasantry, the emergence of a class of large landowners and the domination of minifundia by latifundia — responses typical to peripheralisation in other regions of the world economy — Dutch mercantile domination in the East Indies produced a class of direct producers on the one hand and a commercial-cum-political elite on the other which derived its power from association with the colonial state and its revenues from circulation through the colonial monopoly on the trade in coffee and sugar.

172

The emergence of petty commodity production

In this chapter I shall discuss the development of the peasant economy from the period of the demise of this particular form of colonialism. At the same time I shall look briefly at a period in the late 1950s and early 1960s when petty commodity production itself seemed to be disappearing in the face of an increasing differentiation of rural producers and the development of rural capitalism. An examination of the conditions under which such a change was possible, and the reasons for the de-evolution which followed, will contribute to an understanding of those conditions necessary to the preservation of petty commodity production on the world capitalist periphery and of its potential transformation, points to be taken up in the final chapter.

The dismantling of Van den Bosch's Culture System and the reorganisation of the colonial economy in the second half of the nineteenth century was the result of an extended struggle between 'liberal' and 'conservative' Dutch interests, which we cannot go into here (see Furnivall, 1949, chs. 6 and 7). Suffice it to say that in spite of the debates over 'native welfare', the crux of the matter was whether exploitation of the colony should be left to mercantilists or to capitalists. While, from the defeat of van Hogendorp's proposals, the liberals had experienced one set-back after another, the tide turned dramatically in 1870 with the enactment of the Agrarian Law which empowered the government to grant leases for periods of up to 75 years to European planters in the East Indies. In the following year the government further empowered Europeans to lease land held by Indonesians on customary rights of tenure (see Furnivall, 1949; Allen and Donnithorne, 1957, p. 25). The gates were now open for the development of capitalism in the colony. The Nederlands Handel Maatschappij (N.H.M.), the main commercial organiser of the Culture System, turned to the financing of private enterprise in the colony, specialising in long-term loans to private estate owners. While most of the early developments took place in Java, the Deli plantation area of northern Sumatra was also opened up by private estate owners before the turn of the century.

In the last three decades of the nineteenth century, then, parts of the East Indies underwent radical change. The Culture System was displaced by individual planters and factory owners. Plantations and processing establishments passed to private Dutch capitalists. While the government retained an interest in the

173

running of the colonial economy, it did so now in the interests of private capital. Moreover, as Allen and Donnithorne show, the main developments in the late nineteenth century took place in the private sector (1957, p. 26).

While the popular image of capitalist development in Indonesia rests on the individual planter, in fact the period of the small capitalist was short-lived. By the turn of the century small planters were gradually replaced by corporate bodies in the estate sector, and financial institutions took greater control of the plantation economy. This is in part a result of the economic depression of the 1880s which, by depressing coffee and sugar prices, forced many planters to sell out to the banks. It was also in this period that the European sugar beet industry entered into successful competition with the colonial cane plantations (Allen and Donnithorne, 1957, p. 27). In this respect, however, it seems likely that the colonial economy was simply falling in with a general trend experienced by capital in the world-economy as a whole towards capital concentration, corporate ownership and the domination of financial institutions – a trend described by Lenin as the development of monopoly capitalism.[1] It is this trend more than anything which explains the movement against the small capitalist stimulated by the so-called Ethical Policy of the colonial government in the early twentieth century.

It was nonetheless the small capitalist, and particularly the planter, who opened up much of Indonesia to the world capitalist economy. The original expansion of the plantation economy was pioneered not by banks or large corporations, but by the small planter in search of his fortune. This is particularly significant for West Sumatra, for while other parts of the colony were opened up to capitalism in or shortly after 1870, West Sumatra was still caught in the commercial restrictions of the Culture System at the turn of this century.

In any case, by the early twentieth century large corporations, financial institutions and the colonial government were firmly in control of the colonial economy. A rapid growth of foreign investment, a large proportion of it from European countries outside Holland, took place in the years between 1900 and 1930. Investments stood at $318 million in 1900 and subsequently rose to

1. Lenin, 1917. But Lenin's thesis is clearly inaccurate with respect to the East Indies, in which individual capitalists, not monopoly capital, pioneered colonial exploitation.

$743 million in 1914 and $1,997 million in 1930 (Allen and Donnithorne, 1957, p. 288). All sugar and chinchona estates and most estate production of coffee and tobacco were Dutch-controlled. More than half the rubber plantations, as well as other sectors, were owned by British, American and other European interests.

The increase in private capitalist control of the colonial economy was accompanied by economic boom and prosperity. World demand and prices for natural rubber increased by leaps and bounds with the spread of the private motor-car. Modern Indonesia's most important export, oil, also found a place in the colonial economy in this period. The Royal Dutch Company was founded in 1890. In 1907 it merged with the Shell Transport and Trading Company of Borneo and by 1911 the operating company of Royal Dutch Shell was producing 1,700,000 metric tons of oil, largely for export. Increases in the exports of coffee, copra, sugar, tea, tobacco, tin and palm-oil products accompanied the growth in rubber and oil in the first two decades of this century.[1] But coffee and sugar, the mainstays of the nineteenth-century colonial economy, gradually gave way to raw materials for world industry. In 1925, for example, rubber replaced sugar as the colony's main export earner. In that year petroleum exports were third, after rubber and sugar, while tin and tin ore were sixth in the table of export earners.

The boom of the early twentieth century was not just felt by plantation owners, but also had a revolutionary effect on the peasants. It is estimated that in 1929 41 per cent of rubber output, 96 per cent of kapok, 48 per cent of tobacco, 73 per cent of coffee and 22 per cent of tea came from the smallholder sector.

Thus in these years the colonial economy of Indonesia underwent major changes. There was a general shift in economic organisation. The European-controlled sector changed from a mercantile system based on forced peasant labour to estates and oil fields owned by corporations, employing 'free' Indonesian labour (contract labour gradually disappeared, and was entirely replaced by free labour on plantations in the 1930s). At the same time, large numbers of small peasant producers became involved in production for the international as well as the domestic market. Secondly, the

1. For statistics on international commerce in this period see Allen and Donnithorne, 1957, appendix IV.

nature of commodities changed. Consumption goods like coffee and tea were replaced by raw materials for the industries of world capitalism. While some processing took place in the colony, industrialisation was largely left to the metropolitan countries of the developed capitalist world. Manufacturing industry was almost entirely absent, although it flourished briefly in the production of import substitutes during the First World War.

How did these over-all changes affect the economy of Minangkabau villages? As I have already pointed out, the fact that the restrictions imposed under the Culture System were preserved in West Sumatra long after they had been lifted in other parts of the colony meant that when small planters pioneered the plantation economy in other parts of Indonesia, they were excluded from West Sumatra. Even today estates are relatively unimportant in the local economy, and Chinese control of distribution and small enterprises — which so often followed the penetration of European capital — is minimal in comparison with other parts of Indonesia.

Forced cultivation in West Sumatra was finally abolished in 1908 and replaced by a tax. In 1912 the restrictive rice policies were abandoned. The lifting of compulsory services led to a gradual evolution of free commodity production in the villages. The effects of this change were greatest, at least at first, not in the Minangkabau highlands but rather in the outlying districts known collectively as the Rantau. The reasons for this are varied, but seem mainly to be related to the differential effects of forced cultivation. Ecological degradation of unterraced farming land (*ladang*) was not so great in those areas not subjected to compulsory coffee cultivation. Partly for this reason, more and better land was available outside the highlands for the cultivation of export crops.

There were other changes which allowed the people of the Rantau to profit from the world commodity boom. In the nineteenth century, in accordance with their policy of preserving the isolation of subsistence communities, the Dutch had prevented contact — particularly trade along routes to the south and east of West Sumatra. The small states on Minangkabau's eastern borders, for example, were 'deliberately left intact in order by this means to put a check on unregulated import and export. And when later on the force of circumstances caused these states to be brought

176

under Dutch rule, even the roads indispensable to the development of economic activity were not constructed' (Schrieke, 1955,
p. 97). Seeing the advantages of cheap smallholder production of
export crops, however, the colonial government in the early
twentieth century sought to open up such areas to commerce by
establishing road and rail links. Korinci, for example, was finally
opened up by a new road in order that its rice surpluses could be
exported (Schrieke, 1955, pp. 99f.).

The Rantau areas followed a similar pattern in these years.
After being opened up to trade, usually by road to Padang on the
coast, rice surpluses were initially exported. Korinci exported
52,000 piculs of rice in 1923 and 54,000 piculs in 1924. As
villagers turned to the production of more profitable exports,
however, rice production dropped. By 1926 Korinci, for example,
exported only 14,000 piculs of rice, a decline accompanied by an
increase in coffee output. Similar increases in the production of
profitable export crops, often accompanied by a shift from rice
export to rice import, took place in Indrapura. Tapan, Painan,
Balai Selasa, Muara Labuh, Pariaman, Talu, Bangkinang, Lubuk
Sikaping and Bonjol – areas all on the fringe of the Minangkabau
heartland.

Rubber and coffee were the major commodities produced in
these areas, with the exception of Pariaman, where villagers
exported coconuts. Coffee exports from the province rose quickly,
from under two million kilos in 1907, to over five million in 1926
and 17 million kilos in 1928 (Huitema, 1935).

Rice cultivation, stimulated initially – as we have seen – by
new markets, also increased. Initial increases in the price of rice
were caused, according to Schrieke, by the increase in trade
itself (1955, p. 99). However, prices continued to rise rapidly,
thus causing some hardship, particularly in the Minangkabau heartland, which was not as suited to production of the more profitable
exports. Schrieke gives the following estimates of rice prices in
the village of Sungai Penuh (1955, pp. 99ff.):

Year	Price per picul
1923	5 shillings
1924	7½ shillings
1925	15 shillings 10 pence
1926	15 shillings 8 pence
1927	24 shillings

This rapid rise is explained in the following way:

High prices for rice are due to still another factor, however. In several places the population is beginning to neglect the difficult process of rice growing in favour of the far more lucrative cultivation of commercial crops. The effects of the abolition of the compulsory cultivation of coffee can be discerned here. A period of declining production, during which people, glad, as it were, to be freed of a compulsion they loathed, discontinued cultivation, was followed by a period of unprecendented revival (Schrieke, 1955, p. 99).

Presumably, the effect of this increase was amplified by a decline in subsistence production, and increased reliance on the market.

The combined effect of the boom in export commodities, and the shortage of land in the Minangkabau highlands, led to large-scale migration to the Rantau areas. Land shortage in the Agam district around Sungai Puar, for example, probably accounts for the large number of migrants in the early decades of this century (cf. Anon., 1917).

While, as we have seen, coffee was produced under the direct control of the colonial government in the nineteenth century, commodity production in peasant villages took quite a different form. Almost the entire output of export crops in West Sumatra came from peasant smallholders. The limited evidence from this period also suggests that peasant productive units were very small, probably varying from individual or kin-based groups to units which employed only a very few wage labourers (Schrieke, 1955, pp. 104f.).

Processing and manufacture were also carried out largely by such small enterprises, using relatively primitive techniques. In 1926, for example, there were only 67 'factories' in the province – places of work which were partially mechanised or used electrical power (Smit, 1931, p. 253). Even by 1931 there were only 227 such factories. Informants of mine in Sungai Puar who had worked as blacksmiths in this period describe a situation very similar to the one today, either with production individualised or with a maximum of four smiths working together. The only large-scale enterprises in which smiths worked were in Sawah Lunto, in a Dutch workshop producing tools for the coal-mines, and in the railway workshops of Solok and Padang. The small scale of peasant enterprise is also confirmed by reports from the

178

small banks set up by the government in accordance with the Ethical Policy to aid 'native' entrepreneurs, which reported that in West Sumatra the majority of borrowers were involved in small business (Schrieke, 1955, fn. on p. 272).

While large numbers of people were directly involved in the market economy, either as producers or as small traders, there were very few large-scale enterprises based on wage labour. According to Benda and McVey, for example, in the 1920s 'Tenancy, population pressure and the proletarianization of coolie labour . . . were absent in West Sumatra' (1960, p. xxi). Those villagers who sought wage labour opportunities in the mid-1920s had to leave the province to work on rubber plantations in Jambi and Kuantan, or on one of the few coffee plantations in Tapanuli (Schrieke, 1955, p. 148).

It is possible to conclude, then, that the growth of free commodity production at the turn of the century took place largely through small-scale, atomised productive units. Although there was some reliance on wage labour, productive units were, by and large, individually owned and run. From the Sungai Puar data it seems safe to assume that this type of peasant production existed not just in the export sector, but also in the production of locally consumed goods such as agricultural implements (from Sungai Puar and Lintau), cloth from Silungkang and Kubang, pottery from Andalas and food crops from most areas where vegetable crops are grown on rice land in the off-season.

The owner of these small enterprises probably also worked as a labourer. He or she supplied the necessary tools and implements, as well as land, which was increasingly alienable due to the relaxation of restrictions by the *suku* and by the end of effective colonial ownership of village land which followed the dissolution of the Culture System.

The means of production and cultivation were simple, there was no mechanisation, and techniques in all likelihood did not differ significantly from those which were used in the nineteenth century or even earlier. Cultivation and production was labour-intensive. If anything, this represented a decline from previous technological levels. While, for example, in earlier periods Minangkabau mined and smelted iron ore in the highlands, these activities have been abandoned in this century. It is likely that other branches of the local economy suffered a similar kind of technological devolution

179

as a result of competition with imported goods and the concentration on particular export crops.

Most scholars agree that the rise of a commercial economy also affected the cultivation of rice for subsistence on lineage land. Schrieke (1955) and Maretin (1961), among others, argue that 'traditional' property relations were gradually giving way to private property in this period. The consensus is that the penetration of a money economy resulted in

the outright sale of family land, with or even without provision for redemption within a given period of time, [which] has not been unknown for a long time now, while pledging of land for reasons outside those [provided for by *adat*], that is to say for consumption purposes pure and simple, is as it were the order of the day, particularly in the so-called '*adat*-conscious' areas, in this case those mainly devoted to rice growing (Schrieke, 1955, p. 108).

He goes on to say that in some villages, such as Air Dingin and Solok, 'all the family land has been done away with and has been transformed into self-earned land as a consequence of pledging' (*ibid*, p. 110). For this reason Schrieke concludes that 'The undivided family property is crumbling to pieces under the pressure exerted by the money economy. Land tenure is growing less certain; economic differentiation is increasing. The restrictions laid down by tradition are becoming an embarrassment' (*ibid*, p. 142).

If, as we have seen, the Culture System led to an intensification of communal rights of possession and increased rates of land redistribution, then the development of free commodity production had the opposite effect on the subsistence community. It was becoming increasingly frequent in these years for families to sell or pawn *suku* land to obtain cash for consumption or to invest in capital to engage in commercial production and trade.

Alongside the local subsistence and peasant commercial sectors of the Minangkabau economy were some capitalist enterprises. Dutch-owned and Chinese-run factories were built in Padang for processing rubber, coconuts (into soap and oil) and the like. There were also a few Dutch tea plantations in the highlands. The colonial government itself hired labourers, many of whom were Javanese, to work in the Ombilin coal-mines. A large cement factory was built in Indarung near Padang, and the government-owned railways hired labourers and skilled workers. Some labourers also worked in the port of Emmenhaven (now Teluk Bayur) through which most imports and exports passed. Nonetheless the predominant form of economic activity in the province was the small-scale peasant-owned enterprise.

The commercial development which has been described for West Sumatra in the years after the penetration of private capital was taken at the time by people like Schrieke to promise expanded, capitalist development. Schrieke implies that the eventual destruction of the system of lineage control of land would be accompanied by increased use of wage labour. It would only be a matter of time before the Minangkabau would develop a European-style economy. However, this discussion of the structure of the peasant economy at the turn of the century could apply equally well to the modern situation. Although it has been pronounced dead or dying (cf. Gough, in Schneider and Gough, 1962; Maretin, 1961), the matrilineal system retains a tenacious hold on agricultural relations. Peasant commodity production remains small-scale and technologically backward.[1] Large-scale enterprise continues to be foreign-owned.

While, therefore, in the early decades of this century capitalism was exported to the East Indies from Europe and America, a second form of economic organisation also grew in places like Minangkabau. Petty commodity production became and remains the predominant form of peasant economic organisation, in contradiction to the arguments of those like Schrieke who maintained that the peasant economy would become steadily more capitalist. The situation described for the turn of the twentieth century, therefore, appears not to be transitional in the usual sense of the word, but seems rather to be a specific product of historical circumstance. Before attempting to get at the important historical changes which made this possible, however, I shall examine an interesting test case, i.e. the period in which Schrieke's predictions indeed seemed to be coming to pass, and the process of differentiation seemed to be destroying the petty commodity economy in some rural areas. In order to understand this situation it is necessary

1. For descriptions of the peasant economy in other parts of Indonesia which present a similar picture of small-scale peasant production and distribution see Geertz, 1963b; Jay, 1969; Dewey, 1962 and Siegel, 1969. Also of relevance are some of the articles in Koentjaraningrat, 1967.

to look first at developments at the national level in the immediate post-Independence period.

In spite of the achievement of political independence in 1950, the Indonesian economy remained largely in the hands of foreign interests. The agreements of the Hague Round Table Conference of 1949, which were the basis for post-Independence economic relations with the Netherlands, were remarkably conservative in the degree to which colonial economic conditions were preserved (cf. Glassburner, 1971, pp. 78f.). Glassburner suggests that a pre-war estimate that only 19 per cent of agricultural capital was in the hands of Indonesians could equally well apply to the im-mediate post-Independence years. Dutch and British plantation interests remained largely unaffected by the transfer of political power. Of 716 rubber plantations in 1956, only 76 were Indonesian owned (Mackie in Glassburner, 1971, p. 31). It is estimated that in 1952 50 per cent of all imports and 60 per cent of exports were in the hands of four and eight foreign-controlled firms respectively. Banking was almost entirely controlled by seven foreign banks, three of which were Dutch (*ibid.*, pp. 79f.).

Post-war Indonesian politicians took as one of their major con-cerns this question of foreign economic domination. Until about 1953 the national government was successfully dominated by a group of planners and politicians who defended this foreign con-trol. Called the Masjumi group by one writer (Sutter, 1959) and the economics- or development-minded group by another (Higgins, quoted in Glassburner, *op. cit.*, pp. 72ff.), they successfully op-posed the demands of more radical nationalists in the early years after Independence. Of this period Glassburner writes: 'from the point of view of economic policy, the years 1950 to 1957 in Indonesia are best understood as years of a hopeless losing battle on the part of a very small group of pragmatic conservative political leaders against an increasingly powerful political op-position of generally radical orientation' (1971, p. 71).

The turning-point in this struggle is usually placed in 1953 with the fall of the Wilopo cabinet. In the following years, it is argued, the radical elements in the national government set a col-lision course with Western interests, which eventually led to economic and political conflict with the Western powers. On the political plane there were the conflicts with the Netherlands over

West Irian in 1957, and the confrontation with Malaysia. On the economic plane the conflict manifested itself in the nationalisation of Dutch plantations in 1957, the 1959 take-over of the 'Big Five' Dutch importing firms, and government plans which sought to build up industries, utilities and services within the public sector (cf. Mackie, in Glassburner, 1971, and Mackie, 1967).

The general effects of this policy 'were momentous. It virtually put an end to earlier notions that private foreign investment would contribute to the development of Indonesia's economy, except in a few special cases like oil and minerals' (Mackie in Glassburner, 1971, p. 51).

I have not here presented a detailed economic analysis of national policy-making in this period. My aim has been to show that while in the earlier years after Independence an attempt was made to preserve the colonial economy as it had operated in the years after the dissolution of the Culture System, for various reasons the Sukarno government's about-face resulted in an increasing withdrawal from the world capitalist system. Nationalisation of foreign enterprise and the creation of other obstacles to the penetration of foreign capital was accompanied by a decline in the volume of foreign trade in the late 1950s. Between 1952 and 1967 imports never reached the 1952 peak of $947.8 million. Between 1957 and 1959 the volume of imports fell from $803.3 million to $481.9 million. Exports also declined in this period, although less dramatically, so that the balance of trade, at least in the early years of Sukarno's policies of 'Socialism *à la* Indonesia' was more favourable than in the early post-war period.[1]

It is generally argued by Western economists that the result of Sukarno's policies was almost unmitigated disaster for the Indonesian economy. The terms selected by Higgins to distinguish between the governments of the two periods — 'economics-' or 'development-minded' and 'history-minded' — are a clue as to the accepted view of the Sukarno regime. Sukarno and his followers, it is argued, were more interested in ideology and their role in history than in sane principles of economic development. Opposition to foreign control of the Indonesian economy was the result of an economically uninformed view of the benefits of integration within the world capitalist economy. This also

1. Cf. 'Indonesian Balance of Trade, 1952–1967', in *Journal of Indonesian Statistics*, II, no. 6.

represents the stand taken by the post-Sukarno leaders who ousted him from effective power in the 1965 *coup*. Economists like Glass-burner argue that between 1958 and 1965 Indonesia was plagued by stagnation in production, high rates of inflation, unfavourable trade balances, high rates of external indebtedness and high rates of unemployment (1971, pp. 426–31).

The brief period of Sukarno's 'Guided Democracy' represents a significant change in economic relations. The Indonesian economy since the turn of the century has been dominated by foreign enterprise and investment in the capitalist sector, and a large peasant smallholder sector was dominated by individually owned commodity-producing enterprises. Did this structural reorganisation of the capitalist sector generate a change in the peasant economy?

Relying as they do on national statistics, economists have been unable to judge the effects of Sukarno's policies on the peasant economy. I want to turn back to the peasant economy of West Sumatra, and in particular of Sungai Puar, to attempt to answer this question.

Transition to rural capitalism in Sungai Puar

I have already suggested that the organisation of smithing in Limo Suku in the first few decades of the twentieth century seems to have been very similar to the modern situation described in earlier chapters. Marsden's description of blacksmithing in nineteenth-century Sumatra shows that there has been very little technological change in at least two hundred years:

But little skill is shewn amongst the country people in forging iron. They make nails, however, though not much used by them in building . . . ; also various kinds of tools, as the *prang* or bill, the *banchi, rembe, billiong,* and *papatil,* which are different species of adzes, the *kapak* or axe, and the *pangkur* or hoe. Their fire is made from charcoal; the fossil coal which the country produces being rarely, if ever employed. . . Their bellows are thus constructed: two bamboos, of about four inches diameter and five feet in length, stand perpendicularly near the fire; open at the upper end, and stopt below. About an inch or two from the bottom a small joint of bamboo is inserted into each, which serves as nodes, pointing to, and meeting at, the fire. . . (1811, p. 181).

While this description is of smithing in a neighbouring area, and while charcoal rather than coal is used in forging, this could almost equally apply to modern smithing in Limo Suku. There has, if anything, been a decline both in the range of goods produced and in techniques, as the following quote from a nineteenth-century traveller in the Minangkabau highlands shows:

> The skilful work of these people in silver and gold work has already been described. They are also very skilful in the manufacture of kris-blades (ceremonial daggers), cannon, and matchlocks — mining, smelting and forging the iron entirely themselves. Marsden says their principal mine was at Padang Luar, a village between Sungai Puar and Bukit Tinggi . . . It was taken to Selimpuwong . . . a small kampong between Mt. Merapi and Mt. Sago, on the road leading northward from this place to Paya Kombo, where it was smelted and manufactured (Bickmore, 1869, p. 472).

Modern Minangkabau smiths, as we have seen, rely entirely on scrap for forging. Not only have mining and smelting techniques been lost — they no longer make weapons. The process of lamination used in kris-making has been largely forgotten.

The places mentioned by Bickmore are all in the vicinity of Sungai Puar. Whether he was mistaken about the location of the forges, whether there were several centres in the nineteenth century or whether the centre has shifted up the mountain-side to Sungai Puar is impossible to say.

In any case there is information from the oldest men of Sungai Puar that by the turn of the century Limo Suku smiths had a long-established tradition of making agricultural implements and horse and buffalo carts. The demand for carts, especially the buffalo-drawn *pidati* was stimulated by the introduction of coffee cultivation. In the nineteenth century these carts were used to take coffee to government warehouses.

The first real evidence concerning earlier forms of economic organisation comes from stories told by the older smiths themselves, who say that 'before' (an unspecified period) all *apa* were controlled by a man known as the *tukang tuo*, a non-working owner of the *apa* who received a share of the earnings. Since it is impossible to know exactly when such a system operated, it is difficult to say whether this was equivalent to the role played by chiefs and lineage elders in collecting rent from mining and other entrepreneurial activities before the Dutch control of the highlands. Opinions in the village differed as to whether the *tukang*

185

tuo acquired his rights through kinship and control of the land on which the *apa* stood, or whether he himself was an entrepreneur who 'invested' his savings in smithing as a way of earning a profit.

While the *tukang tuo* system probably dates from before the twentieth century, there have been changes in economic organisation in more recent times. During the Japanese occupation of 1942, an attempt was made to organise all smiths in a project known as the *Persatuan Tukang Besi Sungai Puar* (the Union of Sungai Puar Blacksmiths). By exempting those who participated from mandatory corvée labour, the Japanese were able to bring together a large number of smiths within a single workshop to produce tools and bayonets for the occupying army.

In the late 1950s four separate enterprises grew up which succeeded in drawing together almost all the *apa* of Sungai Puar. One of these was a government-sponsored cooperative. With government funds and supervision, an electically powered plant was constructed in the village where smiths from Limo Suku and brass workers from another section could learn new techniques. This was part of a government *Induk* (literally 'mother') scheme for establishing local centres to upgrade village handicrafts and cottage industries. P.U.R.A. was not intended to supplant traditional places of work, but to supplement them. Steel goods were produced in the *apa*, but then ground and polished on electrically driven machinery. P.U.R.A. was also intended to teach new entrepreneurial and managerial skills to the craftsmen and women of Sungai Puar. Why P.U.R.A. should have collapsed after only a few years of operation is still a subject for debate among villagers. Some say it was due to corruption among P.U.R.A.'s local managers, others say it was because villagers were too conservative to accept new techniques and others that it was due to the collapse in the market for Sungai Puar steelware.

In the same period a Sungai Puar migrant trader returned to the village and started a new productive enterprise. He hired a number of smiths to produce a variety of goods made from scrap metal and alloy sheet metal. Capital investment was small at the outset, although even before 1958 the managers purchased a number of simple, hand-operated machines. The products of this small industry were originally sold in Bukit Tinggi, although later one enterprising manager managed to find a market in Jakarta for most of the firm's products.

In 1959 during the regional rebellions, operations were shifted from the village to Bukit Tinggi. While Sarasah, as the business was called, was much like other village workshops before 1958, after the move it began to expand. Capital investment and mechanisation increased. In the years between 1954 and 1959 the firm purchased 17 small machines of various types. By 1963 the number had increased to 26 and by 1969 to 36.[1] This movement towards increased mechanisation corresponded with a shift from the production of small articles like mirrors, keys and costume jewellery to automobile parts and light agricultural machinery. Sarasah never hired more than 10 semi-skilled workers. The two managers today have been able, through mechanisation, to keep pace with the increased demand for their products, without having to employ an ever larger work force.

Two other firms, which depended more directly on existing techniques and local forms of cooperation, were also founded in the late 1950s, and both reached the peak of operations in the years 1964—5. By 1972 one of these firms had completely disappeared, while the second has returned to the scale of the typical *apa* enterprise.

The first and larger of these two firms was floated by a large bank loan. With this the manager was able to buy equipment for a number of *apa*. The number of *apa* working with the firm eventually reached 48. Orders were received mostly for agricultural tools, largely from government trading companies. The *apa* units were supplied with raw materials, and given a piece-work payment which was divided among the workers in the traditional way, i.e. one portion to each of the workers and an extra share 'for the *apa*'. By the end of 1965 the enterprise broke down because the manager had difficulty in obtaining labour (smiths began to prefer the older, independent-*apa* system), and because the demand for its products became irregular.

The second firm operated along much the same lines, with ties to about 10 *apa* and a trading contact in Medan in North Sumatra. In 1965 the owner ran into financial trouble, and his enterprise gradually grew smaller. Today it is much like any other *apa*, with between four and five smiths.

A third firm, known as C. V. Perindra, was organised in 1958

1. Information on Sarasah comes from a short thesis by a student from Andalas University (Anurlis, 1970), and a long interview I had with the manager in 1971.

187

as well, although I was unable to get any information on the nature and scope of its organisation (cf. Anurlis, 1971, p. 20).

These developments in the organisation of smithing are highly significant. While techniques did not undergo any radical change, except perhaps in the case of Sarasah, the economic organisation of smithing in the years between 1958 and 1965 represents an important change from the earlier period. While some aspects of traditional forms of payment were preserved, the over-all distribution of earnings was altered. In the case of the village firms, with the exception of P.U.R.A., the manager and financer of the enterprise was not a working smith. Nonetheless, after paying costs he aimed to retain a profit. In effect smiths within these enterprises, including the *nangkodoh*, became wage labourers. The organisation of blacksmithing in this period represents a transition from the small-scale, individually owned peasant enterprise, to enterprises more like capitalist industries in the West. While techniques remained backward, wage labour and profit emerged as aspects of village economic organisation.

Though attempts in that period to increase the scale of smithing enterprises were at least temporarily successful, more recent attempts have largely failed. In 1968 a number of influential smiths and merchants got together to decide on how best to improve the local industry. Preliminary plans were made to form a cooperative, at first just for the purchase of raw materials. The organisers thought that cooperative buying would help to stabilise the price of raw materials and to reduce the likelihood of shortages (temporary shortages of coal and steel often shut down the *apa* for extended periods). It was also thought that the formation of a cooperative with a legal charter would make the trade in steel less susceptible to interruption by police and army interference. While originally 29 *nangkodoh* paid the fee of Rp. 100 each to join the cooperative, it never really got off the ground. It lacked capital even to bring in a single shipment of scrap steel. There is still some hope in the village that the cooperative will be revived.

In 1970 the central government, through the provincial department of light industry in Padang, started a new project to upgrade the local smithing industry at a projected cost of some Rp. 20 million. The aims of this project were similar to those of P.U.R.A. Organisers hoped to introduce new techniques as well as managerial skills to the Limo Suku smiths. On the other hand, the organisers also stressed that the enterprise would eventually be expected to achieve financial independence.

The project used imported steel plate which was cut up into pieces of uniform size by workers in the 'factory' or central workshop. These pieces were then put out to *apa* willing to work with the project. The idea was to produce hoes which were cut and polished in the machine shop, and forged in the *apa*. The *nangkodoh* who elected to work with the project were paid about Rp. 100 for every hoe produced in this way. This money was to cover all costs — labour, tools and materials — except of course the cost of the steel itself.

From mid-1971 to mid-1972 the small factory operated sporadically, on average about two days a week. At any one time there were never more than two, and usually only one *apa* working with the factory to produce hoes. Two or three young men were hired directly by the factory to run the welding and grinding machines, and to coordinate the work done in factory and *apa*. The manager also hired a local electrician to supervise the running of the diesel-powered generator. The manager himself was an employee of the Department of Light Industry who worked in both Sungai Puar and the Department's Padang office.

None of these men ever worked full time with the project, and the young labourers eventually quit work altogether because they never received more than a fraction of the wages promised to them. As time went by the manager spent longer periods of time away in Padang, although in mid-1972 he was still trying to get the project running. By this time the factory had largely shut down operations, at least temporarily. Two reasons were given for this. Firstly, it was said that smiths were not willing to cooperate. While the manager attributed this to the famed Minangkabau spirit of individualism, the smiths themselves told me that the payment offered by the factory was not enough to lure them away from the more lucrative traditional system of producing hoes. I was told by a number of people, including a close relative of the one *nangkodoh* who worked consistently with the factory, that smiths would cooperate only if they lacked funds to carry on with independent production.

A second and equally important reason for the collapse of the project was that the organisers did not seem to be able to sell hoes in sufficient quantity to achieve any kind of financial stability.

This probably explains why wages were not paid in full, and perhaps also the low payment offered to cooperating *nangkodoh*. When I left the field in mid-1972 the project was at a standstill and hoes were being stockpiled. It seemed unlikely that the project could be made to succeed, at least without a regular guaranteed market for the output. I heard about a year later that the factory generator was being used to supply villagers with electricity. It seems, therefore, that at least in this period the project organisers had not managed to solve the problems of introducing larger-scale economic organisation into an economy of small-scale, independent producers.

If nothing else, these changes in the organisation of smithing demonstrate the fallacy of explanations which rely on unchanging and universal characteristics of specific ethnic groups or peasants in general. Swift's explanation of the small scale of economic organisation in Minangkabau, which relies on cultural and personality factors; is clearly inadequate: 'I suggest that the intense competitiveness of the Minangkabau is such that success as part of a group is not satisfying for the personality and cultural drives involved. I see the genius of the Minangkabau as most suited to a quick perception and grasping of short term opportunity, best exemplified in the world of petty trading' (1971, p. 265). Economic scale in Minangkabau seems to be a product of particular historical and economic conditions and not so crudely determined by cultural personality type.

Similarly, to characterise peasant economy and society in general as atomistic is also to ignore the historical specificity of economic forms. The fact that all these enterprises emerged and then declined in the same period is an indication of the dependent nature of variables such as economic behaviour, entrepreneurial initiative and peasant atomism.

While studies of the Indonesian peasant economy tend to be couched in terms other than historical ones, and because other data on economic organisation of the village are largely unavailable for this period, it is not easy to tell whether the changes described for Sungai Puar were in fact more general. In spite of the economists' assertions about economic decline in the years between 1958 and 1965, there is some material to show that, at least in the early years of Sukarno's Guided Democracy, the peasant economy was not entirely stagnant. We know, for example, that in these years the production of cash crops actually increased faster than in the years before 1958. In Table 9.1 I have presented material based on figures in the *Statistical Pocketbooks of Indonesia* (Biro Pusat Statistik, 1959 and 1964–7) on changes in total output of basic cash crops in the periods 1952–6 and 1959–63. For these seven crops production increased more quickly in the later period. Only sugar-cane, nutmegs and kapok, of the remaining crops for which there are data, decline in the later period. Sugar-cane, because it was primarily a Dutch estate crop, clearly suffered because of the nationalisation of Dutch plantations. For all the other crops it is estimated that peasant smallholder production accounted for the large bulk of total output in post-war years (cf. Mackie in Glassburner, 1971, pp. 29ff.).

It was in the same period in West Sumatra that a few entrepreneurs in the village of Silungkang, the home of a long-standing cloth cottage industry, built the first factory in the village which produced cloth using a high level of mechanisation. The Kubang cloth-making cooperative experienced some growth in these years, and several cloth mills were constructed in Padang. All of these large-scale cloth-manufacturing enterprises declined in the late 1960s. Statistics published by the Indonesian government show some growth both in total output and in numbers of people employed in manufacturing industries in these years. The limited data on the state of the Indonesian textile industry as a whole show a marked increase in the number of looms, both hand-operated and mechanical, in the years between 1955 and 1966 (in Glassburner, 1971, p. 319).

Other indications of economic progress, particularly in the rural areas, are the great increase in electricity output between 1960 and 1962, as well as the 52 per cent increase in the number of motor vehicles of all kinds between 1960 and 1965 (Biro Pusat Statistik, *op. cit.*).

In the discussion of Minangkabau petty trading in previous chapters, I referred to low rates of mobility. Very few migrants who set up as small hawkers and pedlars manage to build or buy small shops or *kedai*. My census data show, however, that of those migrants who have purchased shops or *kedai* in the post-war period, almost all did so in the late 1950s.

What all this shows is that at least the peasant sector of the Indonesian economy may not in fact have experienced any great

191

Table 9.1   *Per cent change in total output of seven cash crops in two periods*

Crop	1952–6	1959–63
Coconuts	−10.2	8.8
Coffee	27.3	93.9
Tea	14.6	19.9
Areca nuts	−36.0	9.3
Pepper	194.1	211.3
Cloves	−33.3	41.1
Tobacco	−16.4	16.2

decline in the years following the nationalisation of Dutch enterprises and Sukarno's new nationalist economic policies. While it may be that there was not great economic acceleration in this period, and while of course the hyper-inflation of the mid-1960s was disastrous for all Indonesians, before that time the rural economy may have been experiencing a transformation. While output may not have increased as a result of it, in some parts of Indonesia the peasant economic structure of small-scale, individually owned and operated enterprises was giving way to more capitalist-like economic forms. It may be that this rural transformation was more general than the economists' analyses would have us believe. This of course would require a good deal more research − not just into productivity, volume of exports, prices and the like, but into the social organisation of the peasant economy in this period − before any firm conclusion could be reached.

If this picture of the peasant economy in the late 1950s and early 1960s is accurate, or at least partially accurate, then it becomes necessary to account for the change in historical terms, i.e. to ask why it should be that new economic forms arose in some parts of rural Indonesia all at once, in a single historical period − a period, moreover, in which there were distinct changes in economic policy and orientation at the national level. At the same time, to understand the conditions under which such a transformation took place would shed a good deal of light on the question of the requirements of petty commodity production itself, requirements which were presumably no longer being ful-filled.

The main change in this period was a process of separation from the world economic system. This separation must be understood largely in social terms, for it was based on a political policy, as so many critics have pointed out, motivated not just by economic, but by political and ideological factors as well.[1]

One indication of the over-all process of economic separation is in the decline in imports in the 1950s. Tables 9.2 A, B, and C, selected for their relevance to the products of peasant smithing, indicate the degree to which imports dropped after the national-level policy shift. While there are no figures for 1956 to 1959, and while we cannot rely heavily on these data, they do indicate a trend — a sharp drop in imports of those goods produced by Indonesian blacksmiths. This drop corresponds to an over-all drop in Indonesian imports in this period.

For the Sungai Puar blacksmithing industry, then, a drop in imported goods, due both to financial and to other attempts to discourage imports, opened up a larger market by increasing domestic demand for locally produced goods. Not surprisingly, prices in these years increased, not an unhealthy thing for the development of initially less productive domestic industry. Annual inflation rates, if calculated on the basis of the *Statistical Pocket-books'* group A — a selection of 15 home-produced articles — ranged from 1 per cent to 34 per cent between 1954 and 1961. The comparable range for imported products was from a decrease in one year to an 88 per cent annual inflation rate. Later on the rate of inflation jumped alarmingly, of course. In 1962 it reached three figures, and in the disastrous year 1965/6 prices for dom-estically produced goods increased by over 1,000 per cent (Biro Pusat Statistik, *Statistical Pocketbooks,* 1959 and 1968–9).

1. It is significant here that the regional rebellions in the Outer Islands were fought in the late 1950s against outside — in this case Javanese — economic domination (cf. Kahn, 1974a, ch. 10, Alliband, 1970).

To say that the causes of the economic separation were social is not to agree with Western social scientists who view the opposite trend, i.e. close integration into the world capitalist system, as somehow purely economic. It is a commonly promulgated myth in Indonesia today that economic development is a non-political problem, that there is only one road to development, and that those who criticise development plans are politically biased. For this reason the 'economics-minded/history-minded' dichotomy is an invidious one.

Table 9.2   *Import of steel tools and related products**

A. Hoes, forks and spades

Year	Number	Kilos	Market value in *rupiah*
1951	1,219,774	1,770,030	2,417,931
1952	1,665,132	2,389,578	10,791,974
1953	1,174,364	1,788,614	8,242,317
1954	115,706	205,015	905,014
1955	27,972	435,220	2,027,255
1960	38,766	70,748	1,697,746
1961	785,984	1,126,579	22,972,490
1962	227,751	308,082	5,700,852

B. Sickles and machetes

Year	Number	Kilos	Market value in *rupiah*
1951	72,159	51,758	103,083
1952	128,838	73,011	688,284
1953	22,243	12,594	140,577
1954	46,961	23,038	307,198
1955	144,781	86,040	758,522
1960	583	624	31,511
1961	682	539	38,310
1962	200	156	8,216

C. Household knives

Year	Number (dozens)	Kilos	Market value in *rupiah*
1951	113,746	127,767	1,422,855
1952	101,875	117,674	4,950,664
1953	21,672	26,125	1,100,839
1954	5,602	7,611	176,916
1955	5,069	9,803	199,636
1960	1,144	1,622	185,706
1961	18,085	16,892	1,168,428
1962	3,843	2,296	101,696

**Source*: Biro Pusat Statistik, 1972. *Impor Menerut Djenis Barang*

Initially, the rise in prices and the expanded market for many peasant-produced goods must have had a stimulating effect on the rural economy. At the same time, those with access to liquid capital were able to take advantage of the expansion. Rice prices in the same years also rose gradually. In those years the new employers could hire wage labour and still expect to make a profit — for workers' demands for wage increases, tied partly to the price of rice, could be easily met.

The decline in imports and the expansion of the home market had, then, a favourable effect on the development of the rural economy in the early years of the new economic policies. It is more difficult to say precisely what the effects of the other policies were. The nationalisation of foreign-owned import and export firms and the creation of the state trading companies clearly had a stimulating effect on the growth of the smithing industry, as I have pointed out. It seems likely that the policies of these companies were beneficial to other sectors of the peasant economy as well.

In Chapter 5 I tried to show how Limo Suku smiths are constrained by variables of price, wage and market demand for their products. I pointed out that the small scale and low technological level of the industry could be shown to be 'rational' adaptations to existing price, wage and other structures. Relations with the capitalist sector of the national economy, as well as the world-economy, are thus mediated in some way by the market. Changes in these factors result from a changing relationship to world capitalism. Increased demand and increasing prices for peasant-produced commodities seem to create the conditions necessary for the expansion in scale of entrepreneurial units, and new economic forms which allow for capital accumulation. Profits earned on new smithing enterprises in the 1958—65 period were invested in expanding the size of these units, as well as in machines and other labour-saving devices. The development of capitalist forms in the Minangkabau village economy seems to be related in part to an isolation of Indonesia from the world capitalist system.[1] At

1. The relevance of Frank's general argument that it is domination by the metropolis which creates underdevelopment will be obvious here (Frank, 1969, 1970). Hoogvelt and Child (1973), for example, show how isolation from the world capitalist system created conditions favourable to certain kinds of development in Rhodesia. The case of expansion of Indonesia's peasant economy in response to Sukarno's nationalist economic policies is in many ways analogous to these other cases.

least with regard to the village economy in Indonesia in this period, Sukarno's so-called 'socialism *à la* Indonesia' might be better termed 'capitalism *à la* Indonesia'.

These developments in the domestic economy were choked off by the crippling inflation of the mid-1960s. In their attempts to come to grips with this hyper-inflation, however, economists have often overlooked the economic progress of the early years of the economic reforms. Table 9.3 shows the phenomenal rise in the price of rice which was a contributing factor in the collapse of new peasant enterprises. It will be noted that rice prices in the years after 1960 rose faster than at any other time. It is clear that the new entrepreneurs could not possibly hope to keep paying wages which would allow their workers to buy the basic staple. A return to individualised production and to subsistence cultivation was inevitable, whether or not the new markets for peasant commodities were maintained.

The precise causes of the Indonesian inflation have not yet been adequately located (although see Mackie, 1967). An often overlooked factor in the determination of the high inflation rate was the collapse of the rice economy. It has been estimated that in Indonesia as a whole only 20 per cent of total rice production actually reaches the market (Mackie in Glassburner, 1971). I have already discussed the extent to which villagers in West Sumatra are involved in subsistence rice cultivation. While the village of Sungai Puar may produce only about 20 per cent of its annual rice needs, West Sumatra as a whole seems to be almost self-sufficient in rice. It is also known that in Indonesia yields and intensity of subsistence cultivation are closely related to national economic conditions. In periods of economic difficulty it seems that those who can do so either turn to subsistence cultivation or increase the intensity of cultivation on family plots. Java, in most times a rice-deficient island, actually turned from rice import to rice export during the depression of the 1930s (Allen and Donnithorne, 1957, p. 35). Geertz, in an interesting study of economy and culture in Java (1963a), shows that Javanese peasants react to economic adversity through a process he calls involution. In terms of economic activities, involution refers to increased labour intensity, particularly in subsistence cultivation.

Conversely, it could be argued that in periods of economic expansion a reverse process of decreasing intensity of subsistence

Table 9.3   *Rice prices in Jakarta and Padang (rupiah/10 litres)*

Year	Price in Jakarta	Price in Padang
1954	17.90	17.56
1955	21.13	24.71
1956	28.53	29.47
1957	35.44	26.42
1958	59.33	58.09
1959	53.07	65.30
1960	60.94	74.24
1961	101.04	109.73
1962	304.86	554.88
1963	610.28	733.64
1964	1,616.66	. . .
1965	5,808.33	. . .
1966	47,645.83	. . .

cultivation occurs. The relatively unprofitable activity is abandoned in favour of the production of commodities for which prices and demand are higher. I have shown how in the early years of this century West Sumatran peasants turned first to rice and then to coffee and rubber in response to new markets and higher prices for peasant commodities. The boom in world demand for rubber and coffee allowed villagers in the outlying areas to abandon subsistence cultivation and devote more time to cash crops. As a result, after these areas were opened up to world markets they soon stopped exporting rice. Some areas even began importing the basic staple food.

Without wishing to argue for a determinant relation between labour inputs and price, I would argue that these changes in labour intensity in rice cultivation, and subsistence farming in particular, have an effect on rice prices. I suggested in Chapter 3 that there exists an optimal unit in rice cultivation in Sungai Puar. In other words, it should be possible to delineate a combination of factors, given existing technological levels, which, if changed in any way, would result in decreasing productivity.[1] Increased labour inputs

1. The concept of productivity in peasant agriculture is a difficult one. I have gone into the problem elsewhere (Kahn, 1977). Suffice it to say that while it is common for

both over and under this optimum would result in declining labour productivity.[1] At least in the short term, such changes would not be reflected in national statistics, since there are no reliable estimates of the number of people involved in rice cultivation in different years.

In this way the growth and decline in peasant commodity production would directly affect the productivity of subsistence rice cultivation. As peasants became increasingly involved in the production of commodities for domestic and world markets they would devote less and less time to subsistence agriculture, often leaving subsistence cultivation to those in economically un-productive age groups. If, at the time of this expansion, rice cultivation was too labour-intensive, this initial loss of labour to commodity production would be beneficial in that it would actually increase productivity in subsistence cultivation by reducing labour inputs towards the optimal combination of factors. Without any change in the parameters of subsistence cultivation, a labour drain of the kind hypothesised here would eventually result in less productive rice cultivation, and perhaps a total collapse of the subsistence base of the peasant economy.[2]

If in Indonesia 80 per cent of rice and other staple needs are met through subsistence cultivation in the average year, and assuming that rice cultivation is not revolutionised by short-term growth in the commodity sector, it is easy to see how economic expansion would quickly undercut itself through drawing labour out of subsistence cultivation. Peasant producers rely more heavily on the market, and an increasing number of merchants and wage labourers rely completely on the market to provide them with rice. This results in a hugely increased demand for rice as a com-modity. And yet, as I have argued, the Indonesian rice-producing sector produces rice largely for subsistence. Only a small proportion

productivity to be measured as a factor of land area, thus treating land *per se* as a scarce factor, I prefer to use productivity as a factor of labour input (including labour input represented by tools and other constant capital which, in the case of rice cultivation, includes earthworks, irrigation ditches and terracing).

1. I have recently carried out research into this problem in Negeri Sembilan, Malaysia. Early findings tend to confirm these hypotheses.

2. Elsewhere (Kahn, 1975) I have spoken of a cycle whereby expansion in the commodity sector causes a collapse in the subsistence sector which then chokes off the expansion. I would now rather argue against any inevitable cycle – since it may not be regularly repeated. Also, constraints of this sort on expansion might be overcome either through technological and structural change in rice cultivation, or by a willingness to rely more heavily on rice imports.

of rice produced is actually available for sale. Moreover, it is this group of peasant producers, merchants and wage labourers who, in different times, are also the workers in the subsistence sector. It is clear that subsistence cultivation, especially with the loss of labour to commodity production, cannot fulfil the needs for rice. This may in part explain the rocketing rice prices of the mid-1960s in Indonesia and the collapse of the new enterprises at the same time.

In this chapter I have examined the emergence of petty commodity production in West Sumatra in the first few decades of this century as well as the brief period in which a transition to new forms of peasant economy seemed to be taking place. It remains to point out that in part because of the hyper-inflation of the mid-1960s, and in part because of the new economic policies of the post-Sukarno regime, peasant economic organisation in the late 1960s and early 1970s returned to earlier principles. Again, as we have seen, the peasant economy of areas like Minangkabau is dominated by individually owned and operated enterprise, and by the existence of a highly important subsistence sector. In Sungai Puar in the 1970s the collapse of the government factory is probably a manifestation of these different economic conditions which favour the small-scale producer in opposition to the peasant enterprise.

In the final chapter we shall turn to the major question, the way in which the historical developments described in this chapter led to the emergence of petty commodity production, how petty commodity production is reproduced within the Indonesian social formation, and the circumstances under which such production may in future be transformed.

10

Conclusions: the concept of a neo-colonial social formation

I want now to bring together the threads of the argument in this book in an attempt to develop the concept of a neo-colonial social formation in Sumatra. The aim of such an exercise is to put forward an account of the reproduction and possible transformation of the peasant economy within the wider socio-economic system. This in turn should help us answer some of the thorny questions concerning the causes of underdevelopment in the Indonesian economy as a whole, and in the peasant sector in particular.

The concept of social formation developed in the Althusserian tradition represents an attempt to build a theoretical bridge as it were from the abstract concept of mode of production to concrete situations, particularly those in which capitalist societies seem to incorporate elements of their pre-capitalist roots. The use of the concept, particularly in describing societies on the periphery of world capitalism, remains somewhat problematic and has been subject to a number of criticisms. Writers like Frank and Wallerstein, for example, take issue with any attempt to characterise the societies of the periphery as pre-capitalist when they have long been part of a world-economy. Those writers, like Laclau, Amin and others, who have advocated its use nonetheless appear to agree that apparently pre-capitalist forms are largely a product of capitalism itself, i.e. that they are produced because they are necessary to the reproduction of the capitalist mode of production.

At another level altogether, the concept of social formation as the combination of different modes of production each with the three-level structure of a mode of production in pure form has come in for criticism (cf. Hindess and Hirst, 1977a and b).

The use of such a concept therefore remains fraught with difficulties, and at worst amounts to a rather sterile formalism used simply to classify and label the societies of the periphery.

I will use the term here to refer to the coexistence of different relations of production together with specific political and ideological forms within a single economic system; single in two senses: firstly, that the predominant form of production is commodity production, i.e. the production of exchange values, and secondly, that the circulation of commodities unites all the different enterprises in the system. This concept of an economic totality bears some resemblance to the concept of a world-economy of Wallerstein, who, in discussing the origins of the European-centred world-economy, writes:

It was a kind of social system the world has not really known before and which is the distinctive feature of a modern world-system. It is an economic but not a political unity, unlike empires, city-states and nation-states . . . It is a 'world' system, not because it encompasses the whole world, but because it is larger than any juridically-defined political unit (1974, p. 15).

Of course Wallerstein uses the concept in order to establish the primacy of the world-economy in the determination of local economic forms within the totality or, as his critics would have it, to establish the primacy of relations of exchange over localised relations of production (cf. Gerstein, 1977), a primacy which does not necessarily follow from the economic unity implied in the concept of social formation.

The concept of a neo-colonial social formation in which capitalist and non-capitalist relations of production co-exist within the framework of a world market has, I would argue, three basic implications. Firstly, it means that we choose to characterise peripheral economic forms as pre-capitalist or non-capitalist; secondly, it means that we reject any idea of the necessity of specific pre-capitalist forms for the reproduction of capitalism; and thirdly, it means, contrary to the views of numerous writers, that we maintain what is in some sense a dualist position, i.e. we argue that in spite of the apparently systemic nature of a world-economy, non-capitalist forms are nonetheless external to capitalism.

The characterisation of peripheral economics

In stressing the specificity of the peasant economy I have used the concept of petty commodity production. In spite of the fact that

201

the emergence of the peasant economy was largely stimulated by external changes in the capitalist world-economy, I have chosen to specify local economic organisation as distinctly non-capitalist.

It is around precisely this issue that the so-called characterisation debate revolves, although the main debates concern the application of the concept of feudalism or the feudal mode of production to societies involved in a world market. In discussing the second serfdom in eastern Europe, for example, Wallerstein argues that:

It is *not* the case that two forms of social organization, capitalist and feudal, existed side by side, or could ever so exist. The world-economy has one form or the other. Once it is capitalist, relationships that bear certain formal resemblances to feudal relationships are necessarily redefined in terms of the governing principles of a capitalist system (1974, p. 92).

Other writers, on the other hand, have maintained the distinctive nature of relations of production, in spite of their incorporation into a world market, maintaining that eastern Europe in the sixteenth century is better characterised as feudal (see Banaji, 1977; Brenner, 1977).

The same debate has also arisen in the study of the development of a *hacienda* system in colonial Latin America. Frank, Wallerstein and others maintain that Latin America has been capitalist since its incorporation in a world market (cf. Frank, 1969; Wallerstein, 1974), Laclau and others (Laclau, 1971; Martinez-Alier, 1967) advocating the use of the concept of a feudal mode of production dominated by capitalism.

Now, at this level, the characterisation debate is both semantic and formalist. Indeed, as Banaji shows (1977, p. 14), when the participants agree almost totally on the primacy or dominance of capitalism it will never be anything more than sterile taxonomic quibble. I have chosen to become involved in it here firstly, because the apparent underdevelopment of the Minangkabau economy can be explained only in relation to the absence of capitalism, and secondly, because I disagree with the concept of capitalist domination implied in the writings of Laclau, a point to which I shall return.

If underdevelopment refers to low *per-capita* income among a community of peasant producers, then there can be only two causes. The first would be that peasants are subjected to a high rate of exploitation, the second that the peasant economy is technologically backward and yet involved in a world market which contains enterprises of greater productivity. While, as we shall see, Minangkabau producers are exploited to some extent through unequal exchange, the main immediate cause of their low income is low productivity. Low productivity is in turn a result of the simple fact that no one acquires a sufficient surplus of cash to invest in new techniques. The cause of the low level of technology in blacksmithing, as we have seen, is not ignorance of more productive techniques, nor some kind of cultural obstacle to enterprises of scale.

While therefore Wallerstein's idea of a unified world-economy is incorporated within the concept of a neo-colonial social formation, we must take issue with his view that all relationships within it are 'necessarily redefined in terms of the governing principles of a capitalist system' (1974). Petty commodity production emerges and is reproduced necessarily through the operation of a world market. Like other productive systems it is therefore subjected to the principles of a market. However, in no other sense is it subjected to the governing principles of capitalist relations of production. Incorporation into the world-economy means something quite different for the Minangkabau peasant economy. Rather than resulting in a localised accumulation of surplus and a development of the productive forces, petty commodity relations of production produce just the opposite, i.e. they ensure relatively equal distribution of income among producers and traders. Rather than resulting in the development of the productive forces, there is, if anything, the opposite tendency, as we have seen in Chapter 7.

To adopt a concept of a neo-colonial social formation therefore leads us to characterise peripheral economic forms as non-capitalist. Unlike Laclau, however, I would argue that accepting this position must also lead us to question any attempt to explain the presence of specific pre-capitalist systems in terms of their role within the reproductive circuit of capitalism.

Pre-capitalist economies and the reproduction of capitalism

Many writers who adopt the concept of social formation with respect to societies of the periphery nonetheless explain the emergence of these forms largely as a response to certain postulated 'needs' of capitalism. Amin, for example, argues that peripheral modes of production are 'subjected to the distinctive purpose of dominant capital. . .' (1974, p. 360). Laclau takes a similar stand when he argues that capitalism must create/preserve pre-capitalist forms of organisation on its periphery in order to ensure a supply of cheap labour, which in turn offsets the declining rate of profit at the centre (1971). Meillassoux appears to explain the existence of pre-capitalist forms in Africa in much the same way:

One can therefore establish in general that when a worker is engaged both in subsistence production and as a wage worker in the capitalist sector, he produces at the same time labour rent and surplus value in the domestic economy for the capitalist sector over and above the exploitation of the producer's labour power by the capitalist (1975, p. 173, my translation).

Indeed, for Meillassoux pre-capitalist forms benefit capitalism not just by generating surplus in this way – they also have the added advantage of blocking class unity and preserving the subjugation of the peripheral labour force (Meillassoux 1975, pp. 145f.).

As Banaji has pointed out, explanations of this kind differ only in a formal way from those offered by Frank and Wallerstein. For the latter, apparently pre-capitalist forms on the periphery acquire their distinctive character from their incorporation within the capitalist market, whose ethic is maximisation. Whether therefore one postulates a declining rate of profit or a need to maximise profits, the implications are much the same – the world-economy is shaped by a single rationality (attributed to capitalism), that rationality is diffused to all enterprises within the system and all economic forms must be shaped to perform the single function of off-setting the declining rate of profit, supplying cheap labour, maximising capitalism's total surplus, etc.

Such a theory of imperialism has certain major shortcomings. Firstly, in attempting to derive a single driving force behind all capitalist expansion – a force frequently derived from an abstract analysis of the capitalist mode of production – the theories vastly oversimplify the concrete history of European expansion. One need not even criticise the 'tendency' theories of capitalism, as Cutler *et al.* have done (1977, 1978), to falsify such simplistic explanations.

Secondly, and more important from our point of view, such theories suffer all the drawbacks of functionalism by seeking to

204

account for specific social forms in terms of their function. Like other functionalist explanations, these theories fail to explain why one structure and not another performs the needed function.

One of the few writers to have taken issue with functional theories of imperialism has been Pierre Philippe Rey, who consistently maintains that capitalism seeks to transform the world after its own image, and does not, as the 'unequal development' theorists would have it, purposely seek to maintain non-capitalist forms on its periphery. That it has not succeeded in entirely destroying these forms is not a result if its own 'ill will', but, on the contrary, is the result of the fact that 'the previous social and economic structures which it must destroy . . . have proved themselves to be infinitely more resistant than were precapitalist structures in Europe . . .' (1973, p. 11). While it is not necessary to accept Rey's diagnosis entirely, it is important to maintain the spirit of this conclusion, i.e. that there is no reason why precapitalist structures should be necessary to the reproduction of capitalism in general, although their 'resistance' may equally stem from the benefits which accrue to certain fractions of the bourgeoisie as from the 'cultural Lag' implied by Rey.

To see that this is the case, let us return to the Sumatran situation, and the role of petty commodity production in the reproductive circuit of capitalism. I have argued elsewhere (1974b) that within the Indonesian social formation there is a flow of value, a form of surplus, between peasant producers and the hegemonic capitalist class.

It is possible to illustrate this process of surplus transfer by the case of individual production in West Sumatra. Let us take the example of the rubber producer, who grows rubber as a commodity on his own land. Let us assume that rubber producers have access, through their wives, to subsistence plots and domestic labour which yields an average of one half the subsistence needs of each family. Given a large number of independent individualised producers, and hence a competitive system of pricing, the over-all tendency in rubber prices will be such that individuals receive just enough money to reproduce themselves and their families. In other words, the price of rubber, under free competition, will be determined by the subsistence needs of the producers plus the cost of reproducing tools, raw materials, replanting of rubber, land preparation and other constant capital inputs (see formula (ii),

Chapter 7, p. 137). Because of the existence of real income in the form of rice which comes from outside the market system and hence is not monetised, the total price of production of rubber will equal:

$$C + V - S \tag{i}$$

where C is the value of constant capital, V the cost of reproducing labour power and S the average value of the producers' labour power which is reproduced through non-commodity forms of subsistence production. In our hypothetical case, then, the cost of production of rubber, measured in values, will be below the value of rubber produced by 25 per cent.

To see that this process whereby costs revolve around a social average in fact operates, we can take the case of a hypothetical producer who possesses less subsistence land than the social average. If he is to reproduce himself according to average subsistence levels he will have to sell his rubber for more than do those who own average or higher than average amounts of subsistence land. Given a freely competitive market, however, he will be forced to accept the same price for his rubber, and hence his over-all income will be lower. The same situation will hold for all individual producers within the economy, provided that socially average levels of subsistence production are achieved in all sectors of the economy. Just, therefore, as actual costs of production all consistently fall below the value of commodities, so the tendency will be for prices of production to fall below the level of exchange values which would prevail in the absence of a subsistence sector.

Any exchange which takes place in the economy will, therefore, result in a flow of value. The export of rubber, for example, generates a transfer of surplus from petty commodity producer to capitalists. The division of this surplus between industrial capital, which benefits through cheap raw materials, and finance and merchant capital will, of course, depend on the relative power of the different capitals (see Kay, 1975, pp. 86ff.). In any case, in buying these products capitalism as a whole, wherever it is located, receives a surplus equivalent to S, i.e. the socially necessary labour time expended in subsistence production in the dominated economy.

Another transfer takes place when the products of domestic factories are sold on the world market, if domestic wage levels are

206

affected by the existence of the subsistence community. If there exists a sufficiently large labour force seeking work in domestic industry, then wages will also be lower than the cost of reproduction of labour power. Competition for jobs means that factory owners can reduce wages to a level equal to $V - S$. Emmanuel's formulae (1972, p. 64) fit this particular case. This analysis, however, goes beyond Emmanuel's, because it does not take wage levels as an independent variable. Wage levels are socially and historically determined, and one aspect of this social determination is the access to subsistence goods produced outside the exchange economy in Minangkabau.

I do not want to suggest that this is the only mechanism of unequal exchange under neo-colonialism. Trade monopolies, of the kind used in earlier formations by merchant capital, would achieve similar effects, as would debtor—creditor relations whereby the indebted peasant is forced to sell his products below market value. However, in such cases, also it would be usual for peasant commodity producers to find other ways of reproducing their labour power, a function fulfilled in Minangkabau by the subsistence community. Meillassoux (1975) describes a similar situation in West Africa in which the subsistence community functions to produce a migratory labour force subsisting on low wages.

As this discussion shows, therefore, petty commodity production in Sumatra has been drawn into the reproductive circuit of capitalism. Significantly, an effect of this is to favour the reproduction of the peasant economy as well, by drawing off available surpluses which might otherwise be accumulated locally, and in some cases by reproducing the hold of merchant capital or the local state over the peasants.

However it is possible to conclude from this neither that pre-capitalist relations of production are necessary to capitalism, nor that the emergence of petty commodity production in Minangkabau can be explained simply as a response to the demands of capitalism. If, for example, rubber were grown on highly productive plantations, capitalism would benefit in the same way from cheap commodities. Even without increasing productivity, there are other ways — as Meillassoux, Laclau and others have shown — whereby capitalism could assure itself of a supply of cheap labour.

207

As this example shows, the existence of, as well as the specific form taken by, non-capitalist relations of production within the neo-colonial economy can be explained neither by reference to their role within the reproductive circuit of capitalism nor by any single postulated 'need' generated by the capitalist mode of production. Moreover, the existence of petty commodity production is equally dependent upon the world market. In short, in this case the creation of the world market economy is a precondition for, but not the cause of, all the different forms of commodity production within it.

The question of dualism

Andre Gunder Frank, in his attack both on modernisation theory and on the accounts of Latin American feudalism provided by some contemporary Latin American communists, chose to focus on the concept of dualism. The idea that certain sectors of the Latin American economy were in some sense outside the capitalist system was of course inimical to Frank's theory, as we have seen. Significantly, many of Frank's critics nonetheless share his antipathy for analyses that smack in any way of dualism. Laclau, therefore, is in substantial agreement with Frank's attack: 'Dualism implies that no connections exist between the "modern" or "progressive" sector and the "closed" or "traditional" sector. Yet we have argued that, on the contrary, servile exploitation was accentuated and consolidated by the very tendency of entrepreneurs . . . to maximise profits; the apparent lack of communication herewith disappears' (1971). Without wishing to argue for the complete separation of sectors, I would nonetheless argue that to employ a concept of articulation, as does Laclau, one must accept to some extent the dualist hypothesis. Clearly, Minangkabau peasants are closely involved in a world-economy, as we have seen, by being directly tied into a single exchange network. And yet, by maintaining the distinctive nature of localised productive relations, we are by definition maintaining that a degree of dualism exists. The above statement to the contrary, Laclau's position cannot correspond with Frank's. How could it be otherwise when he places so much stress on the distinctive nature of relations of production in the periphery?

To maintain that sectors of a world-economy are in a sense

both non-capitalist and outside capitalism is of course not to accept explanations for this offered by dualism theory, resting as they do on concepts like cultural lag, traditional resistance to change, peasant irrationality and the like. On the contrary, purely ideological explanations of this phenomenon are no more complete than economistic ones. If, following Rey, we argue that at least certain fractions of the dominant bourgeoisie are struggling to impose the capitalist mode of production in the periphery, then the explanation for the existence of pre-capitalist relations of production is dependent upon the state of the class struggle in all its forms.

The feudalisation of the Minangkabau and Javanese peasantry which culminated in the Culture System can be used to illustrate this point. The period from the van Hogendorp proposals to the enactment of the Agrarian Land Law of 1870 was a period of struggle during which the liberals attempted to overturn the mercantilist policies initiated by the V.O.C. The persistence of non-capitalist forms in Sumatra and Java on the periphery of the European capitalist economy in the nineteenth century is a simple reflection of the strength of a colonial class committed to mercantilist policies, and the ability of that class at a political level to resist liberal reforms in the colony which threatened to undermine its economic position.

A similar argument must be advanced in order to explain the reproduction of petty commodity production within a neo-colonial formation. On the one hand, as we have seen, the conditions necessary to its existence are supplied by the operation of a world market, and the mobility of labour and techniques in Minangkabau itself. On the other hand, these conditions are themselves the consequence of the state of class struggle. Peasants, as Indonesian history clearly shows, are a force to be reckoned with, resisting expropriation and hence the destruction of petty commodity production. However, it is not peasants alone who benefit. In many parts of Indonesia, and in parts of Minangkabau itself, merchants are strongly bound up in the commodity economy, making profits through mercantile monopolies ensured by credit/debt relations, or through State trading companies. Indeed, peasants who produce for a foreign market produce over 25 per cent of the nation's foreign exchange and a large proportion of government revenue, a system ensured in the 1950s by discriminatory exchange rates which favoured importers of consumer goods as opposed to exporters of raw materials (Mackie, in Glassburner, 1971). Those forces which oppose the complete capitalisation of the Indonesian economy are therefore extremely strong, and include political groups from the whole range of the political spectrum. An explanation of these forces would, as the concept of social formation implies, rest to a great extent on features in a world-economy which are distinctly local — localised economic/ class relations, the local distribution of political power and ideologies which are themselves strongly tied to locality.

To sum up the argument so far, then, a concept of a neo-colonial social formation is particularly appropriate for the analysis of the Minangkabau peasant economy. It makes it possible to understand the specificity of localised, non-capitalist relations of production, and hence of specific localised forms of accumulation; it provides a non-functionalist account of the creation or persistence of these non-capitalist economic forms; and it allows one to weigh up those features of the local economy which are externally and those which are internally generated in a non-dogmatic way. Finally it provides the concept of a world-economy in the Wallerstein sense (whereby all enterprises are linked into a systemic exchange network) without reducing the whole world to a single form of economic rationality.

Transformation of the peasant economy

In the preceding chapters I have been concerned to outline the structure of a particular form of peasant economy. At the same time the aims of this study have always been broader, in that I have argued that in addition to analysing the operation of a given economic system it is also necessary to place it in space and time, to account for its existence in a particular part of the world in a specific historical conjuncture. To this end it was deemed necessary to present a structural analysis of the petty commodity economy in order to discover the preconditions necessary to its appearance in history, and to examine the specific historical developments which have given rise to it. Put another way, I have always been concerned not only to present a static picture of the functioning of a peasant economy with a given set of apparently externally imposed constraints, but also to attempt to account for the emergence of that economy and the ways it is maintained in the neo-colonial situation of modern Indonesia.

Clearly, however, for some this is where the important analysis begins. The crucial questions are now political and concern the ways in which that economy can be transformed to eliminate the hardships it causes and to provide the Minangkabau peasants with a more adequate living, as well as to give them a greater say in their own future. In conclusion, therefore, I want to turn briefly to the question of the transformation of the Indonesian peasant economy.

The neo-colonial system described in this chapter may benefit certain mercantile and some industrial interests. The profits it generates, however, are limited by underproductivity and the lack of direct exploitation of the labour force of the periphery. This, it seems to me, is the basic contradiction of this kind of neo-colonialism, and the contradiction between the relations of neo-colonialism and the development of the productive forces has generated, and will continue to generate, class struggle. The struggle, however, will not inevitably lead to the end of capitalist domination, but may simply transform it under certain circumstances. While there are, of course, political forces in Indonesia dedicated to the breaking of capitalism, there are also forces interested simply in overthrowing the present order of neo-colonialism, and bringing in a new order based on the direct implantation of capital — an implantation which may be internally or externally controlled. Such a change would be revolutionary in many ways. It would transform the rural economies of places like Minangkabau, introduce higher levels of productivity and create economic forms more akin to those found in other centres of the capitalist world. Such a transformation is clearly taking place in the modern Malaysian economy, and we can expect increasing pressure in Indonesia for similar changes.

The contradictions generated by neo-colonialism in areas like Minangkabau, then, will not necessarily spell an end to capitalist domination of the Minangkabau social formation, but simply lead to the hegemony of new factions of the international bourgeoisie. The direction of future change depends on the outcome of present-day struggles between the opposed interests of peasants, workers and the varied factions of the international bourgeoisie.

It is of course not possible to predict on the basis of the analyses

211

provided here precisely what will happen in West Sumatra. And yet it is perhaps easier to outline a range of possibilities which could arise out of the present conjuncture. Here we shall examine very briefly certain important changes both at the level of the world-economy and in the local peasant economy.

The new international division of labour

Recently a number of students of the world-economy have detected what seems to be an important shift in the forms and location of accumulation which have important implications for the peasant economies of the periphery. Writers like Warren (1973), Petras (1977) and Friedman (1976) have outlined what appears to be a general trend towards the internationalisation of real capital flows, and particularly to an increase in real capital exports to the economies of the periphery.

The emergence of what some writers have chosen to term the new international division of labour (see Fröbel *et al.*, 1978) has important implications for the theory of underdevelopment, as well as for economic organisation on the periphery of world capitalism. We have already noted Rey's critique of unequal development theories and particularly of the idea that capitalism must preserve pre-capitalist forms on its periphery in order to offset a declining rate of profit. Rey argues that 'except for a specific moment in the development of capitalism . . . pre-capitalist modes of production become obstacles to the development of capitalism' (1973, p. 16, my translation). While Rey's analyses anticipate a transformation of this type, i.e. the emergence of core-forms of capitalism on the periphery, many others as we have seen cannot.

If the developments described by Fröbel *et al.* take place in Sumatra, the consequences will be extremely significant for the peasant economy of Minangkabau. Significantly, if we compare the peasant village in Minangkabau to one in the culturally related area of Negeri Sembilan in Malaysia, where the changes in world economic organisation are much more marked, we find important differences. While the major proportion of rural income in West Sumatra derives from the production and distribution of commodities on a small scale, many modern Malaysian villages have become in effect domestic outposts for manufacturing centres in

Penang, Kuala Lumpur, Singapore and in industrial parks established in small towns and rural areas (see Stivens, 1977; Kahn, 1977). The peasant sector of the economy of Negeri Sembilan has experienced a decline. Rubber and rice, once the mainstay of the local economy, are giving way to wages as the main source of peasant income as migration rates continue to rise.

Fröbel *et al*. have argued that since the 1960s a 'single world market for labor and a single world market in industrial sites now, for the first time, effectively encompasses both the traditional industrial countries as well as the underdeveloped countries' (1978, p. 130).

In Indonesia, of course, economic and political conditions are such that this trend is not yet widespread, in spite of the existence of highly capital-intensive petroleum extraction. And yet it seems only a matter of time before the effects of this transformation of the world-economy are felt in peasant villages like Sungai Puar.

The collapse of the peasant economy

We have already examined the way in which a petty commodity economy tends to generate, through technological change, an increasing number of producers who cannot afford even the relatively small investments necessary to set up as traders. The increasing numbers of landless poor in the urban centres testifies to this relative overpopulation – the consequence of the incorporation of a peasant economy into a world market. One possibility, of course, is that some of this labour will be absorbed into the new manufacturing centres described by Fröbel *et al*., who in fact cite as an important precondition for the emergence of a new international division of labour the development of a world-wide reservoir of potential labour, most of which emerges as a consequence of latent overpopulation in rural areas.

Hence the gradual collapse of the peasant economy – a consequence in part of factors internal to petty commodity production and in part of the technological changes in the world-economy – may feed into new international developments. This, of course, again depends on the state of class struggle in Indonesia. In an earlier period, as we have seen, such an internal change resulted in an emerging transformation of the rural economy and the development of local capitalism. However, conditions have

213

changed, the new administration favours closer economic ties with the capitalist West, and as long as it continues these policies the earlier situation will, in all likelihood, not repeat itself.

The third possibility, of course, is that the growing mass of landless peasants will oppose the capitalist path altogether, a situation which appears unlikely in the immediate future given the wide-scale political repression in the country. Nonetheless, the brutal repression of the Indonesian Communist Party which followed the attempted *coup* in 1965 cannot succeed for ever.

Any one of the three developments — the integration of the peasants into a new international (capitalist) order, the re-emergence of rural capitalism or the development of a socialist economy — appears to be a possibility. The outcome depends largely on political struggles currently taking place in Indonesia. While it is clear that the situation described in this book will not continue, it is not as yet clear which direction those struggles will take.

While the present government of the country appears to advocate the path of integration within the new international capitalist order as the only path for development, I hope to have demonstrated here that, the government's claims to the contrary, policies which aim to promote growth and development are highly political, and that a detailed analysis of the predominance of petty commodity production in the present conjuncture is crucial to the formulation of such policies. Past experience of political movements in Indonesia shows that peasants such as those of Minangkabau are under certain circumstances perfectly capable of understanding this. It is only to be hoped that analyses such as this one will be undertaken in Indonesia itself, in order that Indonesian peasants will be able to have a say in the choice of path to be pursued.

Bibliography

Abdullah, T. (1971). *Schools and Politics: the Kaum Muda movement in West Sumatra*, Ithaca, N.Y.: Cornell University Modern Indonesia Project, Monograph Series.

Ali, S. H. (1972). 'Land concentration and poverty among the rural Malays', *Nusantara*, I.

Allen, G. C. and Donnithorne, A. (1957). *Western enterprise in Indonesia and Malaya*, London: Allen and Unwin.

Alliband, G. R. (1970). 'Upheaval in Sumatra: from Dewan Banteng to the P.R.R.I. Rebellion', Cornell University M.A. thesis.

Amin, S. (1974). *Accumulation on a World Scale*, New York Monthly Review Press.

Anon. (1917). 'Een statistiek in de Onderafdeeling Oud Agam', *Tijdschrift voor het Binnenlandsche Bestuur*, 52.

Anurlis (1971). 'Tindjauan terhadap memperkembangkan industri besi di Sumatera Barat', Fakultas Ekonomi, Universitas Andalas, Padang, B.A. thesis.

Bachtiar, H. (1967). 'Negeri Taram', in R. M. Koentjaraningrat (ed.), *Villages in Indonesia*, Ithaca, N.Y.: Cornell University Press.

Balibar, E. (1970). 'The basic concepts of historical materialism', in L. Althusser and E. Balibar, *Reading 'Capital'*, London: New Left Books.

Banaji, J. (1977). 'Modes of production in a materialist conception of history', *Capital and Class*, 3.

Banfield, E. C. and Banfield, L. F. (1958). *The Moral Basis of a Backward Society*, Glencoe, Ill.: Free Press.

Barth, F. (1959). *Political Leadership among Swat Pathans*, London: Athlone.

Bastin, J. S. (1965). *The British in West Sumatra, 1685–1825*, Kuala Lumpur: University of Malaya Press.

Benda, H. and McVey R. (eds.) (1960). *The Communist Uprisings of 1926–27 in Indonesia*, Ithaca, N.Y.: Cornell University Modern Indonesia Project, Translation Series.

Bickmore, A. S. (1869). *Travels in the Indonesia Archipelago*, New York: D. Appleton and Co.

215

Bibliography

Biro Pusat Statistik (1959, 1964–7, 1968–9). *Statistical Pocketbooks of Indonesia*, Jakarta.

(1972). *Impor Menerut Djenis Barang*, Jakarta.

Bradby, B. (1975). 'The destruction of natural economy', *Economy and Society*, IV, 2.

Brenner, R. (1977). 'The origins of capitalist development', *New Left Review*, 104.

Bruner, E. (1974). 'The expression of ethnicity in Indonesia', in A. Cohen (ed.), *Urban Ethnicity*, London: Tavistock.

Chayanov, A. V. (1966). *The Theory of Peasant Economy*, Homewood, Ill.: Irwin.

Cuisinier, J. (1959). 'La Guerre des Padri', *Archives de Sociologie des Religions*, VII.

Cutler, A., Hussain, A. *et al.* (1977/8). *Marx's 'Capital' and Capitalism Today* (2 vols.), London: Routledge.

Dewey, A. (1962). *Peasant Marketing in Java*, Glencoe, Ill.: Free Press.

Dobbins, C. (1975). 'The exercise of authority in Minangkabau in the late 18th Century', in A. Reid and L. Castles (eds.), *Pre-colonial State Systems in Southeast Asia*, Kuala Lumpur: Monographs of the Malaysian Branch of the Royal Asiatic Society, No. 6.

(1977). 'Economic change in Minangkabau as a factor in the rise of the Padri movement', *Indonesia*, 23.

Ekholm, K. (forthcoming). 'On the structure and dynamics of global systems'.

Emmanuel, A. (1972). *Unequal Exchange: a study of the imperialism of trade* (with additional comments by C. Bettelheim), London: New Left Books.

Esmara, H. (1972). *West Sumatra: facts and figures*, Padang: Institute for Economic and Social Research, Andalas University.

Foster, G. M. (1960). 'Impersonal relations in peasant society', *Human Organisation*, 19.

(1962). *Traditional Cultures and the impact of Technological Change*, New York: Harper.

Frank, A. G. (1969). *Latin America: underdevelopment or revolution*, New York: Monthly Review Press.

(1970). 'Imperialism and underdevelopment', in R. I. Rhodes (ed.), *Imperialism and Underdevelopment: a reader*, New York: Monthly Review Press.

Friedman, J. (1974). 'Marxism, structuralism and vulgar materialism', *Man*, 9.

(1976). 'Marxist theory and systems of total reproduction', *Critique of Anthropology*, 7.

Fröbel, F., Heinrichs, J. and Kreye, D. (1978). 'The new international division of labour', *Social Science Information*, XVII, 1.

216

Bibliography

Furnivall, J. (1949). *Netherlands India: a study of plural economy*, Cambridge University Press.

Geertz, C. (1960). *The Religion of Java*, Glencoe, Ill.: Free Press.

(1963a). *Agricultural Involution*, Berkeley: University of California Press.

(1963b). *Peddlers and Princes*, Chicago: University of Chicago Press.

(1965). *The Social History of an Indonesian Town*, Cambridge, Mass.: M.I.T. Press.

Gerstein, I. (1977). 'Theories of the world economy and imperialism', *Insurgent Sociologist*, VII, 2.

Gibb, H. A. R. (1969). *Muhammadanism: an historical survey*, London: Oxford University Press.

Glamann, K. (1958). *Dutch Asiatic Trade*, Copenhagen: Danish Science Press.

Glassburner, B. (ed.) (1971). *The Economy of Indonesia*, Ithaca, New York: Cornell University Press.

Godelier, M. (1973). *Rationality and Irrationality in Economics*, London: New Left Books.

(1974). 'On the definition of a social formation: the example of the Incas', *Critique of Anthropology*, 1.

(1977). *Perspectives in Marxist Anthropology*, Cambridge: Cambridge University Press.

Gough, K. (1962). 'Variation in matrilineal systems', in D. M. Schneider and K. Gough, *Matrilineal Kinship*, Berkeley and Los Angeles: University of California Press.

Haan, F. de (1897). 'Near Midden Sumatra in 1684', *Tijdschrift voor Indische Taal-, Land-, en Volkenkunde*, 39.

Hall, D. G. E. (1968). *A History of Southeast Asia*, London: Macmillan.

Hindess, B. and Hirst, P. Q. (1975). *Pre-capitalist Modes of Production*, London: Routledge.

(1977a). 'Modes of production and social formation', in *Precapitalist Modes of Production: a reply to John Taylor, Critique of Anthropology*, 8.

(1977b). *Mode of Production and Social Formation*, London: Macmillan.

Ho, R. (1967). *Farmers of Central Malaya*, Canberra: Australian National University.

Hoogvelt, A. M. and Child, D. (1973). 'Rhodesia: economic blockade and development', *Monthly Review*, XXV, 5.

Huitema, W. F. (1935). *De Bevolkingskoffiecultuur op Sumatra*, Wageningen: H. Veen en Zonen.

Jay, R. (1969). *Javanese Villagers: Social Relations in Rural Modjokuto*, Cambridge, Mass.: M.I.T. Press.

Josselin de Jong, P. E. de (1951). *Minangkabau and Negri Sembilan*, Leiden: Ijdo.

Junus, U. (1964). 'Some Remarks on Minangkabau social structure', *Bijdragen*, 120.

217

Bibliography

Kahn, J. S. (1974a). 'Economic Integration and the Peasant Economy', University of London Ph.D. thesis.

(1974b). 'Imperialism and the reproduction of capitalism: towards a definition of the Indonesia social formation', *Critique of Anthropology*, 2.

(1975). 'Economic scale and the cycle of petty commodity production in West Sumatra', in M. Bloch (ed.), *Marxist Analyses and Social Anthropology*, London: Malaby.

(1976). '"Tradition", Matriliny and change among the Minangkabau of Indonesia', *Bijdragen, Koninklijk Instituut*, 132.

(1977). Report to the Social Science Research Council on research in Malaysia, MS.

(1978). 'Ideology and social structure in Indonesia', *Comparative studies in Society and History*, XX, 1.

(in press) 'Mercantilism and the emergence of servile labour in colonial Indonesia', in J. S. Kahn and J. R. Lobera (eds.), *The Nature of Precapitalist Societies*, London: Macmillan.

(forthcoming) 'Trade, double descent and the formation of the Minangkabau kingdom'.

Kantor Sensus dan Statistik Propinsi: Sumatera Barat (1970). *Sumatera Barat dalam Angka*, Padang.

Kat Angelino, A. D. A. de (1931). *Colonial Policy*, The Hague: Martinus Nijhoff.

Kay, G. (1975). *Development and Underdevelopment: a Marxist analysis*, London: Macmillan.

Kessler, C. (1972). 'Islam, society and political behaviour; some comparative implications of the Malay case', *British Journal of Sociology*, 23.

Koentjaraningrat, R. M. (1967). *Villages in Indonesia*, Ithaca, N.Y.: Cornell University Press.

Kroeskamp, H. (1931). *De Westkust en Minangkabau*, Utrecht: Fa. Schotanus en Jens.

Laclau, E. (1971). 'Feudalism and capitalism in Latin America', *New Left Review*, 67.

Leach, E. (1970) (orig. pub. 1954). *Political Systems of Highland Burma*, Boston, Mass.: Beacon Press.

Lee, G. (1973). 'Commodity production and reproduction amongst the Malayan peasantry', *Journal of Contemporary Asia*, III, 4.

Leeuw, W. J. A. de (1926). *Het Painansch Contract*, Amsterdam: H. J. Paris.

Legge, J. D. (1961). *Central Authority and regional Autonomy in Indonesia: a study in local administration*, Ithaca, N.Y.: Cornell University Press.

Lenin, V. I. (1917). *Imperialism: the highest stage of capitalism*, Moscow: Foreign Languages Press.

218

Bibliography

Lenin, V. I. (1956). *The development of Capitalism in Russia*, Moscow: Progress Publishers.

Levi-Strauss, C. (1963). *Structural Anthropology*, New York: Basic Books.

Lloyd, P. (1971). *Classes, Crises and Coups*, London: Macgibbon and Kee.

Mackie, J. (1967). *Problems of the Indonesian Inflation*. Ithaca, N.Y.: Cornell University Modern Indonesia Project, Monograph Series.

Maretin, J. (1961). 'Disappearance of matriclan survivals in Minangkabau family and marriage relations', *Bijdragen*, 117.

Marriot, M. (ed.) (1955). *Village India: studies in the little community*, American Anthropological Association Memoirs, 85.

Marsden, W. (1811). *The History of Sumatra*, London.

Martinez-Alier, J. (1967). 'El latifundio en Andalucía y en América Latina', *Cuadernos de Ruedo Ibérico*, October/November.

Marx, K. (1967). *Capital* (3 volumes), N.Y.: International Publishers.

(1973). *The 'Grundrisse'* (M. Nicolaus, ed.), Harmondsworth: Penguin.

Meek, R. (1973). *History of the Labour Theory of Value*, London: Lawrence and Wishart.

Meillassoux, C. (1975). *Femmes, greniers et capitaux*, Paris: Maspero.

Naim, M. (1971). 'Merantau: reasons and effects of Minangkabau voluntary migration', Padang: Center for Minangkabau Studies.

O'Laughlin, B. (1977). 'Production and reproduction: Meillassoux's *Femmes, greniers et capitaux*', *Critique of Anthropology*, 8.

Parels, B. H. (1944). 'Bevolkings Kofficultuur', in C. J. van Hall and C. van de Koppel (eds.). *De Landbouw in de Indische Archipel*, 's-Gravenhage: W. van Hoeve.

Parkinson, B. K. (1967). 'Non-economic factors in the economic retardation of the rural Malays', *Modern Asian Studies*, 1.

Petras, J. (1977). 'Des paysans par le capitalisme mondial', *Le Monde Diplomatique*, June.

Pires, T. (1944). *The Suma Oriental of Tomé Pires* (A. Cortesao, ed.), London: Hakluyt Society.

Ples, D. (1878). *De Koffij-Cultuur op Sumatra's Westkust*, Batavia: Ogilvie and Company.

Radcliffe-Brown, A. R. (1963). *Structure and Function in Primitive Society*, London: Cohen and West.

Radjab, M. (1964). *Perang Paderi di Sumatera Barat*, Djakarta: Balai Pustaka.

Raffles, S. (1830). *Memoire of the Life and Public Services of Sir Thomas Stamford Raffles*, London: John Murray.

Redfield, R. (1955). *The Little Community*, Chicago: University of Chicago Press.

(1956). *Peasant Society and Culture*, Chicago: University of Chicago Press.

Rey, P. P. (1973). *Les Alliances de classes*, Paris: Maspero.

Bibliography

Rubel, A. J., Kupferer, H. J. *et al.* (1968). 'Perspectives of the atomistic-type society', *Human Organisation*, 27.

Sahlins, M. (1974). *Stone Age Economics*, London, Tavistock.

Said, N. (1970). *Kabupaten Agam*, Padang: Lembaga Penelitian Ekonomi dan Masjarakat, Fakultas Ekonomi, Universitas Andalas.

Schneider, D. and Gough, K. (eds.) (1962). *Matrilineal Kinship*, Berkeley and Los Angeles: California University Press.

Schrieke, B. (1955). 'The course of the Communist movement on the west coast of Sumatra', in his *Indonesian Sociological Studies*, The Hague: van Hoeve.

Schultz, T. W. (1964). *Transforming Traditional Agriculture*, N.Y.: Arno Press.

Sen, S. P. (1962). 'Indian textiles in south-east Asian trade in the seventeenth century', *Journal of Southeast Asian History*, I, 2.

Siegel, J. T. (1969). *The Rope of God*, Berkeley: University of California Press.

Smit, L. A. (1931). 'Enkele gegevens en beshouwing met betrekking tot de industrialisatie van Nederlandsch Indie', *Koloniale Studien*, 17.

Stivens, M. (1977). 'Women and their property in Negeri Sembilan', Paper given to B.S.A. Development Study Group in May, 1977.

Stoler, A. (1977). 'Rice harvesting in Kali Laro', *American Ethnologist*, IV, 4.

Sutter, J. O. (1959). 'Indonesianasi: a historical survey of the role of politics in the institutions of a changing economy', Cornell University Ph.D. thesis.

Swift, M. G. (1965). *Malay Peasant Society in Jelebu*, London: Athlone Press.

   (1967). 'Economic concentration and Malay peasant society', in M. Freedman (ed.), *Social Organization*, London: Cass.

   (1971). 'Minangkabau and modernization', in H. R. Hiatt and C. Jayawardena (eds.), *Anthropology in Oceania: essays presented to Ian Hogbin*, Sydney: Angus and Robertson.

Tanner, N. (1974). 'Matrifocality in Indonesia and Africa and among Black Americans', in S. Rosaldo and L. Lamphere (eds.), *Woman, Culture and Society*, Stanford: Stanford University Press.

Taylor, J. (1975–6). Review of *Pre-capitalist Modes of Production*, *Critique of Anthropology*, 4–6.

Terray, E. (1972). *Marxism and 'Primitive' Societies*, N.Y.: Monthly Review Press.

   (1975). 'Classes and class consciousness in the Abron kingdom of Gyaman', in M. Bloch (ed.), *Marxist Analyses and Social Anthropology*, London: Malaby.

220

Bibliography

Thompson, G. (1976). *Inequality between Nations*, Milton Keynes: Open University Press.

Wallerstein, I. (1974). *The Modern World System*, N.Y.: Academic Press.

(1977). Reply to Gerstein, *Insurgent Sociologist*, VII, 2.

Ward, K. E. (1970). *The Foundation of the Partai Muslimin Indonesia*, Ithaca, N.Y.: Cornell Modern Indonesia Project, Interim Report Series.

Warren, B. (1973). 'Imperialism and Capitalist industrialization', *New Left Review*, 81.

Wertheim, W. F. (1956). *Indonesian Society in Transition: A study of social change*, The Hague and Bandung: W. van Hoeve.

Westenenk, L. C. (1912–13). 'De Inlandsche Bestuur ter Sumatra's Westkust', *Kolaniaal Tijdschrift*, Tweede Jaargang.

Willinck, G. (1909). *Het Rechtsleven der Minangkabause Maleiers*, Leiden: Brill.

Wolters, O. W. (1967). *Early Indonesian Commerce*, Ithaca, N.Y.: Cornell University Press.

(1970). *The Fall of Srivijaya in Malay History*, Ithaca, N.Y.: Cornell University Press.

Glossary of Minangkabau terms

adat: tradition, customary law

apa: forge or other place of work of a blacksmith

baban: a sack, 1 sack of rice = about 20 kilogrammes

bajak: a plough

baralek: a wedding feast or, with a *baralek badatuak*, the feast given for the installation of a *panghulu*

Bodi-Caniago: one of two *adat* systems, the one with a more democratic tradition

Bupati: the head of a *Kabupaten*

camat: the head of a *Kecamatan*

Cultuurstelsel: cultivation system, usually mistranslated as 'Culture System'. A system of colonial exploitation based on forced labour or forced deliveries formalised by Governor General van den Bosch in 1830

Darek (Ind: Darat): the traditional cultural heartland of Minangkabau

Datuak: term of address for a *panghulu*

Dewan Banteng: the group that took control of the provincial government in West Sumatra before the formation of the P.R.R.I.

gadai: pawn or pledge

gala: a title such as the one given to a man on marriage or the title of a *panghulu*

Golongan Karya: a state political party set up by the Suharto regime

harto (Ind: *harta*): property

   harto pancarian   earned or non-ancestral property

   harto pusako   ancestral property

induak samang: boss or merchant who controls a putting-out system

222

jorong (or *jurai*): a village section

Kabupaten: an administrative subdivision of a province

kamanakan: sisters' children, lineage members one generation below ego

kampuang: a neighbourhood or housing cluster, also in some parts of Minangkabau a lineage segment

kapalo kampuang: head of a village section

kapak: an axe

Kecamatan: an administrative subdivision of a *Kabupaten*, the next level above the village

kedai: a small shop or food stall

kodi: a score (20)

Koto-Piliang: one of two *adat* systems, the one with a more hierarchical tradition

ladang: unirrigated agricultural land

lapau: a coffee shop or stall

malakok: to affiliate with or join a matrilineal descent group

mamak: mother's brother; also used for a senior male of a descent group

manggaleh: to sell, to trade as an occupation

  manggaleh kaki limo   to sell one's wares on the pavement, without stall or shop

marantau (Ind: *merantau*): literally to go to the *rantau*, generally to migrate from the home village or village section

Masjumi: a modernist Muslim political party, banned for its supposed involvement in the regional uprisings in the late 1950s

musajik (Ind: *mesjid*): mosque

nagari: Minangkabau village

nangkodoh: head blacksmith, also means ship's captain

P.K.I.: Partai Kommunis Indonesia, the Indonesian Communist Party

P.M.I.: Partai Muslimin Indonesia, a modernist Muslim party which inherited much of Masjumi's support in West Sumatra

P.N.I.: Partai Nationalis Indonesia, the Indonesian Nationalist Party during Sukarno's rule

P.R.R.I.: Pemerintah Revolutionar Republik Indonesia, the Revolutionary Government of the Republic of Indonesia which took over the regional movement in West Sumatra from the Dewan Banteng

pandai basi: blacksmith

panghulu: lineage head or head of a village-level clan

pangkuah: a broad-bladed hoe

papatah: a traditional saying

pasiduoan: to share-crop

pegawai: a government employee or civil servant

progol: ornamental metal goods

pusako: the ancestral heritage of a matrilineal kin group

Rantau: traditionally, the outlying districts of Minangkabau, now
    used to refer to anywhere outside one's home village

rupiah: Indonesian currency; at the time of research 1,000 *rupiah*
    (abbreviated Rp.1,000) was equal to about £1 sterling

sabik (Ind: *sabit*): a sickle

sawah: irrigated rice land or field

suku: a matrilineal kin group

surau: a prayer house; traditionally a house for unmarried men of
    a village

toko: a shop or store

tukang: a craftsman or woman

   tukang ambuih   the smith who operates the bellows

   tukang basi   blacksmith

   tukang jahit   seamstress

   tukang kayu   carpenter

   tukang kikia   the smith who specialises in filing

   tukang tapo   the smith who wields the sledgehammer

urang siak: a holy man

V.O.C.: Vereenigde Oosindische Compangnie, the Netherlands
    East India Company

Wali Nagari: village head or mayor

Index

Index

cooperatives, 186, 188
crafts (artisanal production), 11, 103ff., 157f., 160, 179, 185, 191 (see also blacksmithing)
   carpentry, 107
   crafts and migrations, 117
   progol production, 107ff.
credit, 87, 187
*Cuisinier, J., 162n.
cultural lag, 209
cultural obstacles to growth, 190, 203
Culture System (Cultuurstelsel), 9, 25, 44, 159, 163ff., 172ff., 176, 209
currency (exchange rate), xi
*Cutler, A., 204

decision-making, 92ff., 120
demography, 27ff.
Dewan Banteng, 14ff.
*Dewey, A., 115n., 181n.
*Dias, T., 153n.
*Dobbins, C., 162n.
dual descent, 153
dualism, 3, 165, 208

economic rationality, 98ff.
*Emmanuel, A., 207
endogamy and exogamy, 46f.
estates (plantations), 9, 11, 173ff., 182
ethical policy, 174, 179

falling rate of profit, 144, 148, 204
fatalism, 24, 99
fetishism, 90, 134, 149
feudalisation, 156, 161ff., 172
feudalism, 134ff.
fishing, 11, 12, 120, 128
floods, 63
forces of production, 85, 145, 203, 211
foreign investment, 174f., 181ff., 195
*Foster, G., 99
*Frank, A. G., 3, 156, 195, 200, 202, 204, 208
*Friedman, J., 3, 62, 212
*Fröbel, F. et al., 212f.
*Furnivall, J., 155n., 156n., 158, 163, 173

*Geertz, C., 5, 24n., 59, 61n., 115n., 126, 164n., 166, 181n., 196
*Gerdin, I., 127
*Gerstein, I., 201
*Glamann, K., 155
*Glassburner, B., 11, 12, 182, 184
gold, 156, 158f.
Golkar, 21ff.
Gotong Royong, 68

*Gough, K., 151, 181

Haj, 23
*Hall, D., 156n., 162
Haluan, 14n., 15
Hari Raya, 46
harto pancarian, 26, 86 (see also adat)
harto pusako, 26, 50, 52 (see also adat)
*Hindess, B. and Hirst, P., 133, 200
*Ho, R., 61n.
Hogendorp, D. van, 159, 163, 173
*Hoogvelt, A. and Child, D., 195n.
*Huitema, W., 164n.

Imam, 24
income
   per capita, 13, 202
   of smiths, 92, 98
Indarung cement factory, 180
independence, 182
inflation, 184, 193, 195, 199
inheritance, 53ff.
involution, 126f.
irrigation, 59
Islam, 5, 23f., 26, 31, 161f.
Islamic Parties, 14, 22

Jakarta, 31f.
Japanese occupation, 11, 82, 84, 86
Java, 166, 173, 180, 196
*Josselin de Jong, P. E. de, 40, 48, 50, 151
Journal of Peasant Studies, 127

Kadi, 24
kamanakan, 45, 52, 168
*Kat Angelino, A. de, 166f.
Kaum Muda, 10
*Kessler, C., 24n.
Khatib, 24
kingdom in Minangkabau, 8, 9, 153
kinship, 25, 39ff.
   bilaterality, 46
   family, 51
   groups (suku), 40ff., 168
   and labour organisation, 91f., 108
   and property, 52ff.
   and residence, 28, 45f., 49ff.
*Koentjaraningrat, R., 181n.
*Kroeskamp, H., 153, 156n., 157f., 162n.

*Laclau, E., 202f., 204, 207f.
lamination, 85
land
   alienation, 26, 55
   colonial tenure, 166
   distribution of, 72ff., 128f.
   property in, 52ff., 58, 180

226

Index

CAMBRIDGE STUDIES IN SOCIAL ANTHROPOLOGY

General Editor: Jack Goody

* Also published as a paperback